"There is a growing realization that a materialistic science-without-consciousness is not just an incomplete and erroneous view but a dangerous one as well. In *The Collapse Of Materialism*, Philip Comella shows why. As he reveals, there are many areas within science that have been largely ignored that demand a fair hearing—not least of which is that the 'matter' upon which materialism rests cannot be understood without reference to mind. If we are successfully to respond to the global challenges of this century, a vision akin to Comella›s is required—a view in which sentience, mind, and consciousness are central."

—Larry Dossey, M.D., author of *One Mind: How Our Individual Mind Is Part of a Greater Consciousness and Why It Matters*

"In *The Collapse of Materialism*, Philip Comella presents a well-argued, strongly documented, and immensely readable critique of the world view we have come to associate with modern science. In addition, he proposes a bold new cosmological hypothesis that he finds hospitable to the concerns of both science and religion. I strongly recommend this thoughtful book to anyone interested in these philosophically important matters."

—Gary A: Cook, Professor Emeritus of Philosophy, Beloit College

"For years, we have been led to believe that the universe traces its roots back to the Big Bang, a cataclysmic explosion of ethereal energy that resulted in the formation of the planets, stars, and everything in-between. Suppose, though, that the cosmos wasn't, in fact, borne of a random eruption—but rather stems from the ever-evolving imagination of a multi-dimensional dreaming mind? Such a drastically different perspective would no doubt change the way we see not only ourselves, but also our place in the infinite realm of the universe. A highly recommended read."

—Dominique Sessons, Apex Reviews

"Philip Comella addresses some of the most important questions of our time concerning the nature of life, the limits of science, and the need for a new worldview."

—Tim Freke, author of *The Mystery Experience*

"This work, developed over decades of research and personal inquiry, is, indeed, what it sets out to be: a new message of hope in our troubled world. This book should be required reading for any soul who longs to know why we are here and how we can make our highest Real Dream come true."

—Emanuel Kuntzelman, president and founder, Greenheart Transforms

"As a mystic who has personally experienced pure consciousness and the quantum 'reality' scientists claim cannot exist, this book was an eye-opening voyage through the inner realms of material science and the tangled web scientists, cemented in the bias of preconceived beliefs, have woven in an attempt to deny the true fabric of our shared 'reality.' A must read for anyone who seeks to better understand not only how the rift between science and spirit occurred but why Philip Comella's point-by-point arguments tear down the wall materialism has formed around the truth of our world . . . our human existence . . . and our perception of reality."

—Carol Romine, author of *Avatars of Consciousness Awaken to Your Divine Destiny*

"With impeccable logic steeped in meticulous research and deep philosophical understanding of the historic unfolding of materialist science that has limited us and religious belief that has separated us, Philip Comella shows us a way to move beyond the crumbling assumptions of a bygone age and embrace the quantum discovery of the essential role of mind in conscious creation.

—Dianne Collins, Creator of QuantumThink® and author of the award-winning bestseller, *Do You QuantumThink? New Thinking That Will Rock Your World*

"In *The Collapse of Materialism*, Philip Comella demonstrates the inconsistencies in the materialistic worldview, and provides possible bridges to the future in which he sees that mind and matter may no longer be seen as separate. If the implications of this book are truly understood then it represents nothing less than a scientific revolution."

—Manjir Samanta-Laughton, M.D., international speaker and author of *Punk Science and The Genius Groove*

THE
COLLAPSE
of
MATERIALISM

VISIONS OF SCIENCE
DREAMS OF GOD

PHILIP COMELLA

Cover and interior design by Frame25 Productions
Cover photograph © Shutterstock.com

Published by:
Rainbow Ridge Books, LLC
140 Rainbow Ridge Road
Faber, Virginia 22938
434-361-1723
www.rainbowridgebooks.com

If you are unable to order this book from your local
bookseller, you may order directly from the distributor.

Square One Publishers, Inc.
115 Herricks Road
Garden City Park, NY 11040
Phone: (516) 535-2010
Fax: (516) 535-2014
Toll-free: 877-900-BOOK

Visit the author at:
www.thecollapseofmaterialism.com

LCCN: 2009943126

ISBN 978-1-937907-21-1

10 9 8 7 6 5 4 3 2 1

Printed on acid-free paper in the United States

To the new world.

CONTENTS

Part 3: Material Science Lost in a Dream World

Section 1: The Big Bang as Metaphor

*Section 2: Quantum Theory as the
Physical Science to a Dream World*

A NEW JOURNEY FOR SPACESHIP EARTH

Imagine that you are a passenger on a rocket ship hurtling through outer space. Commanding the ship are scientists and religious leaders who have assumed the responsibility for flying the rocket to a new homeland. One day you wake up, look out the window, and wonder whether the pilots are heading the ship in the right direction. You begin to doubt whether you have paid enough attention to the route they have taken and you slowly get up the courage to enter the pilot's cabin and ask them a few questions about where exactly the ship is heading. After all, you only have one chance to make it home.

Today we all ride a rocket ship: the planet Earth. The journey we are on is called life. Like the rocket ship, the leaders of science and religion direct the way we carry out our lives, and we rely upon those leaders to take us to a better place, whether we call it the promised land, heaven, or simply a land of peace and prosperity.

For most of the voyage, we have sat quietly in the back of the ship as we have let others, whom we believe to be smarter than we are, guide us along this journey. But like the passengers on the rocket ship, many of us are beginning to realize that because we only have one life to lead, we should start asking a few questions about our route and destination.

The group commanding our own rocket ship follows a system of belief called scientific materialism. In this view of the world, matter is the ultimate reality; the universe (or universes) arose from a random, purposeless explosion; and God is dead. We may not know it—since we are sitting in the back of the ship and not paying much attention—but this mind-set is controlling the flight of the ship, permeating our culture and society. We are clearly not heading toward any sort of promised land.

Materialism separates us from Mother Nature, other people, and God. It fixes us into categories—race, religion, nationalities, political parties—that mask the fundamental unity of all humankind.

It is time to set spaceship Earth on a new journey. It is time to challenge the thought leaders who have set the ship's guidance system following the methods of materialism, and who are heading this planet toward disaster.

So hold on to your seats as we challenge the core principles of scientific materialism and show that we can take another, more sensible route. We can instead steer this great ship toward a place that does not separate us, but unites us; that turns the mystical belief that we are One into a scientific truth; and that fulfills both the visions of science and the dreams of God.

A Word about Endnotes

This book advances what some may view as a radical perspective toward the world. It is certainly different. But the reason this book's ideas may appear radical is that our current worldview, based upon materialism, is radically wrong. I am a lawyer by trade, and we are taught to document, by citation to authority, propositions made in support of an argument. I have done that here through the use of endnotes. The endnotes also serve as a means of showing that the ideas in this book, though framed in a new light, are deeply grounded in intellectual history. In addition, since much of this book consists of a critique of the failings of modern scientific theory, I thought it would help to provide citations to the sources of those theories for readers who may want to look a little more closely themselves. Ignore the endnotes or use them as you see fit. In the end, they are there to show that although the ideas in this book may at first seem radical, the reader may find that they also concern the very world in which we live.

THE REALIZATION THAT TOGETHER WE DREAM THE WORLD

Reality is an illusion, albeit a very persistent one.
—Albert Einstein

When future historians write the chronicle of our age, they will tell the story of a people rising to the realization that together they dream the world. This realization—or enlightenment—will start slowly and then gain momentum as the evidence supporting it builds and other explanations for the world begin to fade away. As the realization grows, it will mark the beginning of a new world, one that reflects humankind's highest dream: a people united in body and in spirit. This new world will be joined together by a higher truth, a transcendent purpose, a unified way of thinking that connects our souls with the galaxies spiraling high above in the distant cosmos.

This is the story of a people growing up believing that they live in a material world where Mother Nature radiates such grandeur and power that only some almighty external force—the big bang or God—could possibly be responsible for it.

Through the ages the story unfolds, as people raise their eyes to the heavens, wondering by what miracle a world of such deep solidity and order stands before them. At the same time, a group of logical, hard-minded thinkers, taking nothing on faith, adopt the view that they must reason and experiment their way to the truth; scientific methods must prove theories correct or they have no validity.

But the appeal to God and the search for scientific truth lead to no unified theory; religion and science exist in different realms, and the two seldom communicate using the same language.

Without a unifying law for humankind, we wind up competing against those who act, look, or pray differently than we do. As the most severe sign of ignorance, some people kill innocent others in the name of God and trumpet the achievement to their blind followers.

This practice cannot go on, as someday we will come to understand that a greater purpose joins us. But the only way to achieve true unity is for a critical mass of people to acknowledge an overriding principle that transcends the historical belief systems that have led us here. This principle must reorient science, philosophy, and religion toward a higher plane, but the principle cannot be an abstraction or a vaguely expressed feeling. The unity principle must be accepted as both a scientific and philosophical truth; it must create a new scientific paradigm while satisfying the soul-deep yearnings and soaring aspirations of religion.

This unity must yield a worldview more coherent and logical than what modern material science or Darwinism offers. It must blend philosophical insights with the empirical facts of science; it must drive toward the final scientific revolution because it will explain more with fewer assumptions—the truth that remains after all opposing theories fall away.

And so we gradually ascend to the truth: We are the creators in a universe issued from the soul, bursting from the core of the one Mind, not from a big bang or the hand of a heavenly father. Instead, the truth stands in front of us: *We are the one mind*, and we are dreaming this world. *We are God*, and we, with infinite dreaming power, have dreamed a world of such overwhelming power and solidity that we have fooled ourselves into thinking we are not dreaming. We are indeed a young God. Like a God-child, we imagine that the outside world we see—the stars in the sky, the trees in the forest, fields of grass, winding roads, and other people—exist independently of our beings, as if we are moviegoers watching the world go by on a big screen. Detached from the world we create, we pull back from taking full responsibility for our dream home.

This book challenges the material science worldview, which holds that far from being a dream, our world is actually a giant machine composed of tiny mindless particles operating on their own power with no care for mind or soul. This worldview controls how we look at the world and how we act in the world. It is based upon the great assumption that an entire universe of matter exists outside of the mind and beyond the mind's control. As I describe in the chapters that follow, when we dispense with this unnecessary assumption, we find the key to unlock the explanation for why we are here.

It is time finally to answer this question, so that we can get on with the vital task of making this home of ours a truly better and more peaceful place for all the world's people. It is time to set our sights on the only goal that will unify us, a goal that shines silently overhead in a place at the end of science that we will someday know to be heaven.

PART 1

Revolution to the Truth

Chapter One

THE NEXT SCIENTIFIC REVOLUTION

Govinda: *What you call a thing, is it something real, something intrinsic?*
Is it not only the illusion of Maya, only image and appearance?
Your stone, your tree, are they real?

Siddhartha: *This does not trouble me much. If they are illusion, then*
I also am illusion, and so they are always of the same nature as myself.
—Herman Hesse, *Siddhartha*

THE TIME HAS COME to start the next scientific revolution.

Scientific revolutions become necessary when the existing worldview becomes outdated and is forced to give way to a new perspective that better explains the natural world and human experience. Now is such a moment. Our current worldview has exhausted its usefulness, and we must replace it with one that has a deeper and broader foundation.

The material science worldview today controls our outlook toward the world and ourselves. It determines how we spend billions of dollars in scientific research, treat bodily illnesses, interpret religious texts, and view other people and our own bodies. It controls everything we do— everything we say and think. It is the theme of the movie and the plotline of the story; it defines our character, determining our lines, beliefs, and wants. It is the prism through which we see the world, the gloves we use to handle it, and the earpiece that filters the sounds we hear.

The material science worldview is based upon a simple, though massive, assumption: this view of the world assumes that the trillions of tons of matter apparent in the world—from our own bodies to the galaxies far out in space—exist independently of the mind and operate beyond its control. This worldview has led us to a place filled with conflict, hatred, war, disease, terrorism, and environmental degradation. The material science worldview is based upon a false assumption and must be overthrown.

But before beginning the attack on the material science worldview, we need to define a few terms.

Mind and External World

This book uses the terms "mind" and "external world" as the terms are generally used, particularly in the field of philosophy.[1] Mind and external world can be understood in the following manner.

Close your eyes and try to block out all sensations of everything outside you; disregard everything you see, hear, smell, touch, and taste. Block out the sky, clouds, trees, grass, other people, your body, and anything extended in space. Proceeding in this manner leaves nothing but what we feel inside. Inside we have thoughts (ideas), emotions (happy, depressed, lonely, etc.), and something we call willpower, or striving. The source of these inner sensations is the mind.[2] Everything outside the mind, everything we experience through the five senses, *including the five senses*, is the external world[3] or nature.

Note something important here at the outset: The external world, or the world outside the mind, includes the body. This point may seem obvious, but it is still critical to understanding how science made a wrong turn on the way to uncovering truth. Later we drill down deeper into this fundamental problem. For now, however, simply be aware of the following: the body and nature—trees, grass, sand, the sky, and all of outer space—exist on the same level; they are both *external* or *outside of* the mind. The dream nature of the body and the world thus cancel each other out, and they are real to each other. This point is the core principle of the Real Dream worldview advanced in this book. Those in the midst of a dream lose themselves in it and imagine that the world they experience is outside of the mind. Is this not the purpose of a dream?

Using these definitions, the mind is not the human brain; wash this thought from your mind. In a dream world, the human brain is a physical translation of the mind, as if a grand animator sought to draw a three-dimensional image of the workings of the mind. This approach explains the incredible complexity of the brain, and also solves the so-called hard problem of consciousness,[4] which is how, during the course of evolution, consciousness could possibly have arisen from dead stuff. The answer is that it didn't; rather, the three-dimensional image of the brain arose from the dream-creating power of the mind.

If you are having a hard time with this new perspective and find it difficult to let go of your grasp upon the material world, then stop. For this one moment, consider an alternative viewpoint. Consider this new outlook a wild hypothesis—an out-of-the-box supposition—but consider the theory with an open mind and judge it after all the evidence is available. Then make your decision.

Material Science

"Material science," as used in this book, identifies the body of knowledge based on the view that the external world—the stars in the sky, the cells of our bodies, our senses, and all the atoms in the universe—exists independently of the mind and operates beyond its control. Under this viewpoint, the external world (nature) is a giant machine programmed to run according to natural laws. Material science, importantly, assumes that the external world exists independently of the mind and then conducts investigations as if this assumption were true.[5]

Worldview

A worldview is a set of beliefs upon which we base our outlook toward the world; these beliefs make up the lens through which we see the world.[6] Worldviews are buried so deep, however, that we often fail to realize we have one. This book is about the worldview that sits at the base of our mind's eye, an ingrained lens that leads us to view the physical world and our bodies as distinct from our thoughts and emotions instead of as a reflection of them. A worldview also can be called "metaphysics" or "philosophy." One way to understand a worldview is to imagine that you are a child who has yet to form any firm opinions about the world. You look at the world purely. The sum total of beliefs and opinions that build up in your mind over the years forms your worldview.

The core elements of a worldview are established by how people define their place in the universe, their relation to nature (or the external world), and their relation to God. For example, in the material science worldview we learn that man is a descendant of a one-celled bacterium that slowly evolved out of a "hot dilute soup" roughly 3 billion years ago.[7] In the eyes of material science, human beings have no privileged status in the animal kingdom; we are closer to apes than to God.[8]

Nature, according to material science, works according to blind, impersonal laws.[9] Natural forces are objective and care nothing for the plight of the human race. The external world confronts man as an alien creation; mind evolved from matter through random, purposeless laws. Because the external world, under this viewpoint, is utterly distinct from mind, mind has no control over matter. Different human beings, as products of objective natural laws, are totally separate creatures—"robot vehicles."[10]

Because material science is based on facts that can be observed and tested, the concept of God is either left out of the picture or pushed so far back in time that God becomes irrelevant.[11] God therefore remains an object of faith but not of scientific study.

The material science worldview stands in stark contrast to the Real Dream worldview. In the Real Dream, the human body is the mind's best image of a physical form to engage in the process of life. As the only self-conscious creature, a human being is the mind aware of itself, and therefore capable of controlling its own destiny. Nature is not a peculiar creation that incidentally supports life; rather, nature and the mind evolve together as subject (dreamer) and object (dream). Nature works according to peculiarly personal laws and is the scenery against which the mind of God lives. In the Real Dream, we do not experience the same external world because one world exists independently of separate minds; *instead, we experience the same world because we have one mind and participate in the same dream.* This united mind is God; at the dream's ultimate source rests one person in whom the dream originates. God can thus be known and is the primary subject of scientific study. The world, as a projected three-dimensional scene in the one Mind of God, becomes a scientific truth in the Real Dream worldview or—in terms of logic—the major premise from which we can deduce other features of our world.

I am not saying that the world is partly a dream or like a dream. I am not saying the world is a dream on Tuesdays and Thursdays but a material contraption the rest of the week. Nor am I using "dream" as a metaphor or figure of speech. To the contrary, as discussed in further detail below, the materialistic conception of the universe that begins with the big bang theory and ends in Darwinian evolution is in fact a physical metaphor of the mind's struggle to escape from the dark void—from *nothing.* The entire universe— from the DNA molecules that make up the genetic code in our bodies to the far-flung galaxies that make up the universe—are *appearances, projected images,* of an external, physical world. But because we, too, are appearances, this external world is real to us; we live in a world of spirit, and we are also spirits.

And we are not just any spirits. Rather, we are three-dimensional spirits taking up space and existing as the final creative act of unlimited dreaming power. The conception of God we have in our minds—this great, infinite being that many people believe rests at the base of reality— is the source of the dreaming power. The energy of God fuels the dream. Look outside and there you will see a striking example of the power of the mind of God: a force we have misunderstood and therefore utterly failed to appreciate.

Some readers may view this thought as a crazed outlook—insane, ludicrous, or fantasy. Fine. In my view, the big bang theory is fantasy. Let us have a debate: let us see which worldview—that of material science or the Real Dream—better explains our world. Is this not what science is all about? Or should we simply hand material science the trophy before the contest has begun?

Our current worldview is disastrously wrong. It is based upon a model of reality that scientists devised to enable them to conduct experiments in the physical world. At some point in the process, however, scientists mistook the model for the reality. Now they find themselves entangled in a series of Gordian knots trying to explain how a physical, mechanical model—a gigantic stage setting—sprang from nothing on its own power and formed itself into the scenery of endless beauty standing before us.

Let me be direct on this point: The greatest intellectual mistake of our era is the assumption that the practice of science can only be undertaken if we assume that a "real world" exists independently of human perception or the mind. Scientists, from Albert Einstein to Steven Weinberg and Lisa Randall, command the universe to exist independently of the mind so that they can practice their particular type of science. Materialists want to clasp the universe in their vise grips, place it under the lens of the microscope, and have it hold steady to get a good view; they want to detach the physical specimen from the viewing apparatus and study the thing as it is in itself.

Scientists can indeed study the world as if the physical world were really independent of perception, but it in the end it's not. You study a reflection of the mind—a self-portrait, not a randomly placed stage setting put in place by the big bang. The universe does not listen to the command of materialists, but can only exist in one way: as an outcome of the dreaming power. The scientific mind's demand for a real, independent world is an expression of the mind's deep desire for a real world to appear in front of it. The presence of the physical world has answered this desire, but the world can never be separated from the desire or the mind that created it. *We have the world we desire. Now the task is to understand it properly so that we can build a better world, here, now.*

And so it turns out that we live in an enchanted world, a world that should not be here, but somehow is.

Science must thus be reoriented. Rather than look at the world as created from the ground up (or from the inside out), from particles to human life, we need to view the world as being created from the top down: from the three-dimensional dream forms to the inner world. This subtle change in perspective explains the mathematical harmony of the atomic world, from electrons orbiting the atomic nucleus to the laws of chemistry and the DNA molecule.

I write this book to convince the reader that the material science worldview is wrong. But the success of my undertaking depends upon the degree that you open your mind to the possibility of a new perspective. As you read the following pages, try your hardest to throw off your preconceptions. Wring them dry from your mind, and think clearly, like a child, with a fresh outlook toward a new world to experience.

True Science

Because of material science's dominance, "material science" is believed to be synonymous with "science," as if no other worldview possesses legitimacy. The independent-world assumption of material science has penetrated our mindset to such a degree that anyone who takes an opposing stance is viewed as engaging in something other than science.[12] Material science is the enemy of the dream; it rebels against a mind-centered world.

We can all agree that we deeply believe in a world outside of our bodily senses, and we want it to operate regularly and not with the caprice of a nightmare. After acknowledging the intensity of this belief, we next need to ask how it is possible for this particular world to exist. No matter how deep and strong the belief in a mind-independent world, we still need to address how such a world came to stand before us.

Science is the "state or fact of knowing;" it is "systematized knowledge derived from observation, study, and experimentation carried on in order to determine the nature or principles of what is being studied."[13] Science is a collection of what we know about the world.

The first inquiry in building a body of knowledge, or science, is to determine what we are capable of knowing. The question of what the mind is capable of knowing is a central topic in the field of philosophy known as epistemology.[14] Material science is based upon a brand of philosophy that assumes the mind can know about a world independent of the mind, and therefore holds this independent world up as the chief area of inquiry. In other words, material scientists study the assumption of a mind-independent world, but the mind has already delivered this same world to us in the form of a dream—an internally projected, three-dimensional image.

As we shall see, whether the mind can indeed know anything about such an independent world is one of philosophy's most controversial topics; put differently, material science has never proven that a world external to the mind actually exists, or whether our minds are capable of knowing such a world. Material science, in short, simply *assumes* that such a world exists.[15] In material science, the independent existence of the external world is "pure hypothesis," an "object of faith."[16]

Facts become part of science only if they are collected systematically, or according to the scientific method.[17] A scientific fact must be testable.[18] If a statement such as "All Martians have green eyes" is not testable, it cannot have the status of a scientific fact. These statements may form an object of belief or faith, but they have no place in a scientific theory.

The scientific method, however, is based on more than observation and testing. Critical examination of the assumptions used in a theory is also part of the scientific method.

This revolution thus begins with questions: Is the underlying assumption of material science true? Is this assumption necessary to explain the world? Assumptions weaken scientific theory. Under a principle known as Occam's razor, the fewer the assumptions made in a theory, the better the theory.[19] The best scientific theory, therefore, uses no assumptions but explains the world with what we can know.

The total matter in the universe is estimated at 10^{53} kilograms, the equivalent of a billion trillion suns or 10^{80} atoms.[20] Material science assumes that all this matter exists external to the mind. Using Occam's razor, a theory not making this rather large assumption must be considered a better explanation of natural events than the material science worldview. The Real Dream makes no such assumption, and as we shall see, offers a much broader explanation for the world's phenomena than material science.

On the other hand, we can decide not to question the underlying assumption of material science. We can forfeit the debate to material scientists and let them go on explaining the world to us. After all, many of us were raised not to question fundamental beliefs. We question opinions held by our teachers, law officers, political leaders, and football coaches, but we have been taught not to question the great assumption of the material science worldview. Most of us, in fact, probably believe it is beyond question. After all, who are we—mere laypersons—to question the opinions of Nobel Prize–winning scientists who have surely thought about these things?

History shows, however, that the failure to question doubtful beliefs has led entire cultures to accept what are today considered naïve, if not ludicrous, ideas. At one time the Earth was flat, Atlas supported the planet on his shoulder while standing on the back of a tortoise, gods lived on Mount Olympus, and a mysterious ether filled the universe. Soon we will add to these antiquated viewpoints our belief in a material world of self-operating atoms.

Chapter Two

A PROBLEM OF PERSPECTIVE

For philosophy, the real difficulty lies in the spatial and temporal multiplicity of observing and thinking individuals. If all events took place in one consciousness, the whole situation would be extremely simple.
—Erwin Schroedinger

THROUGH OUR FIVE SENSES we experience a three-dimensional solid world that works according to the laws of nature. Objects as large as stars and as small as atoms follow patterned and predictable movements. The force of gravity is the same on Earth as in the distant heavens, and light moves at a constant speed throughout the universe. All the 10^{80} elementary particles that make up the stars in the sky come from the same patterns, and those 10^{20} stars all burn fuel following the same mathematical formula. In living things, we find the same remarkable molecule handing out instructions for how the organism grows and develops. We naturally believe that the material making up the world, as well as the laws governing its movements, originate outside of us—far out among the galaxies or deep within the atom. We live in this world, and we can hardly imagine any other kind of place.

But we are looking at the three-dimensional picture we call the world from the wrong perspective. We assume that because the stars in the sky, sweeping hills, grassy plains, other people, and all the things in the world appear outside of our bodily senses, they also exist outside of what we are. We assume that our essence is a body and not a mind.

Think about this for a moment. Somehow we know that we belong in this world, but we have little idea how such a place is possible. Rather, we do our best to avoid this question and simply take the world at face value. The world appears to exist outside of our bodies; therefore, for all we know, it does. This way of looking at things is implicit in everything modern science teaches, from the creation of the universe (the big bang) to the way our bodies age and life ends.

But suppose this viewpoint is wrong. Suppose that our essence is not a material body, but instead a mind that sits behind both the body and the world outside, a mind that creates the body as well as the scenery we call the world. This is the dream perspective, since any world in which the body and surrounding scenery are mind-created must be a dream.

This alternative perspective is not entirely new. In the seventeenth century, French philosopher René Descartes found that he could doubt every fact about the world, including that a real world existed outside his mind, except for one fact: his ability to think and to doubt. "I think, therefore I am," Descartes says, and it is true each time he says it.[21]

But what is he? He answers:

> Only a thinking being, that is to say, a mind, an understanding, or a reasoning being, which are terms whose meaning was previously unknown to me . . . What is a thinking being? It is a being which doubts, which understands, [which conceives], which affirms, which denies, which rejects, which imagines also and which perceives.[22]

Under the full weight of doubt, Descartes found he is nothing but a thinking being, and only that fact is beyond doubt. The world outside, including his body, might just be a dream.

But upon reaching this point in his reasoning, Descartes concluded that God would never make him believe that a world beyond the mind existed unless one really did. He reasons that because God has given him a "very great inclination to believe that these ideas come from corporeal objects, I do not see how we could clear God of the charge of deceit if these ideas did in fact come from some other source than corporeal objects. Therefore we must conclude that corporeal objects exist."[23]

Descartes, then, could not bring himself to think that God would make him believe in a world beyond his dreaming mind unless such a world really existed. But what if Descartes had not appealed to an external God to restore the outside world that doubt had put into question? Might then Descartes, and in fact anyone following his line of reasoning, have concluded that the world really is a dream?

Our current worldview rebels against this line of inquiry, as modern science reverses the dream perspective. We take it for granted that mind comes before matter, that the big bang—an explosion of matter, space, and time—is the creation event, and that mind emerged from material particles during the evolutionary process.

From the vantage point of material science, we are led to see the world as a motion picture that projects itself at us, not from us. Because, in the current scientific worldview, neither our mind nor that of some unknown Supreme Being contributes to creation, modern scientists must make the incredible assumption that matter miraculously appeared from nothing on its own power and somehow became programmed with the laws of nature. Then, in a miracle hard to exaggerate, this matter somehow became alive and evolved into the life-forms we see today.

It might be time to consider the dream perspective more closely.

Chapter Three

A RESPONSE TO THE MAIN OBJECTION

Socrates: *The question I imagine you have often heard asked—what evidence could be appealed to, supposing we were asked at this very moment whether we are asleep or awake, dreaming all that passes through our minds or talking to one another in the waking state?*

Theaetetus: *Indeed, Socrates, I do not see by what evidence it is to be proved, for the two conditions correspond in every circumstance like exact counterparts.*
—Plato, *Theaetetus*

THE STRONGEST ARGUMENT AGAINST a dream world is a simple one: The world appears much more solid, coherent, regular, and *real* than any dream we experience at night. We compare our night dreams with the public world; we conclude that the former is a fleeting phantom, and the latter, a granite rock.

In arriving at this conclusion, however, we have not considered whether dreams may vary in power and quality. Instead, overwhelmed by the forceful presence of the public world, we jump to the conclusion that night dreams and the public world are wholly different realities.

Let us suppose that they *are* different realities: this fact does not make one a dream and the other a self-operating machine. Rather, it may make one a low-powered dream, and the second an infinite-powered dream.

The truth is that we have no way of going outside this world to compare it to some more real world, because there is no other world. We can only compare *this* world to other visions of an external world—night dreams, hallucinations, and mirages. The waking world, the one we see outside the window, is no doubt a more coherent, solid world than images created by an individual mind, but how do we know that the solid world is not also mind-created? This world may represent an infinite mind's dreaming limit.

Because our own mind has poured itself into creation, we come to associate what we are with our bodies. From this vantage point, it is easy to believe the world is not a dream because what we are is so completely bound up with our bodies, and *we seem so solid and real.*

Today we compare our night dreams with the real world and suppose that the real world cannot be a dream. But perhaps we have not thought this subject through far enough.

A Simple Inference

Suppose both the dreams we have at night and the public world share a similar source: the mind. Suppose both are produced internally. To answer the question of why the public world stands before us with so much more power than a night dream, we need take only one step.

We usually view the world as if one, independent, natural world stands outside a multitude of separate minds (or people), as if we, the human population, are members of a theater audience watching a movie on a screen.

If the world is a dream, however, this setup is incorrect. Instead, the reason we all perceive the same natural world, or the same scenery outside the window, is not because one world exists outside separate minds (or brains), but because we all have the same mind and are participating in the same dream. We are all part of a dream in progress, a *story acted out on the grand stage of the universe.*

This approach enables us to offer a simple explanation for why the public world is so much more powerfully real than a night dream: whatever dreaming power our separate minds exhibit while asleep is combined in the public world; in sleep this dreaming power works dreamer by dreamer; during the day while awake, the dreamers, by necessity, unite in the dream.

We, in short, are dreaming creatures, products of a great mind. The great dream represents the dreaming power pressed to the wall of infinity; night dreams are splashes of water in the great ocean dream.

Does this concept of combining dreaming powers appear odd? Compared with the current material science worldview—with its inflationary big bang, dark matter, dark energy, wave-particles, superstrings, virtual particles, black holes, many-worlds, and strange quarks—the theory presented in this book—that the world is a product of the one, united mind of God—will come to feel perfectly natural.

Science, in fact, regularly combines the power of individual sources to calculate a total power, such as the gravitational pull of a galaxy of stars or the computing power of linked microprocessors. In surmising that the world standing before us is a product of the combined dreaming power, we have only taken what we know is possible—the power of the mind to project a three-dimensional image—and then used this known power to explain the presence of the world.

Chapter Four

THE CONNECTION BETWEEN
MIND AND MATTER

Unless there is a gigantic conspiracy involving some thirty University Departments all over the world, and several hundred respected scientists in various fields, many of them originally hostile to the claims of the psychical researchers, the only conclusion the unbiased observer can come to must be that there does exist a small number of people who obtain knowledge existing either in other people's minds, or in the outer world, by means as yet unknown to science.
—Arthur Koestler, *The Roots of Coincidence*

EVERYDAY EXPERIENCES SHOW that it may not be wise to dismiss out of hand the notion that we dwell in a dream world. In a dream world we might expect to find a connection not only between the mind and its dream, but between apparently separate minds. We would not be robots sliding down slotted tracks, but rather separate forms flowing from a single creative source. In this world, it seems, we should periodically experience a connection between the mind and its world.

Material scientists, however, perceive no connection between the brain and the outer world, and therefore believe these two things have no means of communicating.[24] In philosophy, the viewpoint that the world exists exactly as we perceive it is known as *naïve realism*.[25] Naïve realism is the view that "what you see is what you get." All questions about what the mind is capable of knowing or how the world can exist are put to the side. The world is taken for what it appears to be: a solid, self-sustaining machine.

Naïve realism gives us a stage-prop world. In this world we look outside of ourselves for the secrets to life—far out among the galaxies or deep within the atom. Because naïve realism seems so sensible and obvious, material scientists base most of their theories upon it. For example, Nobel Prize–winning scientist Steven Weinberg writes that most physicists adopt a "rough-and-ready realism, a belief in the objective reality of the ingredients of our scientific theories."[26] Material science then becomes the quest to correlate theory with an assumed, mind-independent world.[27]

Adopting naïve realism as a foundation, however, leads material scientists into endless quagmires. To begin with, many human experiences put into question the notion that the external world stands absolutely detached from the mind. These events include those where the mind projects an external world mistaken for the world at large (night dreams and hallucinations), where separate minds communicate through no physical means (telepathy), or where the mind alone affects an external object (mind over matter) or the body (placebo effect). Material science offers no explanation for these events because it detects no physical connection between the mind and the external world; consequently, material science has no theory to account for so-called paranormal events. Steven Weinberg expresses this viewpoint clearly: "We do not understand everything, but we understand enough to know there is no room in our world for telekinesis [mind-over-matter] or astrology. What possible signal from our brains could move distant objects and yet have no effect on any scientific instruments?"[28]

Of course, when Weinberg says "our world" he means the world of material science—the worldview in which the external world is assumed to have an existence independent of the mind. But before basing an entire world outlook upon this assumption, it may first help to determine if the assumption is true. Material science's conventional response to paranormal events is to conclude simply that they cannot occur regardless of the supporting evidence, or to assert that scientists someday will find a physical explanation.[29] This approach to dealing with unusual events weakens the explanatory power of material science theory. A complete scientific theory should explain the full range of human experiences, not cast off a large portion because some events do not fit a preconceived model.

By comparison, the Real Dream easily accounts for paranormal events. The regularity and solidity of the world is traceable, in the final analysis, to our need for a regular and solid world. Paranormal events become not unexplained phenomena in a mechanical world, but rather disruptions in an ordered dream world. Paranormal events occur infrequently because that is the way we want it; we do not want to live in a world of horror. Studies show that an individual mind's ability to shake reality out of its normal operational mode is marginal[30] or weak.[31] Indeed, if any one person were capable of disrupting the world at large from its normal operation, the world might then become a real nightmare.

The following discussion is neither intended as a comprehensive survey of paranormal events, nor as an argument that any one of these events actually occurred as reported. Instead, the discussion shows that when considering these events as a whole, we might not want to so easily discard the notion that a *real* connection may exist between mind and matter, thus again putting into question the validity of material science's great assumption.

Chapter Five

THE MIND'S ABILITY TO DREAM

*Creations of an individual mind may reasonably be called less
substantial than creations of a universal mind.*
—Sir James Jeans, *The Mysterious Universe*

STANDING BEFORE A UNIVERSE filled with matter, material scientists face the eternal mystery of explaining where all this stuff came from. We face no comparable mystery, however, over whether the mind has the ability to conjure up a three-dimensional world during dreams and hallucinations. In our world, we know dreams are possible.

Night Dreams

Night dreams form part of the world's fabric. They are the most common instance of the mind's ability to create a world of its own. Sometimes we know we are dreaming; on other occasions we fold into the dream and fool ourselves into thinking we are not. While in the midst of a dream, we are convinced the dreamed world has an external existence. Its source appears outside of us; we do not usually believe the dream is self-produced. And, importantly, that is the point of dreaming. The mind wants to lose itself in the self-created world—a pail of water thrown into the ocean. The mind wants to mix into the dream world, and the picture it sees expresses its thoughts and desires.

Night dreams have neither the stability nor coherence of the public world. But during a night dream the dreamer knows no better; left with a dark world at night, the first act of the mind is to conjure up a private world. We do not fight off the dream but rather desire it. Dreaming comes naturally.

Material science believes that our experience during waking hours occurs against an external world detached from the mind. But we gain similar experiences at night when the mind creates its own external world. Anyone who has experienced a nightmare and awakened trembling, fearing the horror's return, knows that night dreams can present a real experience.[32] The mind is perfectly capable of furnishing its own external world; in dreams the mind furnishes both actors and stage.

Night dreams vary in intensity and vividness; some are soft shadows, fleeting images. But others arrive with such convincing presence that they erase the borderline between dream and reality. Sigmund Freud described a thirty-year-old man who distinctly recalled a dream he had when only four, a year after his father died. In the dream, the clerk holding his father's will gave the boy two large pears, one to eat and one to save for later. The second pear rested on the windowsill in the living room. After waking up, the boy was so sure what he dreamed actually happened, he stubbornly asked his mother to give him the second pear he believed still rested on the windowsill.[33] According to some accounts no dreams are as real as those involving the sensation of flying. Havelock Ellis, in his book *The World of Dreams*, relates the experience of the French painter Raffaelli, who often dreamed of gliding through the air like a bird, and was so convinced by the reality of the experience that upon waking he often dove out of bed in the hope of reenacting his dream-flight. "I need not tell you," the painter remarks, "that I have never been able to succeed."[34]

That night dreams occur and that they sometimes carry the emotional force and presence of waking experience are two facts that few people question. But at night only our mind produces this realistic three-dimensional world. No external scientific force is present at that moment to install a three-dimensional world in front of us. Material scientists believe that the brain at night makes a copy of the real, waking world. But in the Real Dream another explanation is readily available: waking life, too, is a dream, but a dream we all share in. Waking life is the public dream; our night world, the private dream.

This approach not only avoids the mystery of how the human brain—a supposed chance product of Darwin's mindless version of evolution—duplicates physical reality, but it also helps explain how our night dreams sometimes connect to the waking world. In a common story theme, *Sports Illustrated* reported awhile back that:

> The night before the woman's figure skating final, Mary Scotvold had a dream. She dreamed that Nancy Kerrigan, whom Mary coaches with her husband, Evy, doubled her opening triple jump, the flip in that competition. Then, instead of falling apart, as Kerrigan had done in her marred performance at the 1993 world championship in Prague, Nancy pulled herself together to skate a clean program the rest of the way. Mary awoke Evy and related the dream to him.[35]

And, of course, Kerrigan "skated just like in the dream."[36]

Charles Dickens reported a similar dream in his personal journal:

> I dreamed that I saw a lady in a red shawl with her back toward me. . . . On her turning around, I found that I didn't know her and she said, "I am Miss Napier." All the time I was dressing next morning, I thought—what a preposterous thing to have so very distinct a dream about nothing! and why Miss Napier? For I have never heard of any Miss Napier. That same Friday night I read. After the reading, [there] came into my retiring-room Miss Boyle and her brother, and the lady in the red shawl whom they presented as "Miss Napier!"[37]

Although we can categorize all events such as these as mere coincidences or nature's oddities, we should remember that drawing a connection between a thought in the mind and a natural event is common not only to the paranormal but also to the way scientists develop theories about the world. Every time a scientific theory is proven valid, such as

Newton's theory of gravity, we might ask how a thought in the mind comes to correspond with an event occurring in an external world supposedly detached from the mind? How does theory manage to correlate with an independent natural event? Those who have studied how scientists devise theories point out that no systematic rules exist "by which hypotheses or theories can be mechanically derived or inferred from empirical data. The transition from data to theory requires creative imagination."[38] In other words, scientists commonly connect a theory to a natural event through intuition and insight, not through logical deduction. Professor Hempel relates an account of a scientific discovery that has much in common with precognitive dreams:

> The chemist Kekulé . . . tells us that he had long been trying unsuccessfully to devise a structural formula for the benzene molecule when, one evening in 1865, he found a solution to his problem while he was dozing in front of his fireplace. Gazing into the flames, he seemed to see atoms dancing in snakelike arrays. Suddenly, one of the snakes formed a ring by seizing hold of its own tail and then whirled mockingly before him. Kekulé awoke in a flash: he had hit upon the now famous and familiar idea of representing the molecular structure of benzene by a hexagonal ring. He spent the rest of the night working out the consequences of this hypothesis.[39]

Nobel Prize–winning physicist Niels Bohr is reported to have been inspired to formulate his solar-system version of the atom through a night dream, and Albert Einstein is said to have arrived at his universe-shaking realizations through mystical visions.[40] Material scientists call these episodes "Eureka!" moments, sparks of genius, happy accidents . . . but in them we find a feature common to precognitive dreams: a vision occurring only in the mind is later reflected in the public world. But why does science call one theorizing and the other fantasy?

Material science believes that no connection exists between mind and matter, and surely none between night dreams and the public world. If the world is a dream, however, then we necessarily share the same mind because it is a world common to all of us. At night the individual mind may more easily share in the collective mind of which it is fundamentally a part.[41]

Night dreams say something about our world. During the night we project an external world that makes us believe it has an independent origin; we play a game on ourselves. What makes us believe similar events do not take place during the day? Our dreaming mind at night stands in the same relation to a night dream as our awake mind stands to the public world. Is not the difference between our night dreams and the daily world only one of degree? In the morning after a bad dream, we wake to realize we were only dreaming; the nightmare never happened. In a new morning, we may awaken and realize the greater dream stands before us.

Hallucinations

Hallucinations show the power of an individual mind. During a hallucination we compare a reality indisputably caused by our own mind with a reality we believe exists apart from our mind. In a hallucination the mind of one person somehow fabricates an image mistaken for the world at large.

The German writer Johann Wolfgang von Goethe, then twenty-four years old and having just visited his lady friend in another town, reports that on the way home one day,

> One of the strangest experiences befell me, not with the eyes of the body, but with the eyes of the spirit, I saw myself on horseback coming toward me on the same path dressed in a suit such as I had never worn, pale-gray with some gold. As soon as I had shaken myself out of this reverie the form vanished. It is strange, however, that I found myself returning on the same path eight years afterward to visit Fredericka once more and that I then wore the suit I had dreamt, and this not by design but by chance.[42]

Several features of Goethe's vision stand out. The figure that Goethe encountered occupied three-dimensional space in the same sense as normal objects; though we cannot compare his vision with reality, we know that the hallucination seemed real enough to fool Goethe. He further sensed that the vision had its source in "spirit," not the eye's retina, as if his inner self projected the external image. Indeed, as the authors of *Phantasms of the Living* report, some hallucinations cause percipients to "rub their eyes"[43] in the hope of making the image disappear, though usually to no avail.[44]

The author Aldous Huxley, who had the ability to hallucinate during deep trance states, once produced a vision of his wife so lifelike that he was seen conversing with his imagined mate.[45] In *Phantasms of the Living*, we learn of similar strange accounts of painters who "after carefully studying a sitter's appearance, could project it visibly into space, and paint the portrait not from the original but from the phantom." One painter took such an interest in his imagined subject that "he requested anyone who took up a position in front of it to move."[46] A common approach to dealing with hallucinations is to conclude that everyone who has ever had one is out of their mind. But that strategy hardly solves the problem. The question is how the mind of one person, even in a state of insanity, is able to project a world mistaken for the world at large.

Hallucinations are known to occur during states of psychological turbulence, including insanity. *Scientific American*, for example, reports that schizophrenia caused one woman to see dinosaurs in the street and live animals in her refrigerator.[47] In a famous case concerning the effect of severe sensory deprivation on the mind, workers trapped in a mine cave-in for fourteen days reported seeing the pope five thousand times, doors to both death and paradise, and other visions.[48] Ingesting hallucinogenic plants, such as peyote, has long been known to blur the distinction between dreams and reality.[49]

In the book *Hallucinations*, Oliver Sacks recounts numerous instances of powerful hallucinations experienced under a wide variety of illnesses and mental states. He recounts everything from simple hallucinations of geometric shapes and glowing, pulsating orbs, to lifelike figures acting out scenes, pigeons flying through the air, eighteenth-century garden landscapes, spiders, crocodiles, and a romantic dalliance between a woman and a phantom nighttime suitor. The hallucinations can occur with eyes open, in blindness, in people with migraines or Parkinson's disease, while entering sleep or awakening, and under other conditions. But what should strike us most deeply about hallucinations is that the false reality is projected by something inside of us out into space and into a form that is "compellingly three-dimensional."[50]

A well-known example of a hallucination is a thirsting man in the desert visualizing a mirage of cool spring water off in the distance. The mirage appears real to the perceiver. It fits neatly into the rest of the vision; the spring is as real as any other portion of the natural scenery. It seems as if the same source projects the mirage and the natural scenery. The thirsting man stalks the mirage because it seems so real.

Material scientists perhaps would rather not be put to the trouble of explaining hallucinations.[51] No material scientist believes that the mind creates the public world or any part of it. Rather, these scientists, as we will see in more detail in part 3 of this book, believe that impersonal, mindless forces created the physical universe and all life-forms, including the human brain. Put differently, these scientists believe that the evolution of the universe came toward the human mind, not from the mind. The human brain and starry sky stand as isolated parts of nature's scenery, with scientists believing that no message from the brain can ever cross the distance to a natural object.

For those who doubt that the world is a dream, I suggest dwelling on the reality of hallucinations. How can the mind duplicate physical reality?

When material scientists attempt to explain how hallucinations are possible, they confront a two-tiered puzzle. First, they must explain how the mindless processes of Darwinian evolution created the intelligence of the human brain. Then they must explain how this piece of gray matter *uses the same imagery as nature to re-create a part of physical reality.* The Real Dream avoids these puzzles: the brain and nature are both dream images originating in the mind. The private hallucination is a product of an individual mind; the public world results from the universal mind.

In the naïve realist picture, the world exists as it appears: rock solid and unalterable. Unusual events remain a mystery to naïve realists. These events, particularly those showing a connection between mind and matter, disrupt its foundation. Internal thoughts, emotions, and the human spirit have no effect on the naïve realist world. Human experience shows, however, that the world does not always function as a machine operating solely on its own power. It is not a picture we watch on a movie screen; rather, we are the scriptwriter and actor in this drama.

Synchronicity

Present a material scientist the problem of explaining how the mind re-creates a part of nature's scenery in a hallucination, and he discusses the complexities of the human brain. He knows hallucinations are possible. But ask the scientist how two minds communicate without speaking, or come to share in the same dream or hallucination, and he will measure you for a straitjacket. Material scientists have no place in their theories for telepathy because in their worldview the minds of two people cannot talk to each other. Events such as the following, recounted in *Phantasms of the Living*, cannot occur in material science's world:

> Colonel Lyttleton Annesley . . . was staying in my house some time ago, and one afternoon, having nothing to do, we wandered into a large unoccupied room. . . . Colonel A. was at one end of this long room reading, to the best of my recollection, while I opened a box, long forgotten, to see what it contained. I took out a number of papers and old music, which I was turning over in my hand, when I came across a song in which I, years before, had been accustomed to take a part, "Dal tuo stellato soglio," out of "Mose in Egitto," if I remember right. As I looked at this old song, Colonel A., who had been paying no attention whatever to my proceedings, began to hum, "Dal tuo stellato soglio." In much astonishment I asked him why he was singing that particular air. He did not know. He did not remember to have sung it before; indeed I have not ever heard Colonel A. sing. . . . I told him that I was holding the very song in my hand. He was as much astonished as I had been, and had no knowledge that I had any music in my hand

at all. I had not spoken to him, nor had I hummed the air, or given him any sign that I was looking over music. The incident is curious, for it is outside all explanation on the theory of coincidence.[52]

Minds are not supposed to talk to each other, according to material science, yet they do. Often the shared thought is as simple as the song on our mind, where to eat dinner, or what to buy a friend for a birthday. We all have them but pay little attention. For example, in reading the book *His Excellency* by Joseph Ellis I came across the word "ukase," which I had never heard or read. The next day, in taking the elevator to work, I noticed a "word of the day feature" on the elevator information screen: the word of the day was "ukase," a Russian word meaning a government directive.

Material science has no place in its worldview for these events. Because it detaches mind from matter, it must treat coincidences between two events, such as Colonel Annesley humming the song his friend was reading, as statistically independent, like two separately spun number wheels. This approach makes coincidences mathematically possible, but it hardly accounts for those occasions when coincidences pile on top of each other, and the related events seem to flow from one script. In these unique moments we find scientific instruments incapable of drawing a full picture of the world we experience.

In 1952 psychologist Carl Jung published a paper titled "Synchronicity" that analyzed these oddities of life and attributed them to the workings of an unconscious mind. One story in his paper is taken from a collection by Camille Flammarion and concerns a certain M. Deschamps who, when a young boy in Orleans, was given a piece of plum pudding by M. de Fortgibu. While in a Paris restaurant ten years later M. Deschamps saw plum pudding on the menu and ordered it. Unfortunately, the last plum pudding had already been ordered by none other than M. de Fortgibu, who happened to be in the same restaurant. A good many years later, our hero, M. Deschamps, was invited to share in a plum pudding as a rare treat. As he was eating it, he commented that the only touch missing was the presence of M. de Fortgibu. Just at that moment the door opened and an elderly gentleman walked in; it was none other than M. de Fortigbu. He had apparently gotten the wrong address and mistakenly walked in on the party.[53]

Another story Mr. Jung relates is from a collection compiled by Wilhelm von Scholz concerning odd lost-and-found cases. In this story, a mother took a picture of her son in Germany's Black Forest. She then brought the film to Strasburg to be developed, but shortly thereafter World War I began and she was unable to pick up the developed photographs. Two years later the mother, intending to photograph her daughter, purchased film in Frankfurt. But she found the film oddly double-exposed: underneath the new film was the picture she took of her son in 1914.[54]

In the eyes of the material scientist, these intriguing coincidences are freakish events of no importance in their mechanical world; in a dream world they are the rule, not the exception. They show the dream of God unfolding with meaning, intrigue, and even humor. In an evolving dream world, for events to seem connected and reveal meaning should not appear unusual. During special moments we sense an overriding purpose to life, some connecting theme holding us together, a script written in our souls that we follow without knowing why. On these occasions, life shows it has a hidden story line, an unfolding drama of its own.

But in highlighting these minor coincidences of life, we may tend to overlook coincidences of a much grander variety. May not it seem coincidental, for instance, that we today rest on a planet balanced perfectly in the midst of a universe of stars, the lucky beneficiaries of natural forces all nicely programmed to make life possible and the future predictable? Is it not coincidental the way earth's life-forms all seem adapted to their environments, like glove in hand? Can male and female imagine better mates? We can thus raise the stakes when analyzing life's coincidences. Plum puddings, lost rings, and repeating themes play a small part in this story. Looking out at the world we may ask: Are we just coincidentally synchronized with the universe, or has indeed the world evolved as one dream?

Chapter Six

MIND OVER EXTERNAL WORLD

With our thoughts we create the world.
—The Dhammapada

IF THERE IS NO CONNECTION between mind and matter, then the mind alone should have no influence upon the external world. We may concentrate with all our might or pray from the bottom of our hearts, the material scientists hold, but these feelings will never touch the world. Many common events, however, put this viewpoint into question.

Positive Thinking

When we approach a task with confidence, whether walking up to a three-foot putt or going on a job interview, we attempt to influence bodily actions by thinking positively. We try to be decisive, focused, and self-assured; we concentrate on the task at hand and get psyched. Often, however, we go further. Testing the limits of confidence, we think positively not only about the actions of our own body but also about the operation of the world external to our bodies. In sports, we may seek to "will" the ball into the hole or visualize it falling through the net. Often we may enlist the help of a friendly crowd to join in, as golfer Johnny Miller recounted when he needed a putt on the last hole to stay in tournament contention: "On that birdie I made at 18, something told me I had to make that putt. I told everybody, 'I'll hit the putt, you have to make it go in.' I got everybody with positive vibes, and they willed it in. It lipped in."[55] Of course, Miller may have spoken with tongue in cheek, but why not test whether "positive vibes" can make things go our way? Such is the nature of scientific experimentation in the Real Dream.

Positive thinking shows the mind taking command of itself and stepping up to the challenge of controlling its own destiny. In material science, self-confidence is a good quality but little understood. In the Real Dream, self-confidence is the method that a dreamer uses to take command of one's own dream. The confident person approaches a task with self-understanding and positive thoughts, as if she knows destiny is in her hands.

Sports competition provides ample illustrations of the power of positive thinking. We regularly read about athletes entering the "zone," a place where concentration and confidence reach such a height that the player exerts inordinate control over his body and the target. We read about basketball players who, for a short time, "can't miss," or the long jumper who leaps an unheard-of distance, but then never does it again.

In these moments, the mind focuses on the target and nothing else exists in the world but the ball and the hoop; here, it may be said, the player taps the power of the mind and enters the dream phase where events occur according to aspiration and desire, and are not subject to normal physical limitations. After scoring fifty-six points in a basketball game, Michael Jordan explained the feeling:

> I was in a zone, and it's hard to judge when you're in a zone.
> . . . I was hitting everything. Everything seemed in rhythm,
> there was no hesitance at all. I always knew what I was going
> to do, and I utilized it all. . . . It's just a great feeling. You see
> the basket very well, and you don't see anything else. I don't
> even know how to describe it.[56]

Visualizing a successful outcome, playing the game beforehand in our mind, and willing positive results are all part of sports competition. The Real Dream explains the periodic success of these methods; material scientists say that we are wasting our time. To these scientists, the athlete's zone is but another metaphor for a yet-to-be-discovered chemical reaction.

Only a short step separates a successful person's confidence or an athlete's zone from a form of extrasensory perception known as *psychokinesis* or *mind over matter*. In approaching the problem of whether mind alone can affect physical objects we should note that we have the strongest evidence for the most difficult part of the puzzle: we know that in dreams and hallucinations the mind conjures up a three-dimensional world often mistaken for the world at large. A mind that paints the picture should also, under the right conditions, be capable of altering it.

Scientist and author Dean Radin and others have taken the next step and conducted experiments testing the effect of a hypothetical field consciousness or group mind upon physical events. The question is whether focused attention by a group of people can alter an otherwise random sequence of events. The instrument Radin uses to test this ability is the Random Number Generator, which, as the name suggests, is a machine programmed to produce numbers randomly, or with zero order. One feature of consciousness that he observes from a review of Western and Eastern philosophies is that consciousness "injects order into systems in proportion to the 'strength' of the consciousness present." Radin writes, "When a group is actively focused on a common object, the 'group mind' momentarily has the 'power to organize.'"[57]

He ran the experiment during such high-interest events as the Academy Awards, the O. J. Simpson verdict, and the Super Bowl. The experiments show that during high-interest moments, when the attention of large masses of people was concentrated on one event, the randomness of the numbers generated measurably decreased, as if the RNG was detecting the focusing of a unified consciousness. Not every experiment works, but Radin reports that chief among the features that distinguish a successful experiment from an unsuccessful one is where the participants experience an "unusually warm or close feeling of togetherness, where emotional willpower is directed toward a common goal rather than personal achievement."[58] Why should this focused attention alter the operation of a random number generator?

Mind over Body

In the field of medicine, we find the best example of how material science controls the way we think. Our bodies appear to exist apart from the mind, so we assume they really do. Once we reach this conclusion, we come to believe that the mind cannot directly affect the body because they are two separate substances existing on different planes of reality. No physical connection is believed to exist between either the mind and nature, or the mind and body. To French philosopher René Descartes, the modern-day source of the concept that the mind and body are distinct entities, nothing was more certain than his own existence as a thinking being; external bodies, including his own, existed on some different level.[59]

Material science approaches a sick body as if it existed independently of the mind. When something goes wrong in the body, when it becomes ill or begins to age, material science treats the body with methods that work from the outside in, from the skin inward to the mind. We spread cream on wrinkled skin, take chemical pills to kill bacteria and viruses, and cut the body open to work on broken and unwanted parts. Each of these healing methods is premised on the view that the human body is a physical entity with an existence external to the mind. Medical science believes that because the illness originates in bodily parts, those parts must be rearranged or treated to eliminate the disease.[60] As medical doctor Jerome Frank writes, "We fondly expect someday fully to comprehend the human being as a complex machine controlled by a computer in the skull. Disease will then be merely a derangement of the machine's functioning produced by noxious environmental agents in interaction with inborn or acquired vulnerabilities or errors of metabolism."[61] If a body is ill, a part must be broken or worn down, just like a used car. Heart valves must be replaced, blood vessels unclogged, tumors removed, hair transplanted, noses reshaped, wrinkles smoothed.

But here an observation is in order. When we feel sick or get a disease, not only do we experience physical symptoms in our body (sneezing, coughing, high temperature, rashes, swelling, redness, etc.), but we also do not *feel* well. Our thoughts are negative, our emotions depressed, our will weakened. No one in medical science would dispute the notion that bodily illnesses negatively affect the mind.

Material science, as we have seen, believes that our thoughts, wills, and emotions have no effect on the external world, and the body is certainly part of the external world. Under the tenets of material science, the mind cannot affect the body any more than willpower can alter the course of a jump shot. To material science, the external world is supposed to be disconnected from mind. The human body appears on the screen of an arcade game, and only the knobs marked "physical cures" alter the picture; those knobs marked "spiritual cures" we twist in vain. They are there only to humor us.

Here then we find an inconsistency. Material science says that mind cannot affect matter, that mind alone cannot heal a withered hand. How then does the diseased hand affect the mind? Why do bodily diseases make us feel bad? Material science seems to have built a one-way street: physical illnesses negatively affect the mind, but the mind can have no beneficial effect on the body.

Placebo Effect

Material science theory states that a healthy mind cannot heal the body, but its own medical findings reveal the opposite: The mind plays a significant role in how well a healing method works. Perhaps the best example is the "powerful placebo."[62] Scientific treatments have a specific effect on the body. They include drugs that produce a generally predictable response in the body (pharmacological drugs) and modern surgical techniques that rearrange, remove, or replace bodily parts.[63] Consistent with the material science viewpoint that the body is a molecular machine, pharmacological drugs are intended to remedy a specific molecular derangement, in the same way that oil fixes squeaky metal joints in a car door.

Placebos, in contrast, are make-believe or sham medical treatments with no scientific basis.[64] In pill form,[65] they have no active ingredient; although they may have the appearance of a pharmacological drug, they are usually nothing more than milk sugar.[66]

If it were only possible to heal the body by treating the body, then placebos—fake medicine—would never work. By definition, they contain no active ingredient; taking milk sugar to cure arthritis should be like swinging at a baseball without a bat. Milk sugar has no scientifically proven effect on tumors, herpes, asthma, or other bodily ailments.

Placebos, however, have been found not only to heal the body but also, at times, to work nearly as effectively as materialistic treatments.[67] One series of studies covering more than one thousand patients showed that 35 percent reported significant relief from a variety of ailments after treatment with a placebo.[68] In another study of over fourteen thousand patients with illnesses from headaches to multiple sclerosis, 40 percent reported relief from placebo treatment.[69] In a study on the analgesic (pain-killing) effect of placebos, it was found they were over 50 percent as effective in reducing pain as the potent drugs morphine, codeine, and Darvon, among others.[70]

Under the right conditions, placebos and the materialistic drug can reverse their expected effects. Two regular users of the hallucinogenic drug LSD were given placebos when they thought they were getting LSD; they experienced hallucinations anyway. They then were actually given LSD but told they were given a placebo; they experienced no hallucinations.[71]

Researchers have studied placebos under double-blind test conditions which reveal the powerful effect that expectation and belief have on the healing process. In these instances, doctor and patient both believe the drug is real and not a placebo. The researchers selected a number of treatments that the medical community at one time believed effective, but that were later found no more effective than placebos. In other words, a treatment once accepted as scientifically legitimate was later found to be, in effect, a "sham."[72] As the researchers point out, these circumstances furnish conditions where the "beliefs and expectancies of both doctors and patients were maximized."[73] At the time doctors administered the treatment, not only did the patient and doctor believe in the treatment, but so did the medical community at large.

In compiling the results based on five different medical treatments, the researchers found that 70 percent of almost seven thousand patients treated reported positive results. Or, put another way, a sham treatment improved the bodily health of almost three in four patients treated.[74] The researchers concluded that under actual clinical conditions, where both the patient and doctor have some faith that the treatment will work, belief, expectation, enthusiasm, and other nonscientific effects "exert considerably more influence than commonly believed and reported in many controlled research studies."[75]

In what is probably the most reported placebo case, doctors treated a patient suffering from a long-term asthma condition with a new wonder drug. The new drug seemed to work: when it was used the condition subsided, and when it was discontinued, the condition returned. The patient's doctor, desiring to test the placebo effect, then substituted a placebo without telling the patient; as expected, the condition returned. Having shown that the new drug worked and running short of supply, the doctor asked the pharmaceutical company for a new shipment. The company informed him that because of the positive response it had received from the drug, the company had never in fact sent it; the first shipment was a placebo.[76] But a problem persists in material science circles: "The placebo effect is a phenomenon still in search of a model or theory."[77]

Medical science's study of the placebo effect is only the most modern example of "how strong belief heals."[78] Only in the last century has medical science concluded that the body consists of a complex arrangement of molecules and that diseases can be viewed as derangements in the body's molecular makeup. If modern science is correct—that only molecular-based cures have scientific validity—then, as Arthur Shapiro notes, "Whatever beneficial effects accrued to man's first medication could only have been due to the placebo effect."[79] Western medical science believes it alone understands the body, and further believes it has a monopoly on the means to heal a sick body. Consequently, if some other healing method works, it must be as a result of the mysterious placebo.

In the material science worldview, a patient who confronts a disease without a medically approved cure stands naked: the patient's thoughts, beliefs, and willpower are left alone to battle the illness. But these internal states (the mind) are not supposed to have a positive effect on the body. The placebo effect shows, however, that these internal states can cure physical ailments.

Over time we should find that our reliance on materialistic cures, such as chemicals, surgery, and radiation, will be greatly lessened as the medical community more fully appreciates the power of the placebo. But then, as we will see in later parts of this book, we will need to take the next step and realize that, in the end, it "takes a village" to cure any human problem, including disease. Our modern, materialistic worldview not only separates our minds from our bodies, but separates us from each other and weakens the power of the united mind to improve the world.

The Power of Belief

In material science's mind-set, the body is a machine composed of genes that control a person's evolution[80] and health. As modern medicine demonstrates a connection between the *belief* in a cure and its effectiveness, so modern biology is beginning to demonstrate that both the environment and a person's belief system affect bodily genes. Our beliefs, not genes, determine who we are and what we will become.

In his book *The Biology of Belief*, Bruce Lipton writes about his transformation from a card-carrying materialist, conditioned in the body-as-machine paradigm, to a holistic thinker, unable to ignore medical findings that "cell life is controlled by the physical and energetic environment and not by the genes." Genes, he says, are "simply molecular blueprints used in the construction of cells, tissues and organs. The environment serves as a contractor who reads and engages these genetic blueprints and is ultimately responsible for the character of a cell's life."[81]

Despite mounting evidence that the physical body is not a self-operating machine, material science continues to ignore its own medical findings and design a continuing assortment of medical treatments and drugs treating the body as a machine. But if our beliefs determine who we are, then is our belief that we are machines taking us down a doomed road that we have unwittingly paved ourselves? We are, in fact, spirits operating under the delusion that we are machines, a misguided belief that we need to overcome.

The Human Genome

Next we come to the Human Genome Project, the successful mapping of the genes making up the instructions for the physical body. One of the dreams of the Human Genome Project was to associate human characteristics with individual genes. If the body is a machine, like an automobile, then we would expect the parts of the body-machine to correlate to features of a human being, from physical features to personality, intelligence, emotions, and consciousness itself. Keeping with the machine model, one would expect that the more advanced the organism, the greater the number of genes, in much the same way that an Apple MacBook is far more intricately designed than an abacus.

But the Human Genome Project produced the opposite result. Needing about one hundred thousand genes to account for the human body, scientists uncovered only twenty-three thousand, which happens to be less than rice (thirty-eight thousand genes), sea urchins (twenty-six thousand), and little more than a fruit fly (seventeen thousand).[82] Being human is obviously more than the number of one's genes.

Another goal of the Human Genome Project was to associate variations in DNA sequences with diseases. If those with the same disease have the same genetic disorder, then modern drugs or medical treatments may be devised to repair the genetic error and thus cure the disease—if not now, then perhaps in future generations.[83]

If the body is a machine, then it would make sense that once physical illnesses are linked to common variations in DNA sequences, the repair of these genetic errors would cure the disease. But data from the Human Genome Project does not support this hypothesis either. As Stephen Hall reports in *Scientific American*, many leading geneticists are abandoning the common variant/common disease hypothesis. Hall quotes Walter Bodmer, one of the pioneers of the project, as saying, "The vast majority of [common] variants have shed no light on the biology of disease."[84]

In other words, the simple picture—that because genes are the fundamental parts to the machine-body, diseases should be reflected in distorted DNA strands—is not holding up. Illnesses do not translate into the language of the body, but seem to have a deeper, more complex origin.

Perhaps the source of the disease results from the mind's misalignment with its true dream-nature, rather than from a misalignment of machine parts. Are we prepared yet to take a broader view of the source of human illnesses?

To the Bottom of the Problem

So now we must make a choice. We can continue minding our own business and go on reading newspaper accounts of material science's ongoing efforts to explain all natural phenomena—from the placebo effect to the origin of life—as the random interplay of tiny particles. We can sit and tap our fingers on the table, waiting patiently for the day when scientists will have diagrammed all the working parts to their great machine-world and will manipulate them to our benefit, when perhaps the true wonder drugs will appear on the shelf of the corner store: Fountain of Youth power shots, IQ-boosting head sprays, cancer-inhibiting lotions, and perhaps even a pill to make us better people.[85] Yes, we can choose to wait.

Or we can take a different approach. We can leave open the possibility that material science may be looking at this whole picture in the wrong way. Perhaps the assumption of an independent world has served its purpose and is starting to cause more problems than it is worth. Perhaps we do not need it anymore to explain the world. The time may be here to remove the mold from its setting and let our creation stand up on its own. We can continue questioning the assumption of material science and see where this new approach leads. After all, we have nothing to lose.

In the next stage of questioning, we try to get to the bottom of the problem, which means entering the field of philosophy. The discussion on philosophy shows that despite the efforts of some of history's greatest thinkers, the relationship between mind and matter remains a subject of deep controversy. The next part of this book argues that because philosophy failed to explain the external world (or matter) as a product of mind, material science came to build a body of knowledge upon naïve realism. Rather than questioning how a world beyond the mind is possible, these scientists simply take what they see at face value. To them, the world appears to exist external to our mind, and therefore it does. We shall seek to uncover why philosophy failed to solve the problem and how material science came to make its great assumption. Then, in part 3, we begin the attack on material science's leading theories.

Here the reader is forewarned: The material science worldview is indeed deeply ingrained in our minds. Accordingly, to uproot this opinion, we need to dig down into the ideas that ground our current worldview. But if we want to achieve our goal, we must start at the bottom and work our way up. Let's begin.

PART 2

The Failed Hypothesis of a Mind-Independent World

Chapter Seven

THE ORIGIN OF THE DEBATE

But we're never gonna survive, unless . . . We get a little crazy.
—Seal

Your theory is crazy, but it's not crazy enough to be true.
—Niels Bohr

WHAT CAME FIRST, mind or matter? The big bang or the Mind of God? The question of whether the world is, at its most fundamental level, mind or matter is one of the long-standing—and still unresolved—questions of philosophy, and of humankind generally.

Whether the world began in the mind or in a big bang is the most fundamental question we are capable of asking. But for discussions on this topic, one must consult obscure philosophy books. Not only does it seem crazy to doubt the existence of an external physical world, but most of us are too busy living in the world to wonder how it got here. Whether the mind's ideas and images represent something actually existing outside the mind appears academic, if not irrelevant.

Reflecting this attitude, materialists do not often bother with philosophical arguments. Instead, they take what they see at face value and go about explaining the world. The world appears to consist of big massy particles (rocks, plants, dirt, etc.) that in turn are composed of smaller massy particles. When scientists pulverize a rock it breaks into small pieces; carrying this approach to its logical conclusion, material scientists theorize that if they cause particles to collide with tremendous energy, they should wind up with the most fundamental parts of reality, and therefore understand it.

Put differently, the staggering intellectual fortress that is modern science rests upon the most naïve of notions: material scientists take for granted a universe filled with freestanding matter and energy without considering whether such a place can possibly exist as they imagine it. *In other words, modern scientists have accepted materialism without even thinking whether it is—or can be—true.*

Going forward, we will see that material scientists have hardly established that matter came first. Rather, they have adopted this viewpoint because they think it is a necessary assumption for carrying out the work of science. The only competing worldviews are those advanced by religion, where the search for truth ends at foundational religious texts, whether the Rg Veda, the Upanishads, the Torah, the New Testament, or the Qur'an. These texts may—and in fact do—contain truth, but because they are viewed as the products of God, their findings are considered beyond question or criticism, contrary to the scientific method.

"Science," as noted earlier, has thus become synonymous with "material science." Every research program that assumes the secret to life is waiting to be found deep within the atom or far out in space, instead of deeply inside of us, is based upon the truth of the material science worldview. Billions of dollars of government money and university grants fund research programs advancing the doctrines of material science; these teachings—from the big bang to dark matter to Darwinian evolution—fill university textbooks and curriculum as if there is no other conceivable way to think logically about the world. The Large Hadron Collider, the Hubble space telescope, the Wilkinson Microwave Anisotropy Probe, the International Space Station, and a host of other multibillion-dollar machines are built on the assumption that the material science worldview is correct, that matter came before mind, and that by exploring the outer limits of the material world we will finally happen upon ultimate truth: the Theory of Everything.

Material scientists do not claim victory, however, because they have proven the truth of the great assumption. Rather, they believe that the assumption must be true because secondary theories—such as Newton's laws of motion, Einstein's theories of special and general relativity, quantum theory, and the laws of chemistry—work in practice. But this leaves open two critical questions: First, *why* do the theories work? Second, is there another way to explain the same phenomena without making the great assumption of material science?

The dominance of material science began with Isaac Newton (1642–1727) and Galileo (1564–1642), who devised accurate theories about the workings of an assumed material world. Newton assumed that an independent world of matter exists. His laws of motion accurately predict the movement of this matter out in the world. Therefore, matter external to the mind must exist.

But as we will see in part 4, this viewpoint is quite ironic; at the same time the scientific establishment proceeds as if Newton's classical independent world really exists, its leading theory of the physical world—quantum mechanics—compels the conclusion that Newton was wrong and no such mind-independent world is actually out there. Rather, the majority of quantum theorists, including many of the theory's founders, believe that an inextricable link between mind and matter exists.

Furthermore, even leaving aside the devastating impact of quantum theory upon Newton's classical worldview, simply because a theory predicts that the external world follows ordered movements does not mean that the material world exists on its own power.[86] Rather, because this supposed external world of mindless stuff does in fact follow mathematical patterns, numerous uncomfortable questions arise for material science; for example, how did mindless particles become infused with the laws of physics? How can the human mind be so accurate in predicting the movements of a completely independent world?

In fact, the more mathematically ordered the physical world, the *lower* the odds that the material science worldview is correct. Its theories operate to disprove the material science worldview. By definition, material science resorts to no mind or intelligence to order its world. Without an intelligent organizing force, material science must explain how dead and dumb particles managed to arrange themselves into constant mathematical patterns on their own power. This is no simple task.

The *model* of material science, an assumed independent world that material scientists use to conduct their experiments, actually proves the truth of the Real Dream: only a world answering to the commands of a mind can fall into the mathematical patterns we see throughout the world. "Eureka" moments, it turns out, result from the scientific mind finding a harmony first put into place by the united mind of God.

Only in the Real Dream do we find a way for the physical three-dimensional world—the leaves on trees, endlessly patterned snowflakes, orbiting planets, spiral galaxies, the genetic code, and so on—to have a direct connection to a possible organizing force: specifically, our own mind, the only intelligent power in the cosmos of which we have direct knowledge.

Chapter Eight

THE SOURCE OF THE BELIEF IN
AN INDEPENDENT WORLD

Life is one great dream of a single dreamer in
which all the dream characters dream too.
—Joseph Campbell

MATERIAL SCIENCE'S CURRENT STRANGLEHOLD on our worldview results
not from the logic of materialism but because no one has come up with
anything better.

In part 3 of this book, we compare material science's explanations
for the world's existence with those that follow from the Real Dream.
In the next three chapters, however, we first need to take a detour and
find the source of our belief in an independent, self-operating, external
world—and a distinction here is important. Of course, an external world
exists. The question is whether the external world we experience exists
independently of the mind and operates beyond its control.

The question of how we came to believe in a mind-independent
world begins with our perception of the world. Most of us take the external world for granted. We do not question how such a world is possible,
or whether what we perceive outside of us can possibly exist in the form
in which it appears. We see a tree, a house, the moon, the stars. They
appear to exist outside of us. Therefore, they do. That is all we need to
know. After all, we are living in this world, on this stage, playing our

parts; we do not typically question how it is possible for this external world to exist as it appears, or ask about the source of this appearance. We are too busy living and surviving to wonder how or why we are here.

In naïve realism, we assume that our perception of an external object exactly corresponds to something independent of the mind. Put another way, we assume that our senses give us accurate information about ultimate reality. This thought is actually simple: When we look at a rose, for example, we naturally attribute all its qualities—color, shape, texture, size, motion, and fragrance—to something existing external to the mind. The sum total of an object's qualities make up what we experience as the object.

But it's not as simple as that. Some of history's greatest thinkers have examined the source of the belief in a mind-independent world, and have shown the problem admits of no straightforward solution. Because the deep, philosophical inquiry into the origin of the belief in an external world led to no clear-cut solution, the simplistic approach still carries the day: modern science continues to adopt a naïve realist explanation for perception of the external world. Material scientists assume the external material world as given, without concerning themselves with the knotty problem of how it got there.

The Apple Tree

Imagine that nothing exists in the universe except you and an apple tree. Question: Does the apple tree exist outside of you? Answer: Of course it does; in order to have the experience of perception there must be space and distance between you and the tree. Next question: Does the tree, with all of its qualities, exist outside of your mind? This question is different.

We know that in night dreams, hallucinations, and mirages, our own mind conjures up a three-dimensional image of something that exists external to the mind. Therefore, the tree could also be a mind-projected reality. The apple tree could be part of the mind—not an independent, external object that impresses itself upon the mind through the use of the bodily senses and the nervous system.

We can also approach the question by breaking down what we call the perception of the apple tree into its component parts, or qualities.

With our eyes we perceive one tree shape and the colors of green and brown, along with the redness of the apples; with our hands we can feel the roughness of the tree bark; we taste and smell the freshness of a just-picked apple; and we hear the wind rustling through the branches.

Now the question may be asked: Which of these qualities actually exist in the tree, and which qualities does the mind contribute to the perception of the tree? Philosophers in the seventeenth and eighteenth centuries confronted this question and came to a remarkable conclusion: The existence of an independent, material world is a matter of belief or of habit, not of experience or reason. In other words, we believe in an external world more because we deeply want one, not because we can ever prove it exists outside of the mind's dreaming power.

John Locke's Blank Tablet

John Locke (1632–1704) considered the question and concluded that some qualities of an external object exist out in the world, and others form in the mind. Primary qualities—solidity (or hardness), extension (three dimensions), figure (shape), number (how many), and motion (moving or stationary)—are actually part of an object external to the mind.[87] Secondary qualities, in contrast, are not actually part of external objects but are formed in the mind from powers in the external object.[88] These secondary qualities are color, sound, taste, and smell.

Locke's conceptual division of qualities into two categories, primary and secondary, and his description of perception correspond to how modern science believes that perception occurs.[89] Under the worldview of material science, the brain receives perceptions of the external world through our senses. Science tells us, for example, that light shines on a tree and reflects its image into our eyes, which the nervous system sends to our brain and converts into a picture of a tree. Taste, scientists say, is caused by chemicals in food that trigger sensations in our tongues that again interact with nerves and send taste messages to our brain; sound emits waves that the brain hears as music. In each instance, the same pattern emerges: science assumes that something outside of our minds causes the experience of an external world.

Locke leaves us with two key observations about how the mind gains knowledge. First, we can only have ideas of external objects; second, all knowledge derives in the first instance from sense experience.[90] But a serious problem arises at this point.

The body is outside of the mind in the same sense as other physical objects, such as the apple tree, are also outside the mind; therefore, under Locke's reasoning, everything we say about the natural world is also true about the body. Our perception of the body is received in the mind. In empiricism, one idea (the body) receives sense impressions from another idea (e.g., trees, air temperature, rain).

But Locke does not divide the body into primary and secondary qualities. Instead, like a true empiricist, he puts his total faith in the bodily senses, as if the body is an independent, self-contained sensing device—like a deep-sea submarine—designed to record information about the external world. He assumes that the body, and all five senses, exist independently of the mind exactly as they appear. Once he assumes that the body exists independently of the mind, a natural step is to conclude, as material scientists do generally, that the rest of the external world also exists outside the mind. Having put his faith in the bodily senses, Locke is already out into an assumed external world; he already assumes that the mind can know something other than its ideas (his body), contrary to one of his central premises.[91] In other words, empiricism, the bedrock theory of knowledge for science, is internally inconsistent as it places the body and the world external to the body on two separate levels of reality. It assumes the body exists exactly as it appears (naïve realism) but then uses the bodily senses to determine what qualities of an external object are, in fact, outside of the mind. This naïve form of empiricism, therefore, will never succeed as a theory of knowledge. Body and nature must be viewed on the same level.

When we recognize that the human body, just like the rest of the world, is known only through the mind, we can reach the conclusion that the body's purpose is to experience the world. That is why we dream: to lose ourselves in the dreamed world. With this realization, true knowledge can only lie internally, because only the mind can be the source for the dream.

Bishop Berkeley Finds the Answer

Bishop George Berkeley (1685–1753) quickly exposed Locke's error of dividing the features (qualities) of external objects into two groups, one subjective and the other objective. Berkeley pointed out that what Locke called primary and secondary qualities are all qualities of one thing. The taste of an apple, for example, is inherent in its substance and figure; the color red is wrapped around one motionless apple.[92] Berkeley refutes Locke's separation of secondary and primary qualities through several arguments, but they reduce to one point: If the mind can only know its ideas, then we can have only ideas about the world; we can never know something existing outside of the mind. The belief that something exists independently of the mind is only that: a belief. We can never know something external to the mind because we are locked within the mind. When we reach outside with our hand to prove the firmness of our world, we are reaching out with a hand also perceived only in the mind; our hand is part of the dream.

Like Descartes, Berkeley observed that in dreams, madness, and similar states we have images of external objects in our mind, though no independent bodies exist. As Berkeley wrote, "If there were external bodies, it is impossible we should ever come to know it; and if there were not, we might have the very reasons to think there were that we have now."[93]

After having done away with the belief that external matter exists, Berkeley faced the issue of what causes the ideas of external things in our mind. Since the cause of these ideas cannot be a material substance, the cause must be nonphysical or spiritual. But this spiritual source, according to Berkeley, is not the human mind, because things that the senses perceive are not dependent upon a person's will.[94] Accordingly, Berkeley reasons that there must be "some other Will or Spirit that produces them," and this spirit is none other than God. As Berkeley states:

> All the choir of heaven and furniture of the earth, in a word, all those bodies which compose the mighty frame of the world, have not any subsistence without a mind; that their being is to be perceived or known; that consequently so long as they

are not actually perceived by me, or do not exist in my mind, or that of any other created spirit, they must either have no existence at all, or else subsist in the mind of some Eternal Spirit: it being perfectly unintelligible, and involving all the absurdity of abstraction, to attribute to any single part of them an existence independent of a spirit.[95]

In the eighteenth century, therefore, Berkeley glimpsed the truth: The universe is a dream in the one mind some call "God."

The Paradox of Idealism

Berkeley's philosophy, however, harbors a paradox. If all qualities making up the world exist in the mind, then don't each of us have a different world? In whose mind does the world ultimately originate?[96] The view that the entire world is in the mind of any one percipient is known as *solipsism* or *subjectivism*. Solipsism is the theory that the self can be aware of nothing but its own experience and internal states.[97] Subjectivism, as the term suggests, is the theory that all knowledge is subjective, and whether an external real world exists can never be known.[98]

Professor Mary Whiton Calkins articulates this line of criticism against Berkeley:

I unchallengeably know only myself and my experience. From this it follows . . . not merely . . . that alleged material things are really my ideas but also that God and my fellow-men are my ideas. In a word, the metaphysical universe narrows to myself and my own experiences. . . . I have no more right to infer the existence of other selves than to infer the existence of non-mental objects. Yet, on the other hand, the passivity of my perception, indeed all my involuntary experience, forces me to admit the existence of something other-than-myself. The idealist is thus [Berkeley's critics assert] involved in a hopeless contradiction. On the one hand he insists that he is certain of himself and his own experience. Yet, on the other

hand, because of his directly experienced passivity, he is forced
to admit the existence of something besides himself.[99]

Berkeley expressed the truth but the problems remain: If each of us
only knows our own mind, then how can we ever share the same world?
If the answer is that we all dwell in God's mind, then where is God?

As we have seen, the Real Dream worldview answers the question by
concluding that we share the same world not because one independent
world operates outside our mind, but because we share the same mind.
We all participate in the same dream. We are a river flowing along an
endless course. If we fold our dream back up and reverse time, we all
would be one. But our dream rushes headlong in the opposite direction:
our goal is to defeat the fear of being the only one. Finally, the paradox
of solipsism can be solved if an ultimate source of the dream—a god-
creator—exists. This may appear to be a strange statement anywhere but
in our own world, as most religions contain the idea of a father figure or
godhead. As modern science searches for the ultimate elementary particle
and a theory to unite the particles and forces of nature, so in the Real
Dream we look and wait—in concordance with many of the world's religions—to find the ultimate source of the dream.

At this point, we may note, the new science and the old religious
traditions converge, for the missing piece to the puzzle in the Real Dream
worldview is not the most fundamental particle but the ultimate source
to the dream: the God in the heaven of the Mind.

Hume and the World's Double Existence

David Hume (1711–1776) went still further, asking, How is it that
people insist on believing in the independent, continuous existence of
external objects even though "nothing is ever present to the mind but
perceptions"?[100] If the mind knows only its ideas, then why does everyone
so naturally believe that something exists beyond our mind and perceptions? Hume did not question the existence of independent bodies; he
took that fact for granted.[101] Instead he sought to find the source of the
belief in external, independent objects.[102]

Hume considered three possible sources for the belief in independent objects: the senses, reason, and the imagination. He concluded that the senses cannot cause the idea of an independent existence. Senses only produce perceptions, and no perception produces the idea of independent existence. The objects we see—trees, sky, grass—*are* the perceptions. These perceptions furnish no idea of independent substance but produce only the ideas of qualities in our mind. To believe that the senses give us the idea of a continued existence is a contradiction because such a belief suggests that the senses continue operating after they have stopped operating.[103] When we perceive a sunset we can attest to the splendid scene, but when we look away or close our eyes, the senses yield no perception of a sunset—just as a camera stops taking pictures when the shutter closes.

The senses only give us one perception of each object, such as a tree. The senses do not produce the idea of both the original tree and a copy that we see. "A single perception can never produce the idea of a double existence, but by some inference either of reason or imagination."[104]

Nor, according to Hume, can reason lead us to believe in independent bodies. When we apply reason to the idea of independent bodies, we meet the same barrier we just encountered: we know the world only through perceptions and cannot reason ourselves beyond them.[105] Reason does not compel the idea of an independent, continuous existence in the same way that two plus two equals four, or that "I think, therefore I am" is true each time we say it.

Having eliminated sense experience and reason as sources for the idea of independent existence, Hume is left with one remaining source: the imagination.[106] Because neither senses nor reason produce the idea that material bodies have a continued and distinct existence, Hume concludes the imagination alone "seduces" us into believing in the continued and independent existence of objects.[107]

But Hume realized that the belief in a continued, independent existence "has taken such deep root in the imagination, that 'tis impossible ever to eradicate it, nor will any strain'd metaphysical conviction of the dependence of our perceptions be sufficient for that purpose."[108] On this issue, people ignore the philosopher and trust their senses. Despite the uncontested view that the mind only has perceptions, humankind continues to adopt what Hume calls the "vulgar" approach: the independent existence of external objects is simply taken for granted.[109]

In the Real Dream, belief in an independent world is deeply rooted because we are embedded in the desire for an external world; an external world is the paramount desire of the mind. The constancy and coherence of the external world are not properties of independent things, but rather core demands of the united mind. We do not just imagine a world; we are imagination. We, in a word, are in the midst of a dream, happily immersed in the belief that we and nature exist exactly as they appear. No one wants to get shaken from this dream.

Once we accept the world as a dream, all questions about the independent existence of the external world vanish; we get the solid, clockwork universe we desire. The mind is no longer a movie screen blindly accepting images from an external source and converting them into coherent pictures. Instead, the unconscious mind itself is the projecting source, and one with bottomless creative powers. The independent world is no mere abstraction, but our wish come true.

Chapter Nine

THE SOURCE OF THE BELIEF IN A SELF-OPERATING WORLD

The external world of physics has thus become a world of shadows. In removing our illusions we remove the substance, for indeed we have seen that substance is one of our greatest illusions.
—Sir Arthur Eddington

OUR BELIEF IN AN independent world may indeed be nothing more than a belief. Neither sense experience nor reason leads us to the necessary conclusion that a world independent of our perceptions exists. As Berkeley said, the world may in fact be a dream in the mind of God.

But not only does material science tell us that the external world exists independently of the mind, it also preaches the dogma that the world operates outside of the mind's control. Natural laws, we learn, are products of objects—speeding light rays, spinning electrons, spiraling galaxies—not of the mind.

In empiricism, upon which material science is based, all knowledge is derived from sense experience.[110] If no sense impression corresponds to an idea, then the idea, such as a winged horse, is fantasy. This approach lays the groundwork for the scientific method. To elevate a statement about the world—such as "All objects fall at the same rate"—to the status of a scientific law, the statement must be testable. Some sense experience (such as dropping objects of unequal weight from a leaning tower) must support the truth of the statement.

Material science attributes the order and regularity of natural events to external objects. Scientific laws are laws of material objects; they are properties of things, not of the mind. The concept of law brings with it the idea of necessity. We consider it a law of nature that the sun rises in the morning; that rain falls down, not up; that the properties of chemical elements are constant throughout the universe; and that light always travels at the same speed. Material science states that the external material world, the picture moving across the screen, follows these laws of nature. The mind plays no role in organizing reality. We watch the natural world flow by on the screen and believe that something behind the screen imparts necessity to events. These necessary connections between events (such as the sun's rays heating our skin) underlie natural law and the uniformity of nature.

We claim to know that the sun will rise in the morning. But from where do we derive the idea of necessity? Where is this law written? What is the source of our belief that we live in a lawful world, a world that operates according to fixed rules and patterned movements?

David Hume also got to the bottom of this problem. He first concluded that, unlike the propositions of math (two plus two equals four), events occurring in the world are not logically necessary. If events in the world, such as the rising of the sun, are not logically necessary, Hume asks, then what is the basis of a scientific law? Why do we say that the sun must rise tomorrow, rather than next week, or perhaps never? Where, Hume asks, do we get the idea that one event (morning) will necessarily follow another event (night)?

He concluded that experience and not reason must be the source of the idea of necessary connection between cause and effect. But then, from what sense impression does the idea of necessity originate? When we see a certain event, such as a boy eating bread, we naturally believe that the bread possesses some power or energy that produces another event: nourishment. But viewing this scene with a blank, passive mind, we might ask, What in this experience necessarily leads to the conclusion that bread nourishes?[111] Experience imprints no idea labeled "necessity" upon our mind.

Search as you may for the idea of a necessary connection out in the world, you will never find it. You may find constant conjunction[112] or succession,[113] but you will not find through sense impressions the idea of necessity. Therefore, the idea of necessary connection underlying cause and effect comes neither from reasoning nor from experience. What then is the source of these necessary connections underlying natural law? According to Hume, the source is habit and custom.[114] Through experiencing the constant pairing of event following event, the mind comes through habit to believe that, indeed, the same sequence of events will recur. "All inferences from experience, therefore, are effects of custom, not of reasoning."[115]

If we assume that the world is detached from the mind, a three-dimensional image flowing through time, then sense impressions from this world can give us no certainty that it will continue operating uniformly in the future. Only our subjective belief in nature's uniformity founded on past experience leads us to think that the future will repeat the past, that light will still speed away at 186,000 miles per second, that the force of gravity will not change, and that two hydrogen atoms plus one oxygen atom will always produce one molecule of water.

The Kantian Revolution

Immanuel Kant (1724–1804) was dissatisfied with Hume's answer. Some force stronger than feelings and beliefs, he thought, must guarantee natural laws. Kant recognized that relying solely upon sense impressions to produce knowledge leads to a dead end. Out in the world we find only the constant pairing of events, but no laws linking them together. Kant proposed a new approach. Instead of assuming that the mind is a passive receiver of sense information, he gave the mind an active role in framing experience. Rather than look out in the world for certainty, Kant would find his certainty in the structure of the mind.[116]

Kant said rather than view the world with the belief that the mind conforms to objects, let us invert the picture and suppose that objects conform to the mind. To Kant, the mind no longer is a blank screen accepting projected images from the outside world. Kant rearranged the equipment; for him, the mind converts raw sense data into a coherent experience. Kant asked how can we have certain knowledge about worldly events (such as the rising of the sun) independent of sense experience?[117] If the external world offers no assurance that events will follow natural laws, then maybe the mind will furnish the guarantee. As Hume showed, if the mind is a blank movie screen, we can have no knowledge about the world; metaphysics, the science of reality, becomes a futile pursuit. Physical science becomes a study of beliefs and feelings[118] because nature fails to provide the necessity required to make laws. Kant's metaphysics focuses not on a study of a world detached from the mind, but rather on the forms and concepts that the mind adds to sense impressions to make experience possible.

As Descartes and Berkeley had appealed to God to supply the supporting brace to the external world, Kant, like material science, simply assumed that a world existed beyond the mind. He knew that knowledge was limited to the mind, and for the mind to go outside itself to know an independent world is impossible.[119] But, like Berkeley, Kant understood that man did not create the world; this is the work of the Divine Intellect, which creates its objects.[120]

Kant therefore took the scientific approach: he undercut arguments for the existence of God,[121] and presupposed an independent, material world. Kant replaced an unknowable spiritual being (God) with an unknowable material world (thing-in-itself). Kant accepts the viewpoint that the mind only knows itself. At the same time, he takes it for granted that independent objects, what he calls "things-in-themselves," exist outside the mind.[122] These "unknown occult entities"[123] provide the matter and permanence[124] to experience; the mind contributes the form,[125] and the imagination—working together with self-consciousness—creates the image we see.[126]

The unknowable thing-in-itself furnishes the backdrop to reality but the mind supplies nearly everything else required for a coherent experience. Space, time, causation, reality, unity, and other basic elements the mind adds to experience. Hume could not find necessary causation out in the world; Kant installed it in the mind. An effect necessarily follows a certain cause because our mind can perceive events in no other way.

What material scientists look for out in the world, Kant placed in the mind. The mind organizes reality, not the laws of nature:

> It is we therefore who carry into the phenomena which we call nature, order, and regularity, nay, we should never find them in nature, if we ourselves, or the nature of our mind, had not originally placed them there.
>
> However exaggerated therefore and absurd it may sound, that the understanding is itself the source of the laws of nature, and of its formal unity, such a statement is nevertheless correct and in accordance with experience.[127]

But importantly, Kant's mental forms do not apply to things as they actually are; they only apply to what appears to us on the screen of the theater.[128]

Despite these inconsistencies in Kant's system, he may have had little choice but to assume the thing-in-itself. He defines this thing as something *given*,[129] something assumed present that stands behind sense perceptions. Unless Kant fell back to Berkeley's system and assumed a God in heaven, then Kant, much like material science, had to assume an external world beyond the mind. Reason could not complete the bridge to God; a leap of faith is required to cross that expanse, and leaps of faith have no place in either philosophy or science.

Kant made a political compromise. He remained faithful to the established view that the mind can only know itself, but he also assured his readers that an independent world still existed outside the mind. Because everyone desires an external world, this assumption is popular. But as we shall see, in the centuries following Kant, the modern mind has run off with this assumption and forgotten about the rest of Kant's system. (After all, it is much too complicated.) Modern science flashes back to Locke and naïve realism:[130] natural laws, we are told, are properties of a world independent of the mind. Kant's mental forms become transposed onto the things-in-themselves, those mysterious objects we can never know.

Similarities between Kant's system and the Real Dream worldview may be apparent. It is true that the mind structures physical reality.

Contrary to Kant's system, however, the mind does not structure perceptions coming from a mysterious, unknowable thing-in-itself. Rather, the mind is simply structuring its own three-dimensional, projected world.

Chapter Ten

IDEALISM FAILS TO COMPLETE THE PUZZLE

Nature should be Mind made visible, Mind the invisible Nature.
—F. W. J. Schelling, *Ideas for a Philosophy of Nature*

EMBOLDENED BY KANT'S STATEMENT at the end of the *Critique of Pure Reason* that human reason might soon solve the riddle of existence,[131] later thinkers set out to prove the prediction true. The mission was clear: Discard the thing-in-itself. Mind alone must be used to explain the world. German philosophers Fichte, Schelling, Schopenhauer, and Hegel all made bold attempts at completing the idealist program, and in the end each would fail for the same reason Berkeley did: When one person in the unfolding dream of God attempts to explain the world as a product of the mind, he is dealt only losing hands. If he analyzes the problem from his own perspective, he faces the charge of solipsism.[132] If, like Berkeley, he invokes an Eternal Spirit (or Absolute Being) as the source of experience, as most idealists do, he faces the charge of mysticism.

These idealist philosophers fall short because their Absolute Being is no more provable than the God of religion. Explaining the world as a product of Absolute Mind may fascinate the intellect, but reason offers no proof that this Being exists. Idealism's failure to complete the puzzle of existence opened the gates wide for materialism to try its hand at explaining the world. With no God in sight, material science returns us to the comfort of our senses; the existence of the independent world need no longer be questioned. Any doubts whether the mind is capable of knowing an external world can be put aside. And material science will continue to take the independent world for granted in all its theories.

Fichte's Distant Dream

Once the external world is no longer taken for granted (Hume), or the thing-in-itself assumed (Kant), all that remains is the productive imagination to project external objects. Indeed, in the philosophy of J. G. Fichte (1762–1814), "All reality . . . is brought forth solely by the imagination."[133] External things, he says, are "*nothing more than the product of our own presentative faculty.*"[134] The thing-in-itself is only a thought, and we do not move beyond the mind in thinking it.[135]

In the attempt to deduce the world as a product of the imagination, Fichte naturally started with his own mind. To avoid subjectivism, however, Fichte implied that no one person imagines the world. Rather, the world is rooted in something called the Infinite Life, or the Absolute Ego.[136]

Removing the artificial brace supporting the independent world, Fichte transforms the world into a series of images moving across the landscape. The images, he writes "float past . . . without significance and without aim . . . All reality is transformed into a strange dream, without a life which is dreamed of, and without a mind which dreams it; into a dream which is woven together in a dream of itself."[137] Reason brought Fichte to see the world as dream without meaning. And, like Hume, he faced the question of why we regard the world as more than a dream; why do we suppose, he asks, that something exists outside our mental presentations?[138] Uncritical common sense says that the world exists as it appears. But our mind has the ability to go beyond this naïve thought and discover that the world is a creation of the mind. But why do so few reach this point?[139] Fichte answers that only our "interest" in an external reality upholds the belief. The belief brings us something to touch and enjoy; it gives us something to do.[140]

Fichte viewed his dream world from afar, like a movie on the screen of a drive-in theater; he did not put his heart into the picture. Though realizing that the imagination creates the world, he failed to appreciate that the imagination also creates his body, and the purpose of life is not to watch the world pass by but to dive into the action and lose ourselves in the dream. Fichte ventured to the end of reason, but there he found only faith and a voice telling him his task is "not merely to know, but to act according to your knowledge."[141] In the midst of a dream not of his making, Fichte turns and listens to a voice saying, Act morally, demand a better world.[142]

This world, Fichte concludes, neither reason nor science can fully explain. Rather it can be explained only through the One in whom they are united . . . the Infinite Will who sustains and embraces them all in His own sphere . . . Only through the common fountain of our spiritual being do we know of each other; only in Him do we recognize each other and influence each other. "Respect here the image of freedom upon the earth—here a work which bears its impress." Thus it is proclaimed within me by the voice of that Will which speaks to me only insofar as it imposes duties upon me. The only principle through which I recognize you and your work is the command of conscience to respect you.[143]

Here reason dissolves into faith and mysticism. Knowing that he was not the source for the pictures he saw outside, Fichte looked to a higher power . . . and listened. Act for a better world, the voice tells him. The link between the self and the Absolute, by whatever name it goes, is made by faith and intuition, not by reason. Fichte nobly continued the idealist program but could not finish it. In the end, he rested his case on faith; the source of the dream world remained a mystery.

Hegel's Absolute

Georg Wilhelm Friedrich Hegel (1770–1831) assumed that the world is made from Absolute Mind, not matter; his moving force is therefore not the laws of physical science but rather the law of the mind. Reason is the synthesizing force[144] that strives to make sense of the world. Hegel's object of science is the Absolute, not matter.[145] Purpose,[146] the feature missing from materialistic explanations of the universe, Hegel makes the cornerstone of his philosophy.

Hegel saw the Absolute as a force developing within human consciousness and flowing through human history. When reason is used to grasp ultimate reality (the Absolute), an unusual event occurs. Once God is viewed as Spirit working within the world, then, according to Hegel, reason can take hold of God because it seeks to understand only itself. We need not settle for an otherworldly God that only faith approaches; reason can bring us to know this Being.[147] According to Hegel, the process of self-realization continues until the mind gains Absolute Knowledge, the point at which the mind comes to find it comprises all reality and that it is in the process of knowing the depth of the self.[148]

Hegel believed that the world is developing toward a higher goal, and he marked the progress of the river flow. He is like a film enthusiast who, anxious to view the final picture, rushes to the studio and views the film before it is fully developed. He makes out shadows and images but can see nothing clearly. God had not yet fully developed in nature or in man.

The Mystery Remains

In an idealist philosophy one must presuppose the existence of an Absolute Mind or universal Spirit to avoid the paradox of solipsism.[149] Still the question remains, Where is Hegel's Absolute Mind? Without sense certainty that such a mind or spirit exists in physical form, mystery defines the relationship between humans and God. Reason alone cannot bring us to God; it can only bring us to the edge of a ravine where we look inward for the courage to jump. Hegel showed what reason can say about the Absolute, but how does a living, breathing person connect with this being?

Hegel faced the same problem as other thinkers trying to understand existence in a developing dream. Because God cannot be proven scientifically, and because the world appears beyond the control of any one mind, the world must be assumed as given.[150] Once the world is assumed, believing that it exists outside the control of the mind is natural. When this step is taken, idealism turns mystical because the question of how mind affects matter avoids an answer.

Hegel's metaphysical system ends with Spirit knowing itself as Spirit, where man's alienation is supposed to end. But it does not end there. Man remains alienated even at the end of Hegel's system because the purpose of existence is still not known. The picture cannot be filled in until the ultimate dreamer appears. Until then, humanity remains alienated from its true self because it cannot speak the whole truth with confidence.

In the Real Dream we need not undergo the same struggle to uncover the highest idea. In the back of our mind we see the true idea—or goal—of the cosmos: simply dream with the free mind of a child and reach for the highest star. What is the brightest idea our mind can reach? In a dream world powered by endless creativity and incessant striving, the answer is not surprising, and it has long been in our mind. The idea is heaven, an earthly paradise; this idea is the one toward which human history flows.

Chapter Eleven

THE ILLUSION MAKER

*When we dream we do not know that we are dreaming. In our dreams we may even
interpret our dreams. Only after we are awake do we know we have dreamed. Finally
there comes a great awakening, and then we know life is a great dream.*
—Chuang-Tzu (between 399 and 295 B.C.)

WESTERN IDEALISM[151] HAS MUCH in common with schools of thought
in Eastern philosophy and religion. For example, the Vedanta school of
Hinduism does not deny the "existence of matter, or of solidity, impen-
etrability, and extended figure (to deny which would be lunacy), but in
correcting the popular notion of it, and in contending that it has no
essence independent of mental perception; that existence and percepti-
bility are convertible terms."[152]

According to much of Eastern philosophy, what appears to our
senses as the physical world—the trees in the forest, the birds in the sky,
the planets circling the sun—is maya, an illusion, a second-rate reality.
The world of appearances hides the true oneness of the universe, for all is
Brahman. By searching deeply within the self, a person can realize one's
unity with the Great Self (Atman), and the all-pervasive spirit that is
Brahman.[153] In the famous words of the Upanishads, "That are Thou."[154]
The self is identical to ultimate reality. Humanity is God in disguise.
Hinduism focuses on the means to lay the self over the Absolute, to unite
the two, which necessarily entails detaching oneself from the material
world. In Hinduism, we are not to mistake the world that we see for

the ultimate reality. "All living creatures are led astray as soon as they are born, by the delusion that this relative world is real."[155]

Brahman grounds the world and is that out of which it arose: "From this Self (Atman), verily, space arose; from space, wind; from fire, water; from water, the earth; from the earth, herbs; from herbs, food; from food, semen; from semen the person."[156] Early Indian thinkers realized Brahman or the Absolute was actually the force alive in our dreams, developing as a seed in the unconsciousness of man. In the Katha Upanisad, it is written,

> He who is awake in those that sleep,
> The Person who fashions desire after desire
> That indeed is the Pure. That is Brahman.
> That indeed is called the Immortal.
> On it all the worlds do rest;
> And no one soever goes beyond it.
> This verily, is That![157]

According to the Chandogya Upanisad, "Now, when one is sound asleep; composed, serene, and knows no dream—that is the Self (Atman)," said he. "That is the immortal, the fearless. That is Brahman."[158] And "'He who moves about happy in a dream—he is the Self,' said he. 'That is the immortal, the fearless. That is Brahman.'"[159] The Brihadaranyaka Upanishad states:

> While one is in the state of dream, the golden, self-luminous being, the Self within, makes the body to sleep, though he himself remains forever awake and watches by his own light the impressions of deeds that have been left on the mind.

Everyone is aware of the experiences; no one sees the Experiencer.[160]

These excerpts, from one of the foundation documents to human thought, suggest that the ultimate being is residing in the unconscious mind of humankind; joining us at sleep and lurking in the background, weaving the dream world. Because this ground of being is spiritual, most Indian philosophy is idealist in nature.[161]

Brahman is the illusion-maker—the greatest of magicians—that projects a real-seeming world from its universal mind.[162] "One should know that Nature . . . is an illusion (maya) and that the Mighty Lord is . . . the illusion-maker (mayin)."[163]

To say that the world is an illusion produced by the universal mind (Brahman) strongly implies that the universe is a dream; indeed, some Indian philosophers maintain this view. The sixth-century Hindu philosopher Gaudapada saw no relative difference between night dreams and waking life; both possess reality within the boundaries of the experienced world.[164] "In dreams things are imagined internally, and in the experience that we have when awake things are imagined as existing outside, but both of them are but illusory creations of the self."[165]

Gaudapada's views are similar to those held by the Mahayana school in Buddhist philosophy. This system affirms the primary reality of mind and makes the world of appearances "representation-only."[166] Answering the question of what grounds external objects if only ideas exist, Vasubandhu, author of *The Treatise in Twenty Stanzas on Representation-only*, states, "Place and time are determined as in a dream."[167] "As in a dream, although there are no real objects, yet it is in a certain place that such things as a village, a garden, a man, or a woman are seen."[168] To these thinkers, the dream becomes more than a metaphor; it is the form and substance of waking life.

Both Gaudapada and the Buddhist idealists, like other such thinkers, are open to charges of subjectivism. Gaudapada believed that the world "exists only in the mind of man."[169] If so, then in whose mind does the world dream ultimately originate? Samkara[170] (A.D. 788–820?) avoided the paradox of subjectivism by granting the public world a higher reality than night dreams.[171] Foreshadowing Berkeley, Samkara compares life to a dream[172] but then concludes that waking life is more than a dream: "The things of which we are conscious in a dream are negated by our waking consciousness. . . . Those things, on the other hand, of which we are conscious in our waking state, such as posts and the like, are never negated in any state."[173]

Here Samkara recognizes a fact that Berkeley and Kant later identified: the world seems to be given; it appears to exist beyond our control and does not go away when we close our eyes. The world seems something more than a night dream. Berkeley concluded that the universe is a dream in the mind of God, the great projecting source hidden from our view. In a similar sense, Samkara believed that the world has "no existence apart from Brahman."[174] The physical world originates in the mind of Brahman.[175]

Hinduism, like Western philosophy, tends to straddle the real and the ideal. In daily life we experience a diverse world that we assume is real; in quiet moments of reflection, however, we may sense a unity suggestive of a dream. Hinduism recognizes that the mind may be the source for the world, but resists labeling life the grand illusion; Hinduism looks for reality at the base of the Self. The goal then becomes to immerse the self into the one—to return the soul to its origins and enter a dreamless sleep, the state of mind when illusion did not mesmerize us.[176]

To Hinduism, the uniting of the individual self with the universal self in the depths of being is called *moska* or liberation; in Buddhism, the denial of the self and entrance into the universal flow of life is *nirvana*. In each instance, the individual attempts to escape the churning wheel of rebirth in which material bodies are placed on the Self and then thrown off as the Self seeks perfection.[177]

In Hinduism and Buddhism, the spiritual enlightenment that occurs at moska or nirvana, respectively, is likened to an awakening; "Buddha," in fact, means "an awakened one."[178] In Hinduism, the enlightened one awakens to find that he is part of one world, one universal power underlying appearances. In Buddhism, the enlightened one awakens to find the self is part of the stream of becoming, a never-ending force flowing toward perfection, defeating suffering standing in its path. In each belief system, the term "awaken" implies rising to a higher level of consciousness; man "snaps out" of his fixation on the material world,[179] and feels a greater power lying within.

In the Real Dream, enlightenment occurs along the same path, but instead uses the methods of science and modern, rational thought. We first observe that to claim nature is unreal defines what is real before we learn what is possible. If we claim that the world of appearances is unreal because it only *appears* to exist outside of us, we reject the very world we desire. In a dream, the projected external world answers our need and desire for that world. If we reject the dreamed world and continue demanding a real world outside of the mind, we overshoot the mark; having dreamt the world we desire, the next step is to experience it, not to demand more than is possible.

The One, by whatever name it goes, is indeed universal and all-powerful, but in the Real Dream, the simple reason we have a world is that being the only one is a lonely existence. We are in the midst of escaping from nothing. Both our bodies and nature may indeed be illusion or appearance only, *but they are real to each other*.[180] The body and world play the same game. Such is the nature of a dream. After following Hinduism's directions and realizing the unity of mind, our next task is to use this knowledge and put the finishing touches to the dream. The world not only issues from the One Self, but also is within the Self's control.

In the same way that holding a material science worldview in a dream world ruptures the spirit of the Western mind, so the denigration of the physical world distorts the outlook of the Eastern mind. Know yourself at the bottom of your soul; unite with Brahman; but then come to realize that this world was meant to be everything we desire, not shunted off as a second-rate reality.

In a style that Descartes began, the Western philosopher attempts to reason his way to truth using the methods of mathematics and logic. In carrying this method to its conclusion, we find the mind limited to its ideas. But to avoid solipsism, the world, before the ultimate dreamer appears on the scene, cannot be the product of any one person's mind. Therefore, to overcome this paradox, the Western idealist must presuppose the existence of a mysterious Absolute Being or Transcendental Ego as the source of the world's appearance. The world, under this line of reasoning, radiates from one Absolute Being, and hence is one entity.

Eastern philosophy reaches much the same point but approaches the problem from a different direction. Rather than mark off the limits of knowledge using reason, the Easterners rely upon inner sense to know the world is one. But where Western idealism ends with faith, Eastern idealism ends with mysticism. Unless Brahman is considered a person who is also the Ultimate Source of the dream, appeals to the Absolute will end with intuition and emotion, but not with the sort of empirical proof that the scientific mind demands.

Although materialists have still not shown where all their particles and forces came from, idealists, in turn, have been unable to show where the great dream originates. The mystery of the dream's origin leads us to put the question aside and not worry about it: after all, we have an apparently real physical world facing us, which scientists say arose from a big bang in the distant past.

The perception of the apple tree started with the naïve thought that the tree exists as it appears, *wholly independent of the mind.* As thinkers examined this belief, some concluded that as a matter of simple reasoning, certain qualities—such as color, taste, texture, and sound—could not reside as they appear in the object, but must be added by the mind. Berkeley then observed that one could not separate the secondary qualities from the primary qualities; all qualities of the tree are known only by the mind. Kant, in an attempt to rescue the certainty of scientific knowledge, concluded that mental structures contributed the order to the world, and an unknowable thing-in-itself stood as the independent back-brace to external objects. Upon kicking that brace away, the external world again becomes a dream in the mind of the Absolute. In other words, philosophical reasoning on the perception of the apple tree ends in mysticism, and a belief in the one Mind—or God—that science cannot prove. Without any way to prove the truth, or value, of this line of thinking, the worldview of material science, with its naïve assumption of an independent external world, came to dominate our outlook toward the world.

But material science itself never has shown how its independent material world, filled with trillions upon trillions of tons of matter, is possible. To solve the puzzle, and provide a rational alternative to the material science worldview, we must next show how the Real Dream better explains the world that we see outside our windows. We already know that dreams are possible.

PART 3

Material Science Lost in a Dream World

THE BIG BANG AS METAPHOR

Chapter Twelve

THE ORIGIN OF SCIENTIFIC THEORY

ALL SCIENTIFIC THEORIES ORIGINATE in the mind.[181] The challenge of science is to align a theory with what really happens out in the world. Thus, scientific theory attempts to correlate a mental picture, created in the mind, with an external world presumed to exist outside of the mind.

Trying to Prove More Than They Have To

Material scientists break one of their own fundamental precepts when devising a theory: They seek to prove more than they have to. Occam's razor judges scientific theories according to how much they explain rather than assume. The best scientific theory would therefore rely upon no assumptions but explain the world with what we can know. Such a theory may be said to be more conservative than other theories because it explains events without recourse to unprovable beliefs and assumptions. Thus, if we can explain the world without taking for granted the independent existence of matter, space, and natural laws, we will have found a better theory than the one on which science now relies.

Standing before us is an *appearance* of a natural, independent world. Nothing in this appearance alone tells us that this world actually does exist independently of the mind. Scientists, however, in the big bang and related theories attempt to explain how this hypothetical independent world created itself from nothing. Thus, they create a more difficult problem than actually confronts them. They imagine an independent, material universe, freeze this thought in their minds, and then try to come up with a theory explaining how this incredible, *imagined* mass appeared out of nowhere. It might be easier if scientists did not make the independent-universe assumption in the first place, as this would relieve them from the impossible task of explaining how a mindless, material world arose from nothing and organized itself to the limits of mathematical order.

As all theories begin in the mind, the first step in evaluating their truth is whether the theory speaks of a world standing apart from the mind, or whether the theory speaks only of a world that the mind created. Perhaps, before believing that a theory tells us about a world independent of the mind, we should first decide which type of world more likely exists: a dream or a self-created machine.

If the mind is limited to knowing itself and, in fact, dreams the world, then the testing of scientific theories must occur within a framework in which the unconscious mind first creates physical reality (from atoms to galaxies), and then the conscious mind theorizes about its makeup.

In this new framework, we adopt a much different standpoint than material science. Forces of nature join at the core of the mind, not in the fiery blast of the big bang. Harmony found in the external world is the harmony that the mind put there. Constants of nature, such as the speed of light or the gravitational force, can be explained as functions of the mind's infinite need for regularity, not as mere coincidences resulting from the random shuffling of mindless particles or as a peculiar feature of one special universe out of an infinite number actually created.

The Real Dream does not naïvely separate the mind from the physical world when seeking to explain it. Rather, this new science first seeks to understand the degree to which unifying the thoughts, emotions, and goals of people can improve the physical world, including their bodies, because controlling internal states is how a dreamer controls one's dream.

In a dream, we know we can explain the source of the physical world. Material scientists, in contrast, avoid questions about how this flowing, three-dimensional movement outside of us can possibly exist. They simply take an independent world for granted and then go about their theorizing.

Materialists, in fact, demand an independent world without stopping to wonder whether the mind of God has already answered this wish. But once separating the mind from its hypothetical independent world—or God from its creation—material science must pay the price: physical reality left to itself has no mind,[182] no purpose,[183] and no means to organize itself into the mathematical harmonies that constitute nature.

In cosmology, for example, material scientists attempt to explain how the entire universe, from the farthest galaxy to your closest friend, all arose from a big bang of matter, energy, and space-time—but no mind.[184] Likewise, in the theory of evolution, scientists tell us how all life, and therefore the mind itself, sprang out of lifeless matter through a mindless process called natural selection.[185] In the material science worldview, the mind, whether of God or humanity, plays no part in forming the physical world. The Real Dream worldview concludes exactly the opposite: The mind of God is the origin of both the material world and the scientific theories that seek to explain the world's operation. Scientific theorizing thus becomes much simpler in the Real Dream.

Chapter Thirteen

FROM NAÏVE REALISM TO THE BIG BANG

As we have seen, the viewpoint that the world exists as it appears is known as naïve realism, or what Steven Weinberg calls "rough and ready realism." Naïve realism is an unthinking acceptance of the world as it appears to our eyes. It takes the world at face value. The hard, solid stuff that makes up the world around us—the tree across the street, the back-yard grass, the sky above, and other people—all appears to exist outside of what I am, and therefore it does.

Now if we consider ourselves a physical body, then indeed the tree exists outside of our bodies; after all, that is the point of a dream. But if we consider ourselves a mind, then both the body and the tree exist outside of us; they exist on the same level. We are in the midst of an out-flowing dream, launched into space.

As also noted earlier, a key feature of naïve realism—or materialistic realism generally—is that it separates mind from matter; material scientists can thus use their minds to theorize about how the external world managed to arrange itself into the mathematical harmonies of nature, but the mind can play no role in helping to arrange this world into those harmonies. Put differently, the same mind that created the world is put to the test of explaining it without using the mind. This fact helps explain why *the material science worldview, as we shall see below, has become a multitiered jumble of assumptions, wild guesses, and esoteric mathematical equations, as brilliant scientists seek to explain the creation and workings of a dream world using only particles and mechanical forces.* Since we know that a world was created (as one stands before us), you might think it took a simpler path to being here than through the big bang, inflationary theory, cosmic expansion, antimatter, black holes, and the other material science theories.

The First Atom

The metaphysical system known as atomism[186] follows from naïve realism. Atomism is roughly twenty-five hundred years old, and traceable to the ancient Greek philosophers Democritus and Leucippus.[187] Atomists believe that all the apparent diversity of physical reality, from the colors of the rainbow to the tastes of fruits and spices, can be reduced to complex arrangements of fundamental particles called atoms.[188] What appear as different objects in the world, such as trees, people, and oceans, are simply intricate arrangements of tiny, faceless atoms.

Once scientists assumed that physical objects exist separate from the mind, common sense dictated that if someone breaks them down to their smallest parts, we might understand the world. Having assumed that the parts to reality are independent of the mind, the search for meaning and explanation ventures outward: materialists look for God in a particle.[189]

The only problem is that scientists could break down 10^{53} kilograms of matter and still not answer the question of how these small particles came to be in the first place, nor how they combined to form a universe. We therefore begin by asking material science theorists the most fundamental of all questions: Where did all this stuff come from?

To answer this question, first imagine that we are at the moment before creation, waiting for something to appear on the scene. Patiently we wait. So far, nothing. Science's standard explanation to the source of all this stuff is that the world began as a "singular point of infinite density" some 10 to 20 billion years ago.[190] But what does this mean?

Now imagine that we are looking at the ongoing creation of the universe as a three-dimensional film. Then take all the energy and mass in the universe and rewind the film to the presumed beginning of the universe. As we rewind the film within the material science worldview we are destined to end up with one very small particle: into this one particle we need to fit the mass and energy equivalent to all the stars in the sky. Clearly, this must be a very small—and condensed—particle.

Physicists term this point a singularity, a "dimensionless point,"[191] or a point so small it has no size. Thus, at the beginning of time, according to modern science, the entire universe was folded inside a point billions of times smaller than the head of a pin.

Having rolled the universe up into a point, material scientists then invoke the concept of infinity to explain how all this matter fit into a size-less point. This sizeless point, the theory goes, contained infinite energy.[192] Modern science thus rewinds the film and ends up at an infinitely dense point, something no one has ever experienced, and the existence of which we can trace to only one source: the mind of the material science theorist.

Material science begins its creation theory with a point of infinite density. But what they have theoretically placed into this point is the entire existing universe. Working backward from the observable universe, they outline a simple formula: infinitely dense point + big bang = universe. Note an important point here: We thought science was explaining the creation of the universe, but all it has done is hide a supposed mechanical universe within this densest of all seeds.

We next ask: Where exactly did this infinitely dense point come from? Modern science avoids this question, because the answer would require scientists to explain how near-infinite energy and matter sprang from the void with no help from a mind. Answering this question is critical, though, because the entire theoretical edifice of materialism rests upon the truth of the big bang.

Material scientists offer no explanation. Scientists say they can push back the explanation to the first 10^{-35} seconds or so after the creation event but "what happened at the precise moment of creation is not yet known because unfamiliar physical principles unique to the immense densities and temperatures of that moment mask the initial structure of the universe."[193] The laws of physics break down at the singularity.[194]

Noble Prize–winning professor Leon Lederman of the Illinois Institute of Technology is more candid:

A story logically begins at the beginning. But this story is about the universe, and unfortunately there are *no data* for the Very Beginning. None, zero. We don't know anything about the universe until it reaches the mature age of a billionth of a trillionth of a second—that is, some very short time after creation in the Big Bang. When you read or hear anything about the birth of the universe, *someone is making it up.* We are in the realm of philosophy. Only God knows what happened at the Very Beginning.[195]

And it is not even the quantity of matter that makes the job of the material scientist so formidable: they have no credible basis to account for the creation from nothing of one grain of sand, much less all the stars that fill the heavens.

Material scientists believe that for them to conduct experiments about how the world works, they must assume the existence of an independent world. George Gaylord Simpson, one of the twentieth century's most respected paleontologists, explained this feature of modern science:

The most successful scientific investigation has generally involved treating phenomena *as if* they were purely materialistic or naturalistic, rejecting any metaphysical or transcendental hypothesis as long as a natural hypothesis seems possible. The method works. The restriction is necessary because science is confined to material means of investigation and so it would stultify its own efforts to postulate that its subject is not material so not susceptible to its methods.[196]

Similarly, Harvard University professor Ernst Mayr, one of history's leading biologists, expressed the issue this way:

Despite the openness of science to new facts and hypotheses, it must be said that virtually all scientists—somewhat like theologians—bring a set of what we call "first principles" with them to the study of the natural world. One of these axiomatic assumptions is that there is a real world independent of human perceptions. This might be called the principle of objectivity (as opposed to subjectivity) or common-sense realism. This does not mean that individual scientists are always "objective" or even that objectivity among human beings is possible in any absolute sense. What it does mean is that an objective world exists outside of the influence of subjective perception. Most scientists—though not all—believe in this axiom.[197]

Material scientists believe that to do science—to be truly objective—the scientist must separate mind from the physical specimen under study. Scientists must not allow the influence of Mind, God, or any supernatural force into the workings of the material world.[198]

As noted above, medical science provides a good example of this desire that the mind play no role in affecting the physical world. Scientists believe that the human body is independent of the mind; thus, when something goes wrong in the body—when arteries clog, tumors appear, cancer cells multiply—the medical scientist (or doctor) operates on the physical body by cutting it open, removing diseased parts, and treating it with drugs, lasers, or other treatments which assume that the disease originates in the body. Medical science has done great things for the people of this world and will always serve a valuable function, even in the Real Dream. But the repairs of material science are always *temporary*; they are crutches, patches on a leaking boat, short-term fixes in the mind-created world. *The patient always dies.* We must heal the mind in addition to the soul to fully heal the body, as a host of writers and thinkers have long observed.[199]

And this is a *deep* dream; we infuse the physical world with substance, saturate it with meaning. We can surgically remove a tumor from the brain, but we will never truly *heal* the ailments of the modern world unless we align scientific theory with the nature of the universe. We must live the story we were born to follow and play the roles ingrained in our innermost being: the story of dreamers rising to accept the responsibility of dwelling in a world the mind has created for them.

When scientists look out at the heavens above, they give no thought to the notion that they might be looking at the far reaches of the mind's imagination. Material scientists mistakenly assume that they cannot practice science without making the great assumption. From one perspective there is nothing wrong with separating (or subtracting) the possible effect of mind on matter when studying nature. In fact, such an approach makes sense as a method of gaining knowledge about the world. The question might be framed as follows: In a dream world, how much of the world can be explained or catalogued without recourse to the mind? Like an early explorer of uncharted territory, science serves the valuable function of mapping the world, providing explanations of how the parts work together, cataloguing its regularities and the laws by which it appears to operate.

But many scientists, whether through overconfidence or lack of competition, go much further. Instead of acknowledging that they created a model of an independent physical world in order to study it, they proceed as if a physical theory will one day be capable of explaining how their own model world came from nothing on its own power. In other words, they forget that they have conjured up out of their own mental theories the abstract idea of a physical world. Forgetting this unavoidable fact, cosmologists proceed to tangle themselves up into hopelessly complex knots, trying to explain how dead and dumb matter formed itself into a vision of the mind.

The Big Bang as Metaphor

Somewhere along the path of scientific discovery, science transformed the great assumption—the independent existence of the external world—into a metaphysical theory. And as we have seen, the most telling example of this feature of science is the big bang theory, under which the universe arose from a primordial explosion of all the matter in the universe. The big bang stands in the same relation to material science as the God of Genesis stands to the creation of the world. In the same way that religion has never provided a physical mechanism for how God created a preformed universe, so modern science has never provided a physical mechanism for how the matter in the universe came from nothing.

There is no doubt that the assumption of an independent world originated in the mind, and like any other hypothesis, is much easier to imagine than to explain as a feature of a world outside of the mind.

In other words, it is no easy task to understand how empty space can produce a universe full of matter. Most scientists, in fact, believe that the question is one that science is not capable of answering. John Maddox, in his book *What Remains to Be Discovered*, after surveying the evidence and science's creation theories, writes, "The only prudent answer to the question, 'How did the universe begin?' is that we do not yet know."[200] John C. Mather and John Boslough, in their book *The Very First Light*, write,

> Although the Big Bang is loosely described as the beginning of the universe, or even as a creation event, that has never been a satisfying picture for me. I would like to know what happened before that. Physics has no words to describe creation from nothing, but describes only the formation of one substance to another.[201]

Further,

> What happened to precipitate the Big Bang? Technically speaking, such a question is misleading. It seems to imply a possibility that the universe sprang into being out of nothing at a certain instant that astrophysicists describe as time (t) = 0, the big bang. All that we really can know from extrapolating back is restricted to t > 0 (time greater than 0), so we could say nothing about a creation event itself if there had been one.[202]

Martin Rees, former director of Cambridge University's Institute of Astronomy, in his book *Before the Beginning*, writes,

> Indeed some physicists already claim that our universe evolved essentially from nothing. But they should watch their

language, especially when talking to philosophers. The physicist's vacuum is a far richer construct than the philosopher's "nothing": latent in it are all the particles and fields described by the equations of physics.[203]

What he means is that scientists have to assume something to explain something, which is another way of saying that the big bang explains nothing.

The something of the scientist—assumed or explained—may be matter, energy, fields, or quantum fluctuations . . . but it is always *something*, the same something that scientists have simply borrowed from each other unquestioned, without ever stopping to ascertain if these theories could ever be substantiated.

Although even material scientists admit that they have simply taken as given all the matter in the universe, many still offer their own creation myths. For example, in *The Creation of Matter*, Harald Fritzsch, professor at the University of Munich, recites one such myth:

In the beginning there was nothing, neither time nor space, neither stars nor planets, neither rocks nor plants, neither animals nor human beings. Everything came out of the void. It all began with space and time and a very hot plasma composed of quarks, electrons, and other particles. This plasma cooled off rapidly; protons, neutrons, atomic particles, atoms, stars, galaxies, and planets formed. Finally life sprang up in many solar systems of the universe—in one case, on a planet of a most ordinary star situated in a spiral arm of a galaxy at the rim of a large cluster of galaxies. There, in the course of 4 billion years, plants and animals, and eventually human beings, developed out of the simplest organisms.[204]

In his book *Alpha and Omega*, Charles Seife writes,

In an instant, the nothing becomes something. In an enormous flash of energy, the big bang creates space and time.

Nobody knows where this energy came from—perhaps it was just a random event, or perhaps it was one of many similar big bangs. But within a tiny seed of matter and energy is all the stuff of our current universe.[205]

George Gamov (1904–1968), an originator of the big bang theory, provides another telling look at what material scientists really know about this most important of all moments. In 1951 Gamov published a popular account of the big bang in a book he titled *The Creation of the Universe*.[206] In a note for the second printing of the book, Gamov responded to objections concerning his use of the word "creation" in the title, which suggested a biblical creation. The author replied that he had been misunderstood: "It should be explained that the author understands this term, not in the sense of 'making something out of nothing,' but rather as 'making something shapely out of shapelessness,' as, for example, in the phrase 'the latest creation of Parisian fashion.'"[207]

Gamov acknowledged that he did not use the word "creation" in the normal manner. Material science, in fact, fails to explain how something can come from nothing. But give physicists an infinite amount of matter and energy, and they believe that the rest follows naturally.[208]

Material science will not be bothered with having to explain how this something came from nothing. That question—the most important one we can ask—is outside its scope. Material science responds to our need for a physical world to surround and comfort us: a *Mother Nature*. But if we truly want to find nature's origin, looking 14 billion years backward in time to the big bang will do us no good. The big bang explains nothing as it fails to describe how something came from nothing; it ignores the major question.

Put another way, material science has assumed the independent existence of the external world, and the big bang theory simply camouflages this assumption. Material science gives us one way to look at the world and then tries to convince us it is the only way. But instead of taking matter as given, we can easily go the opposite way and take the mind's dreaming power as given. We have empirical evidence for this power, but absolutely no evidence that a flowing, three-dimensional scene can appear—from nothing—outside the mind.

Something can come from nothing in only one way: through the combined projection power of the mind, or our dreaming-power. This method of creating an apparent world is the only one we know is possible, as we see it evidenced in hallucinations and our nighttime dreams. By extrapolating from these personal world-creating experiences, we can see how the universe at large can be a creation of the united dreaming power of humankind.

Modern science takes exactly the opposite approach to explaining the world we see. Fooled by the apparent solidity and externality of the world—or, in different words, lost in the dream world—scientists imagine that the universe came from nothing on its own power, as if, one fine day, billions of suns burst from the void and rushed toward a world of perfect order.

The task before us is thus clear: We need to explain the object of scientific study— the physical world—as a product of the mind's dreaming power.

Chapter Fourteen

THE BIG BANG EXPLODES

FEW PEOPLE QUESTION MATERIAL science when it takes for granted a universe worth of matter. With this unquestioned assumption deeply ingrained in their worldview, material scientists refer to other observations they claim prove the big bang theory true. As we will see, however, these observations do not prove that something came from nothing and are better explained through the Real Dream.

In 1929, astronomer Edwin Hubble found that the galaxies are receding at a speed proportional to their distance.[209] Put another way, more distant galaxies move away faster than closer galaxies.[210] Equally distant galaxies recede uniformly across the ceiling of the sky, like a college band marching in formation. As noted earlier, working backward from these observations, physicists theorize that in the beginning the universe was compressed into one point, and that today's expanding universe results from a great primordial explosion.

Physicist George Gamov supplied the second fact supporting the big bang theory. As physical evidence for the big bang, Gamov predicted that the blast would leave background radiation against the sky, as a cosmic fossil.[211] In 1965 two researchers at Bell Laboratories, Arno A. Penzia and Robert W. Wilson, detected faint microwave radiation emanating from distant space at a constant temperature of 2.9 degrees above absolute zero, apparently confirming Gamov's hypothesis.[212] So the two facts we are working with are as follows: the universe is expanding at a uniform rate, and background radiation is a uniform 2.9 degrees Kelvin.[213]

Material Scientists Misinterpret the Cosmic Background Radiation

Material scientists argue that the existence of nearly uniform background radiation, spread evenly across the celestial sphere, provides proof for the big bang theory.[214] The thinking is that the primordial event was like the explosion of an infinitely powered globe of light, radiating light in all directions. When astronomers study this light, they believe they are looking at the aftermath of a physical explosion.[215]

But of course, the presence of this faint uniform energy projected across the sky does not prove that something came from nothing. Nor does it prove that the universe resulted from an infinite explosion of space, time, and energy, or that the big bang really happened. Indeed, the cosmic background radiation is better explained as simply the faint background buzzing of the infinite dreaming mind.

In moments of high concentration (such as the athlete's zone), while waking up from a night dream, or simply in moments of peaceful tranquility, many of us experience a subtle sense of mental energy, or "buzzing." If, indeed, the world resulted from an infinitely powered dream, rather than an explosion of mindless matter and energy, then we can expect the inner energy exploding from the dreaming source to project itself to the limits of the mind. We must remember that, in a dream, the edges of the physical universe are in fact the edges of our mind; as we peer out into the far reaches of space, we are peering into the limits of the imagination.

This explanation for cosmic background radiation is better than the big bang theory for two reasons. First, it does not require assuming that 10^{53} kilograms of matter simply burst from the void as a random event; instead it uses the only mechanism known to exist that could create the appearance of a physical world—our mind. Second, it explains why the cosmic background radiation is uniform to a few parts in 100,000.[216] In the material science worldview, it should seem odd how a chaotic explosion of mindless matter and energy could have left such a perfect imprint across the sky, as if some supernatural being ignited a precisely tuned explosion. But we are so conditioned to accept science's mechanical worldview as correct that most people unthinkingly accept the big bang model as true, even though it requires the universe to appear from nothing on its own power. The universe did in fact appear from nothing, but its appearance is a product of the dreaming mind.

This viewpoint does not imply that the cosmic background radiation does not exist or that science's measurements are wrong. Rather, it means that we are locked within the confines of our united mind *in the midst of an infinitely powered dream.* The measuring devices (the radio wave detectors) and the measured phenomenon (the background radiation) exist on the same level; scientists here are using mind-projected bodily senses and instruments to measure a mind-projected physical phenomenon. All we have done here is reinterpret the physical data within a different worldview. Throughout the theories of modern science, we will see that mathematics seems to rule the cosmos, as if the random, mindless pieces of building blocks were first programmed with the laws of Newton and Einstein before being sent on their way to form a universe.[217]

The Uniform Expansion of the Universe

The second physical observation used to support the big bang theory is the expansion of the universe. As noted, Edwin Hubble discovered that the universe was expanding; the farther the galaxy, the faster it is moving away.[218] Applying the cosmological principle, scientists conclude that every observer in the universe should see that galaxies are receding at the same rate; there is no locus point to observe the expansion. As Daniel Goldsmith explains, "If all observers see galaxies in recession, with the galaxies at greater distances receding more rapidly, then the entire universe must be expanding, as the basic agglomeration of matter moves apart throughout the cosmos."[219] Scientists reason that humans arrived on the scene 14 billion years into the expansion, and we are observing a process that has continued at the same constant rate from the time of the big bang.

Material scientists believe that humans have no special place in the cosmos. We are randomly formed collections of stardust adrift on large, round rock floating in space. Our view of the universe from the Earth is not unique; under the cosmological principle, the universe appears the same to any witness no matter where he or she looks. The best example used to explain this picture is the one we've introduced: an expanding balloon. Placing dots on a small balloon and then blowing it up show that the farther away the dots are from each other in the beginning, the faster and farther they will move apart as the universe expands. The balloon has no center.[220]

Thus, material science tells us that, on the largest scale, the universe is homogenous, looks the same to all observers stationed anywhere in the universe, and is growing at a uniform rate.

Assuming all of these observations are correct, how do they prove that the big bang actually happened? To begin with, the observations do not prove that the stars in the sky suddenly burst from the dark void; nor do they prove that they were at one point compressed into one cosmic seed. Instead, material scientists are left to explain how the wildly chaotic event of the big bang could possibly have launched all the matter in the universe with such accuracy that millions of rows of stars are now marching outward at a constant rate. What force is blowing up the balloon with such precision?

Dark Energy Accelerates the Expansion

As material scientists continue their quest to explain the visible universe as leftover matter from the big bang, they confront a growing number of uninvited conundrums. In the simple version of the big bang, an infinite amount of matter flies to the far reaches of the empty universe, filling it with the stuff of which stars are made. This repulsive force, it seems, would eventually be counteracted by the attractive force of gravity. As this colossal mass of matter exploded from the dense seed of the big bang, one would expect the material farthest from the launching pad to speed ahead, as it tries to outrun the attractive force of gravity.[221]

Hubble's original data showed that the universe appears to be expanding, as if the receding galaxies far away are still reeling from the explosive force of the big bang, but the picture is not this simple. In the late 1990s a number of cosmologists discovered that not only is the universe expanding as Hubble observed, but the most distant galaxies are in fact *picking up speed.*[222] What is this mysterious force that is giving trillions of stars a turbo-boost? Material scientists have no idea, but they give it a name: "dark energy."[223] Thus, the expanding debris shot out of the big bang cannon and sent rocketing into outer space is picking up speed from an unknown, invisible energy source.

Dark energy is commonly associated with Albert Einstein's *cosmological constant*. Before Hubble made his famous observations on the expansion of the universe, Einstein applied his gravitational theory (the General Theory of Relativity) to the universe at large, concluding that the universe should either be contracting or expanding. But this result seemed to conflict with observations at the time, which revealed a static universe. Therefore, to offset the attractive force of gravity upon the universe, Einstein added "by hand" the cosmological constant. This constant, which was a product of his equations and not of observation or testing, supplied a repulsive force to empty space to balance the attractive force of gravity and produce the desired static universe. After learning of Hubble's findings that the universe was in fact expanding, the need for the cosmological constant disappeared, leading Einstein to call its formulation his "biggest blunder."[224]

But where Einstein used the cosmological constant to counteract the attractive force of gravity, dark energy accelerates an expanding universe. In both instances, however, the source of the universal repulsive force remains a mystery under material science theory.

Another feature of dark energy also bears mentioning. As the upcoming discussion of quantum theory shows, material science believes that even empty space has energy. The reason for this conclusion follows from the quantum theory, which holds that "virtual particles" pop in and out of existence in the black void of space.[225] Might these fleeting virtual particles be the source of dark energy? When scientists actually calculate the predicted total energy from the virtual particles hiding out in space, they get an infinite answer.[226] Even if theorists subtract out smaller quantum effects, the result is still 10^{120} times greater than all the energy in the universe and 10^{123} greater than the amount of dark energy assumed to be boosting the speed of the expanding universe. In other words, the quantum energy of empty space cannot be the source of dark energy.[227]

The misfit between the observed value of dark energy and what quantum theory says the value should be has been called "the most major mystery particle physics and cosmologists face today,"[228] and is the reason that many physicists subscribe to the incredible notion that we live in not one universe but are part of a vast network of other universes, the multiverse.[229] The thinking is that since our universe has "such an incredibly unlikely value for the vacuum energy,"[230] we must live in the one universe—among an infinite number of others—that just happens to have the right amount of dark energy to allow life to exist.[231] In other words, material scientists are so dead-set against making any compromise to religion that they are willing to accept the incredible notion that a multiverse exists rather than take a fresh perspective on the phenomenon of the physical world.

Dark energy brings into question the completeness and accuracy of the big bang model. The stuff of the big bang is not receding smoothly outward, but is gaining speed as if some mysterious force is giving it a boost. It appears as if material scientists must assume that contained within the original energy present at the big bang was an invisible force that would increase the speed of the galaxies flying off into space. Making matters worse, this dark energy has precisely the strength to allow life to exist, as if something adjusted the dark energy level at the beginning of time just so we can be here, now.

Chapter Fifteen

THE FLATNESS AND HORIZON PROBLEMS

MATERIAL SCIENCE'S BIG BANG theory yields a number of amazing oddities, any of which should inform observers that something is seriously wrong here. Two of these oddities are known as the flatness and horizon problems. But as the following discussion shows, these problems—perhaps better described as coincidences—are only problematic in a materialistic worldview. They are easily explained in the Real Dream worldview.

The Flatness Problem

One of the most remarkable—and little advertised—coincidences in the makeup of the universe concerns the balance between the total gravitational force of the stuff making up the universe and the total repulsive energy driving its expansion. This coincidence has its roots in technical theories derived from Einstein's theory of relativity and studies done on the expansion of the universe. But the problem can be stated simply.

According to material science theory, the big bang propelled an infinitely condensed ball of matter, space, and time out into nothingness to form what we now see as the universe of stars. As noted, the best analogy scientists seem to agree upon is the expanding balloon: the universe started as a tiny pinhead and then miraculously blew up, as space and time stretched their way into the universe. Edwin Hubble then discovered that the universe is expanding, as if the initial big bang force continues to drive the far-flung galaxies farther and farther away. So in this simple picture we have two opposing forces: the big bang repulsive force (and dark energy) fighting against the gravitational attractive force. One pushes, the other pulls. Which will win the cosmological tug-of-war?

To material scientists, this question is important because it tells them something about the fate of the universe. If the repulsive force is greater than the attractive force, then the universe will expand forever, as the galaxies (including our own) gradually drift apart until they lose contact with each other and stars no longer light the night sky. This model is called an *open universe*, graphically represented with the shape of a saddle to reflect the stretching out of space. If, on the other hand, the attractive force of the stuff in the universe is greater than the repulsive force, then the expansion rate of the universe at some point slows to a halt and gradually reverses; the stuff in the universe begins closing inward, like a giant magnet pulling the far-flung cosmic debris toward itself. Eventually, this attractive force draws the matter in the universe back to one colossal point, euphemistically labeled the big crunch.[232] This model is called a *closed universe*, graphically represented by the shape of a sphere to reflect the curvature of space upon itself.

In a third option—a *flat universe*—the repulsive force exactly equals the attractive force, graphically represented by an infinite sheet of paper where neither the repulsive force nor the attractive force has the upper hand in bending space one way or the other.[233]

A rocket's launch into outer space may be used to illustrate these three possible universes.[234] In an open universe the launching force overcomes the Earth's gravitational force and sends the rocket into outer space. In a closed universe the rocket's launching force is strong enough to enable the rocket to break through the Earth's atmosphere but insufficient to free the rocket from gravity, causing it to fall back to Earth. In a flat universe the force of the blast-off is set with such precision that the rocket escapes the Earth's gravitational force with just enough energy to settle into orbit like a satellite.

Now consider *critical density*. The critical density is the precise density of matter necessary to balance the attractive force with the repulsive force—the density that ensures a flat universe. Expressed in terms of matter, the critical density is equivalent to about five hydrogen atoms per cubic meter of space.[235] Thus, if we find ourselves in a universe with five hydrogen atoms per cubic meter of space, as opposed to a near infinite range of other options,[236] we likely live in a flat universe.

It may take a little reflection to appreciate how odd it would be if there were actually the equivalent of five hydrogen atoms of matter in every cubic meter of space and we really lived in a flat universe. Fourteen billion years after the big bang, we'd be living in a universe where the exploding debris from that big bang managed to spread itself so perfectly across space that it balances the explosive force present at the beginning.

Another way to look at the strangeness of any such result would be to consider how finely tuned the conditions must have been at the big bang for the matter density to equal the critical density. The universe's flatness today would mean that the balance of competing forces would have had to be almost perfectly flat at the beginning of time, or else the universe would have already collapsed upon itself or exploded off into infinity.[237] The slightest tilt in favor of either the power of the repulsive force or the gravitational force of the mass density would immediately cause the universe to lose its equilibrium, like a tightrope walker losing her balance, or a pencil tumbling off its point.

As Lawrence M. Krauss states, "If the universe is measurably curved today, cosmologists must accept the miraculous fact that this is so for the first time in the 10^{10}-year history of the universe; if it had been measurably non-flat at earlier times, it would be much more obviously curved than it is."[238] Paul Davies adds, "Unless [total mass] is exceedingly close to [critical mass], the universe would either rapidly collapse back on itself, or explode."[239]

In a similar way, scientists have calculated that in order for the actual density to be within 0.1x and 2x the critical density today, the mass density must have equaled the critical density to one part in 10^{14} one second after the big bang.[240] Extrapolating further back, to 10^{-35} seconds after the big bang, scientists estimate that the mass density must have been equal to the critical density[241] to one part in 10^{49}. Such a universe is indeed finely tuned.

So it would seem impossible for these two independent, random forces—the repulsive force of the big bang and the gravitational mass of matter—to exactly balance. *But they do:* observations show that "the geometry of the universe is flat."[242]

In other words, the big bang—the most chaotic and mindless event imaginable—exploded with a precision light years beyond that achievable by the instruments of modern technology. So material scientists would lead us to believe.

We look out at the picture-perfect world and see that it hangs in balance. Using sophisticated instruments and high-level mathematics we discover that mass produces both an attractive force and the big bang, a repulsive force. Yet these mindless forces cancel out and stay in a precise balance to bring us the world we see. It might be easier to discard the materialistic prejudice and see the world for what it is: a three-dimensional creation of our infinite mind—a world created to respond to our deep desire for harmony.

The Horizon Problem

We customarily use the term *horizon* to tell us how far we can see along a straight line. On the curved surface of the Earth, the limit of the horizon is the point where our straight-ahead vision loses sight of an object that dips below the horizon. Out on a ship in the ocean, on a clear day, one's horizon can be drawn as a circle with a radius extending to the point where the water surface seems to join with the sky.

As noted, the universe not only appears to look the same in all directions but the microwave background radiation is nearly uniform across the cosmos. This should seem odd from one standpoint because it would appear unlikely for the complete chaos of the big bang to have uniformly distributed matter and energy to all parts of the universe, particularly considering that the microwave background radiation at one end of the universe is the same as it is on the other end to one part in 100,000.

But there is also a physical reason why regions on opposite ends of the universe would likely not have the same temperature, mass, or density. Simply put, in the standard model of the big bang, it is impossible for regions of the sky to have communicated with each other outside their horizons. In this case, the horizon is defined as the distance that light could have traveled since the moment of the big bang;[243] scientists calculate that regions on opposite ends of the universe are one hundred times farther than the distance that light could have traveled since the big bang.[244] In other words, the expansion of the universe outraced the ability of light—nature's fastest form of communication—to exchange information between regions rocketing off in opposite directions. Even light could not make up the handicap.

Thus, there is no known physical means for these regions to have shared information, or mixed, since the time of the big bang.

Imagine a global art project in which ten thousand artists around the world are each given one identical piece of tile. They are to paint the tile in the color of their choice. The tiles are to be collected and then formed into a mosaic on the ceiling of a new auditorium. The artists are forbidden to communicate with each other and, in fact, none of them knows who else is participating in the project. They each paint their tiles and ship them back to the art director, who arranges them on the ceiling of the auditorium. Something remarkable becomes apparent: Each artist painted the tile the same color. Arranged across the ceiling, the tiles form a perfect sky of blue. How is this possible if the artists had no means of communication?

Cosmologists face a similar issue on a universal scale with the horizon problem. How is it possible for vastly separated regions of the universe to have nearly the same energy, temperature, and stars if they had no means to communicate? Unless these separated regions of space were able to communicate or mix, there is no known physical mechanism for them to have shared information, much like the ten thousand artists.

In the Real Dream worldview, the horizon problem is easily explained: since the same artist painted the sky, it should all look the same. There are not ten thousand artists, or millions of separate regions of space; there is one sky, one universe, and one author of nature—our united mind.

In material science theory, the horizon problem, like the flatness problem, should raise a big red flag. This degree of symmetry is not supposed to be possible in a mindless material world. The flatness and horizon problems suggest that something more is at work in creating the universe we live in than the blind laws of material science, perhaps even a Mind.

Chapter Sixteen

THE AMAZING INFLATING UNIVERSE

CONFRONTED BY THE FLATNESS and horizon problems, material scientists face a familiar choice: consider a new, all-embracing world model, or simply bolt more parts onto the existing model in the hope it will continue running. Certainly, it would be just too odd in material science's mindless worldview for the infinitely chaotic big bang to have produced a universe of mass and energy perfectly balanced on pencil point, and a sky full of galaxies uniformly distributed across the heavens. Mindless explosions are not supposed to produce worlds of endless order.

Material scientists now believe that they have found a way out of this unwelcome state of affairs. The solution is known as *inflationary theory*. Of all the theories of science, inflationary theory might just be the most outlandish. That so many cosmologists now subscribe to this theory is a commentary on the desperate state of materialistic science. Of course, one would not know this fact by reading popular books and articles on the subject, where the inflationary theory is fast becoming part of the scientific mainstream. It is as if we have compartmentalized our minds to such a degree that we have shut off any independent thinking about the origin of the universe. We close our eyes and hand over the assignment to the scientists with the thought, "Tell us how you think the world was created and let us know when you're done." No matter how absurd the theory they come up with, we take the package and file it on a shelf in the back of our minds; after all, answering the big questions is their job.

Alan Guth, a professor at the Massachusetts Institute of Technology, is credited with coming up with the "spectacular realization"[245] of inflation. As noted, the root of the horizon problem is that at no time in the history of the universe, according to the big bang theory, could the opposite ends of the universe have been in thermal equilibrium (or had the same temperature). Even going back to the matter assumed to exist 10^{-37} seconds after the big bang (an impossibly short period), there was no physical mechanism for this stuff to stay in thermal equilibrium.[246] Guth imagined that the universe started off much smaller—in fact, exactly the right size for light to have traveled across the entire expanse of this early universe. Then, through a theoretical sleight of hand, the universe just so happened to inflate by a factor of 10^{51} in 10^{-36} seconds—and then paused to track the normal expansion of the universe predicted by the big bang.[247] This wild expansion occurred in an unimaginably brief time— one-billionth of the time it takes light to cross the distance of an atomic nucleus.[248] This expansion is far faster than the speed of light.[249]

No words in the English language describe the stupendous nature of this growth rate, and the theory is a sign of the extreme measures that material scientists take to preserve the foundation of their mindless worldview. Instead of considering another force at work in creating the cosmos, they appear content with an inflationary theory they call "natural."[250]

Then the question arises of what drives inflation: Why should the very early universe expand at an exponential rate, and then stop to join the more steady universal expansion we see today? Simply to flatten the universe and place it in thermal equilibrium? To put it mildly, that answer would seem a bit contrived.

Keeping with their mechanical view of the universe, scientists need to invent another force field or two to drive inflation. One of these theoretical force fields is called the "inflaton" field and the other the "Higgs" field[251] (on which we say more later). One field supposedly drives inflation, and the other gives particles their unique masses. The inflaton field is tailor-made to possess just the right features so that it puts the early universe on its hyperdrive acceleration but then suddenly slows down and joins up with the expansion rate of the observable universe. As Alan Guth himself observes, the addition of an energy field with an energy density appropriately flat for driving inflation can be included in any unified theory:

> It must be admitted, however, that the ad hoc addition of such a field makes the theory look a bit contrived. To be honest, a theory of this sort *is* contrived, with the goal of arranging for the density perturbations to come out right.[252]

Further, Guth acknowledges that "inflation does not explain how the universe began, nor does it set out to do so." Instead, given a "speck" of matter, inflation provides a physical mechanism for converting the speck into the universe. According to Guth, inflationary theory "reduces the question of the universe's origin to the question of how we get that subatomic speck."[253] Accepting the inflationary theory comes at a steep price. As Guth laments, with inflation, "Calculations yield reasonable predictions only if the parameters are assigned values in a narrow range" and that "most theorists . . . regard such fine-tuning as implausible."[254]

Indeed, it seems obvious that Guth is right on at least one point: inflationary theory is nothing more than a mathematical contrivance to make the universe obey materialistic theory. Even leading material scientists question the nature of the theory. P. James Peebles gives inflation an "incomplete" grade, stating that it lacks direct evidence and "requires huge extrapolation of the laws of physics."[255] John Maddox, editor emeritus of the influential science periodical *Nature*, writes, "There is no direct evidence that the universe went through a period of inflation."[256]

David Lindley, in his book *The End of Physics*, observes that in place of fine-tuning the initial conditions of the standard big bang theory, the inflationary model requires the fine-tuning of an assumed force field known as the Higgs mechanism.[257] In other words, for inflation to produce the universe in which we live, we have to assume that a roomful of physicists were at the controls of big bang to make sure it exploded in just the right way.[258] As Lindley writes,

Inflation is not the greatest triumph of particle physics in cosmology but its greatest misapplication. . . . With inflation, particle physicists have begun to design theories whose sole purpose is not to solve a problem in particle physics but to make cosmologists happy. Inflation is a nice idea; it would be pleasing if particle physics worked in such a way that it made the universe large and uniform. But there is no substantial evidence that inflation actually occurred, and its biggest prediction, that the universe should be exactly flat, may not even be true. Nevertheless, so enamored are particle physicists of the idea of inflation as cosmic panacea that they have taken to inventing theories that do nothing except make inflation work.[259]

Professor Paul J. Steinhardt of Princeton University, who received the P.A.M. Dirac Medal from the International Center for Theoretical Physics in 2002 for his contributions to inflation, has succeeded in exposing the fatal flaw in inflationary theory. This theory, which was intended to carpet over evidence of fine-tuning suggested by the flatness and horizon problems, itself requires an incredible degree of fine-tuning to fulfill the function that scientists desire. The problem, again, is that the rate and type of inflation necessary to flatten the universe and solve the horizon problem is *far more unlikely* than the "bad" inflation that will do nothing other than scatter matter to the deep reaches of outer space.[260] In other words, cosmologists must hope for a highly improbable, finely-tuned inflation to do away with the distasteful fine-tuning features of the flatness and horizon problems. With inflation, scientists replace one form of fine-tuning with another, and make no progress toward solving the mystery of where the fine-tuning came from in the first place.

We can state a simple principle: Getting matter to organize itself into the symmetries of nature will inevitably lead to a fine-tuning problem, and the fine-tuning problem leads either to the multiverse or, heaven forbid, an intelligent force in the cosmos.

The origin of the problem is that material scientists never explained where the first speck of matter came from, or how it came to form the universe on its own power. Material science made a wrong turn at the beginning of its theorizing, and no amount of corrections along the way-ward journey is getting them on the right course.

Inflation gives believers in a material-based creation something to cling to. Remarkably, despite its contrived and ad hoc nature, inflation-ary theory is now part of material-science orthodoxy and standard uni-versity textbooks.[261] Reflecting a trend in material science, these scientists explain the ordered universe not by calling upon Mind (or God) but by spinning out increasingly elaborate theories that cannot be proven true, but serve the function of making some people believe they are being scientific because they invoke no supernatural agency—by which they mean, "no mind."

In constructing inflationary theory, scientists have roamed far from their common belief in the underlying simplicity of the universe. We are trying to explain what exists, but what exists did not wait for a theory; it simply was. It took the straightest line to being because it happened once and that is all. This is why the Real Dream must be right. It is the simplest theory. It requires no parameters, force fields, or fine-tuning. It requires only one mind—which cannot be doubted—and the ability to dream. No theory can offer as direct an explanation for what exists as can a theory based on the connection between a mind and its dream.

Material scientists, however, constrained by their death grip on a material universe, try to explain everything in terms of matter and energy—regardless of what the evidence shows or how absurd the the-ory.[262] They will ride materialism to the end, regardless of whether they must dispense with logic, reason, or empiricism along the way, so enrap-tured are they with the need to explain the creation of matter and forces by means *wholly independent of mind.*

If you take a wrong turn on the way to a destination, you may soon find evidence of your wayward direction piling up. You start in Denver on the way to Salt Lake City; you may then find it curious that after driving the expected time you find yourself not in Salt Lake City, but in Kansas and then Arkansas. Undeterred by the signs, landmarks, and your compass, you plow on, tossing off these signs of misdirection as errors in highway sign-making, then of the map-maker, as you continue your way-ward voyage to the Atlantic Ocean. You then determine that someone has altered the magnetic pull of the North and South Poles, causing your compass to read the opposite of how you just *know* it should read. Then, like a character in a Dr. Seuss story, you conclude that on this day the stars in the sky must be misaligned, as nothing is right except the thought in your head that you are on your way to Salt Lake City.

And how much easier it might have been to stop early on in your trip and checked to see if you were indeed heading in the right direction.

Material science is no different. Material scientists start off in exactly the wrong direction by imagining, against all the evidence, that the entire material world sprang from nothing on its own power and then formed the world standing before you. Once material science rockets off in the wrong direction, its proponents drift further and further away from the truth. But so focused are they on explaining the world in terms of mindless particles and energy that they just keep adding more sophisticated theories and assumptions to their worldview, hoping that no one notices how far from the right track they have wandered.

Chapter Seventeen

A MATERIAL WORLD THAT SHOULD NOT BE: THE ANTIMATTER PROBLEM

During the 1930s, material scientists gained the ability to make particles collide at high speeds in particle accelerators. By colliding particles at speeds approaching light, these researchers succeeded in smashing material particles into yet smaller pieces. In the meantime, the experiments verified Einstein's prediction that mass is equivalent to energy by actually creating matter out of energy.[263]

Though supporting Einstein's famous equation, these experiments inflict yet another serious wound upon the big bang theory. Nearly every time a particle is created from energy, an "antiparticle" is also made.[264] An "antiparticle" is a particle with the same mass as a normal particle, but an opposite charge.[265] For example, the antiparticle to the electron is known as the positron.[266] When a particle meets its antiparticle, they annihilate each other in a burst of energy,[267] like two superheroes with equal but opposite powers. Reversing the process, a given amount of energy produces a particle/antiparticle pair.

According to the theory, the big bang released infinite energy, which created the particles making up the universe.[268] If laboratory findings reflect what occurred at the big bang, then that infinite energy should have yielded equal parts matter and antimatter. But this is not what happened. Matter, as we know, dominates the universe.

These facts leave material science pondering the rather ironic question of why such a great oversupply of matter exists in the universe, instead of equal parts matter and antimatter.[269] So critical to science is the solution to the antimatter problem that, as one scientist writes, "Once the excess of matter has been established, the subsequent evolution of the universe is comparatively straightforward."[270]

But what if matter did *not* dominate antimatter? What if there were an exact symmetry between matter and antimatter? Well, unless these particles mutually agreed to stay at opposite ends of the universe,[271] they would have long ago destroyed each other and there would be no universe, no Earth, and no human consciousness.[272]

Let us see if we have this straight. First, material science states that at the moment of creation there existed infinite energy compressed into a pinhead. Then, we learn, this infinitely dense point suddenly and for no reason exploded, causing a titanic release of energy and the creation of space and time. But laboratory findings strongly suggest that this infinite energy should have produced a symmetry between matter and antimatter because the blind laws of nature favor neither.[273] Therefore, according to the laws of physics, the present universe is impossible because matter and antimatter should have long ago destroyed each other. Or, after assuming the entire material universe, many physicists are now puzzled over why the laws of nature allow it to exist, as if materialistic theory contains its own self-destruct mechanism.

Two choices confront particle physicists seeking to solve the antimatter problem. They can suppose either that an overabundance of normal particles locked into the universe from the start, or that an unknown physical condition broke an exact symmetry between particles and antiparticles.[274] This last possibility appeals to some physicists because they believe that nature recognizes no distinction between matter and antimatter.[275] Some scientists value symmetries to the point where they even seem to prefer a symmetry to a real universe. As Steven Weinberg states, "One might have supposed, if only on aesthetic grounds, that the universe began with equal amounts of matter and antimatter and therefore with equal numbers of baryons and anti-baryons."[276] According to many scientists, some unknown force had to break the symmetry between matter and antimatter in order for the world to exist.

Breaking the particle/antiparticle symmetry requires violating a physical law known as *baryon conservation*. Physics assigns each elementary particle a baryon number of +1, −1, or 0.[277] Normal particles have a baryon number of +1, and antiparticles have a baryon number of −1. Other particles are assigned a 0 in this counting system. Conservation of baryon number states that in any reaction the total baryon number remains the same before and after the reaction.[278] Scientists initially proposed baryon conservation as a law of nature to explain the stability of matter; unlike radioactive chemicals, normal matter—such as stones, water, and metal—does not spontaneously decay.[279]

To solve the antimatter problem, scientists believe they must explain why a positive baryon number exists in the universe or, put in more common terms, why there is a lot more matter than anti-matter. Material scientists discovered in the 1960s that one of their elusive particles, known as the K^0_L meson, decays somewhat more frequently into antiparticles than particles. This finding provided a small bit of evidence supporting the nonconservation of baryon number.[280] From this limited data point, scientists then speculate that perhaps it is possible for the early particles of the universe to have decayed into one extra particle for every 1 billion antiparticles, precisely the small dominance that some scientists believe is needed to account for the present-day universe.[281]

Many of our leading scientists, therefore, believe that the existence of our universe results from this tiny victory that particles scored over antiparticles in the early days of the big bang.[282] According to material science, if not for the irregular decay pattern of a theoretical particle, we would not be here. Materialists thus take a grand loop: they prize symmetries and, therefore, for aesthetic reasons, prefer equal parts matter and antimatter. But this particular equilibrium leaves us with no world and no scientists. So then, using the power of theory, scientists imagine that something broke this world-denying symmetry, leaving us with the universe of matter. Materialists thus use one theory to rescue us from the consequences of another, as we patiently wait for them to take a different perspective on the appearance of matter in our world.

Chapter Eighteen

TWENTY INVISIBLE UNIVERSES

First material scientists assume a dimensionless point containing the seed for the universe; then this seed explodes into trillions of particles that immediately start following the laws of physics and chemistry. Then it turns out that something programmed the big bang with just the right explosive force to place the stars in the sky into a state of equilibrium. The big bang should have produced equal parts matter and antimatter, leaving us with no universe. Scientists assume that some force broke the perfect symmetry just enough to leave us with the present oversupply of matter.

And it only gets worse. With the possible exception of the inflationary big bang, probably no concept in material science theory is as dubious as the strange form of matter that scientists have invented to explain other observed phenomena in the cosmos.

When speaking of matter, we commonly think of "stuff"—things we see, touch, and feel: rocks, trees, dirt, water—anything that resists a force. Matter, as commonly conceived, is the *opposite of nothing*. When we look out at the world, we might imagine how all the stuff got there— trillions upon trillions of stars, space dust, and planets . . . sands from all the beaches on Earth thrown into the sky to become glowing stars.

But the visible stuff of the universe—those trillions of stars in the sky—make up only 1 percent of the matter that scientists believe constitutes the universe.[283] Hot gases make up another 3 to 4 percent, leaving over 95 percent of the stuff in the universe to consist of mysterious forms of matter and energy that scientists believe exist, but cannot see or touch. According to the theories of modern science, in the shadows of the stars hide twenty invisible universes. That's right: Material scientists, the rulers of our worldview, believe that enough unseen matter and energy exist to form almost two dozen more universes.

Scientists believe that the law of gravity *demands* more matter to exist, even if we cannot see it. Johannes Kepler (1571–1630) was a German astronomer known for deriving three laws of planetary motion.[284] His third law, known as the harmonic law, states generally that the farther a planet is from the sun, the slower it moves. This movement, however, is mathematically proportionate to the distance from the sun. Sixty years after Kepler's finding, Isaac Newton converted Kepler's third law into a formula that can be used to deduce the quantity of matter enclosed within the orbit of a stellar object, such as the Earth or the sun.

By knowing the velocity of a stellar object and the radius of its orbit, one can deduce how much matter Newton's law of gravity states must lie within the orbit, since gravity is essentially spinning the stellar object around a gravitational source. For example, applying Newton's formula to the sun's orbit around the Milky Way galaxy leads to the conclusion that there are 100 billion solar masses (stars equivalent to the sun's mass) within the sun's orbit.

An impressive feature of Newton's law of gravity is that someone can calculate the expected mass within an orbit simply by knowing the velocity of a stellar object and the radius of its orbit. But here a serious problem arises: what astronomers observe in the heavens is not what the math tells them should be there. There are not 100 billion stars observed within the sun's orbit. Rather, the "number of stars falls far short of accounting for the derived mass."[285]

This finding creates a scientific dilemma. Scientific theory is based on observation, or empiricism. Kepler, for example, derived his harmonic law by using extensive observational data collected by the Danish astronomer Tycho Brahe (1546–1601). Observations lead to theory, and observations contrary to a given theory should place the theory in question. But having elevated gravity as a universal law of nature, scientists had to make a choice: either modify the law of gravity to account for the observations or convince themselves that what they were seeing must not be true. *Scientists chose the latter option.* Accordingly, they decided that there must be an invisible form of matter lying out there somewhere in the dark spaces of the universe to make the law of gravity hold true across the cosmos.

Put differently, dark matter inverts empiricism: instead of allowing observations to drive theory, theory determines what we are supposed to see. If we do not see what our theories say should be out there, then the theory is right, and our observations wrong.

Dark matter gives scientists a choice: Place all bets on the law of gravity and imagine that a mysterious invisible force rules the cosmos, or recognize that the law of gravity is not universal. Simon Singh, in his book *Big Bang: The Origin of the Universe*, remarks on how astronomers, despite data showing that Hubble's original measurements of the distance to galaxies were wrong, still refused to question Hubble's conclusions because of his stature in the scientific community. Mr. Singh observes, "A failure to question and challenge such fundamental statements, even when they are made by eminent authorities, is one of the key features of poor science."[286] If we multiply the respect given Hubble's distance calculations in the 1930s manifold, we might have an understanding of the scientific stature of Newton's law of gravity. But the failure to question these theories when faced with contrary data remains poor science.

Scientists first considered it necessary to imagine the existence of dark matter by studying spiral galaxies.[287] Spiral galaxies are vast collections of stars in the shape of a pinwheel. These galaxies, however, cause problems for material science.

Another one of Kepler's laws states that the farther a star or planet is from a gravitational source, the slower its speed. Under the laws of gravity, the outer rings of a spiral galaxy should move slower than the inner spirals, in the same way the outer planets in the solar system move slower than the inner planets.[288] This fact means that the outer spirals should be thrown off into space, and not kept intact as a pinwheel.[289] But observational data shows that the outer spirals move as fast as the inner spirals, in apparent violation of the laws of gravity.[290] We know that the outer rings move as quickly as the inner rings; if they did not, no spiral galaxies would exist in the heavens, yet we know they do.

These are the facts. The outer rings move as fast as the inner rings in violation of the laws of gravity. To supply the missing mass to hold spiral galaxies together, material scientists first imagined dark matter.

Dark matter shows material scientists compounding the error that began when they assumed an external world of matter. Once they anchored this assumption firmly in place, the mind was separated from matter and could provide it no help in forming the world. The known laws of science cannot account for the shape of spiral galaxies. Rather than change their laws or frame of reference, scientists imagine trillions of tons of additional dark matter to hold the universe steady.

But before this theorizing begins, scientists fail to appreciate that they have already imagined one universe of matter; this universe, the one we see outside, seems to stay in place quite well without assuming twenty additional invisible ones.

When an artist paints a mural showing fields of gold, towering mountains, and the twinkling stars overhead, he does not take a ruler to make sure that all the pieces of the scenery are spaced to obey the law of gravity. Rather, he is painting something to express a feeling of beauty; the canvas reflects an internal image of something out in the world. In our world, the creative mind, an infinite source of power resting at the center of existence, projects a world and then places itself in that world.

Finding ourselves in the world, we *demand* order. Our infinite need for a world translates into an infinite need to repel the nightmare of a disordered world. We channel this need into the forms we see, but this force transforms itself into a regular-operating world, a fixed machine; it does not control the spacing of the pieces on the scenery.

Material scientists should stop their wasteful search for dark matter.[291] As their observations show, dark matter does not exist; rather, we are actors in a great story, moving through history as beings on a wave, riding the wings of creation to a higher place.

What is the overriding law in the universe? What law stands at the top of the hierarchy? Look deep inside and ask yourself what you want most: Companionship? Regularity? Constancy? Solidity? A tomorrow?

Something to hold on to? Hume was on the right track when he postulated that at the core of scientific law is our need for a world: a barren, naked, raw need, screaming in the night, praying for something to hold on to. Somehow deep inside, through a miracle we will never understand, something answered this need and projected a world.

Today, we are too young to appreciate the enormity of this miracle. With our tablet computers, cell phones, big-screen TVs, fast cars, and all the dazzling wonders of modern society, everything seems natural and here for us. But we are rising slowly to the realization that we can only be here in one way, and that is through a united dream. Here we will find the source of symmetry and beauty in the physical world, not through the misguided theories of material science.

Chapter Nineteen

THIS ACCIDENT NEVER HAPPENED

The universe looks like a put-up job.
—Fred Hoyle

LET US NOW SUPPOSE for the sake of discussion that material science is in fact on the right track. Through an incredible miracle, a point of infinite density burst from the dark void, and matter overcame antimatter in the first moments of creation. But then another major problem confronts those who seek to continue this line of explanation. How can the mechanical laws of material science bring these mindless particles together into the mathematical forms of the physical world?

We have an infinite point and an explosion, but we lack an important ingredient: the mind or intelligence to guide this creation. The exploding particles are on their own to form a picture-perfect universe. How is this supposed to happen?

Paul Davies helps us put some perspective on both the time it might take for the random shuffling of dead particles to form the world outside your window and the odds against this event occurring. Davies refers to certain predictions made by Ludwig Boltzman (1844–1906), based on the chances that random, floating molecules of primeval gas would spontaneously form universal order. According to Boltzman's reasoning, these mindless molecules would now and then join together to form an organized pair, and over time, another pair would be created and a little more order formed. Bit by bit, the mindless particles would form not just a clump of collected dust but the spiral galaxies, the seven seas, the Alps, human beings, and the rest of creation.

About how long would it take for these particles to form the universe? Davies estimates a length of time in years expressed by a two-level exponent, the number 10 raised to the 10^{80} power.[292] This number is not just 10 with eighty zeros after it; it is 10 with 10^{80} zeros after it. Therefore, the time it would take for these wandering particles to form the universe is 10 raised to the 10^{70} power greater than the age of the universe. In other words, it cannot happen in this world.

Davies also refers to the odds, calculated by Roger Penrose, against the observed universe appearing at random instead of another less inviting habitat, such as a giant black hole.[293] Davies arrives at another double-level exponent, 10 with 10^{30} zeros after it.[294] These odds make winning the lottery a sure thing. Simple arithmetic shows that the chance of our universe arranging itself out of random particles roughly equals the chances of winning the lottery every day in a row for about 10^{28} years.[295] In other words, at the risk of understatement, the odds are that the big bang should have produced one big black hole instead of our universe.

A large number of leading scientists believe that we live in a universe created by nothing other than chance. Many scientists, particularly when allowed to lean on the multiverse, prefer to place their bets on the long odds coming up in favor of materialism, rather than belittle their intellects and succumb to faith in God. But in making this choice, they have not given the miracle of the universe its fair due. We do not live in a two-dimensional, connect-the-dots, stick-figure world in which the odds of any particular arrangement appearing can be calculated with a computer. Instead, we are in the midst of an amazing, three-dimensional, flowing movement riding out into the future. What theory of material science accounts for this 3-D symphony we call life?

Science should not exist simply to perpetuate prejudices, even if most of the intellectual establishment shares them. Material scientists, as the foundation to their cosmological theories, assume an independent universe of matter. Because this assumption requires science to disconnect mind from matter, science is left without an intelligent guiding force to assemble the universe. Thus, science faces mind-boggling odds against these particles forming a universe on their own power.

Scientists have another means to account for the physical appearance of the world—the mind's dreaming power—but to date they have decided not to use it. In dreams we experience the very three-dimensional flow we experience in what we call the real world. Is this simply a coincidence, or do our dreams tell us more about our lives than we give them credit for? Furthermore, is not the mind's dreaming power also a force of nature? Is it not also *natural*? Is it somehow scientific to assume matter and the laws of nature, but unscientific to work with the forces we know exist?

Science's Forces of Strength

Because material scientists have exiled "mind" and intelligence" to the realm of the supernatural, they cannot invoke these forces to organize their mindless particles. But even if we assume that the laws of nature are properties of things and not of the mind, nature gives us only four forces to organize these dead particles: gravity, electromagnetism, the strong nuclear force, and the weak nuclear force. That's it. With these four forces and infinite energy, physicists believe that they can explain the creation of the world.[296] But when we examine these forces, we find science is missing a force or two ilfor the task at hand.

Let us consider the four forces. The strongest force is the strong nuclear force, which, according to physics, binds various subparticles together in the nucleus of the atom.[297] Residual strong nuclear force binds atoms into molecules.[298]

The strong force counterbalances another fundamental force, electromagnetism, in the atomic nucleus. In the classic model of the atom, an electron orbits the atomic nucleus. The electron is negatively charged; electromagnetism keeps the electron fixed in its orbit around the nucleus. The nucleus, in turn, contains the proton, which is positively charged, and the neutron, which has no charge. Material science theory, therefore, pictures the atom as a miniature solar system held together by electricity rather than by gravity.

In this solar-system model, the protons are compressed together in the atom's nucleus. According to the laws of electromagnetism, these positively charged protons should repel each other with terrific force and explode the nucleus. But obviously this does not occur, since here we sit. The atomic nucleus, and hence all matter, is stable because the strong nuclear force overrides the repulsive force of electromagnetism and ensures that protons stay bound together in the nucleus.

The strong force exhibits another beneficial property. It operates within an extremely limited range—only 10^{-13} cm, the diameter of the nucleus.[299] If it operated across an infinite distance, as do gravity and electromagnetism, we all would be stuck together like peas in a pod, and life would be impossible. The strong nuclear force is 10^{38} times as strong as gravity.[300]

Gravity, as we know, holds the planets in their orbits around the sun, the stars within galaxies, and galaxies in their orbits around each other in the universe. Gravity is only an attractive force and, because it is so weak in relation to the other three fundamental forces, requires a huge mass to be important in physical theory.[301] With regard to the strong force, it was noted that we are fortunate that its powerful effects operate only within the nucleus because otherwise we would be pressed together rather uncomfortably. A similar remark may be made with respect to gravity. If gravity were much stronger, stars such as the sun would suffer an earlier death and, according to Paul Davies, the Earth would have been incinerated by now.[302] As a matter of common sense, we could all be thankful that gravity is just an attractive and not a repulsive force. If masses both attracted and repelled each other like electric charges, we might now be caroming off into space rather than circling the sun. In such a world, again, life would be impossible.

Electromagnetism, the third force, encompasses what we know as electricity and magnetism. Electromagnetism, as noted above, holds the electron in its orbit around the nucleus and, along with the strong force, is responsible for the stability of what we know as matter. Electromagnetism operates between charged particles.[303] Electromagnetism spans a spectrum of wavelengths, from radio waves, which have the longest wavelength, to visible light, X-rays, and gamma rays, which have progressively shorter wavelengths.[304] Electromagnetism is the only fundamental force that both repels and attracts other particles. This force helps solidify matter and also has produced enormous practical benefits for modern society. Countless technological innovations, from lightbulbs and telephones to televisions and computers, are based on electromagnetism. Without electromagnetism, atoms could not stay together, and the universe would consist of wandering particles.[305] Chemistry would be impossible, and stars could not shine and give life to planets such as ours.[306]

The last fundamental force is known as the weak nuclear force, which is responsible for the spontaneous decay of certain radioactive nuclei, resulting in the emission of electrons or beta rays.[307] The weak nuclear force has the shortest range of any of the fundamental forces, only—10^{-16} centimeters.[308] Unlike the other three forces, the weak nuclear force is actually a transformation force. It converts a nucleus of certain radioactive atoms into different particles; it does not attract, pull, or repel particles like the other forces. According to physical science, the weak force is responsible for radiation produced by the stars, including the sun. As with the other fundamental forces, the strength of the weak force fortunately is geared to allow the sun to burn its hydrogen fuel at a slow rate. If the weak force were significantly stronger or weaker, life as we know it probably would be impossible.[309]

In summary, the strong nuclear force keeps the nucleus of the atom in one piece. Gravity keeps planets and stars in their orbits and our feet on the ground. Electromagnetism holds the electron in its orbit and allows for the wonders of modern technology. Finally, the weak nuclear force regulates the decay of radioactive elements and the burning process of the stars.

Importantly, scientists express each of these forces in terms of relative strength, range, and their effect on matter. These are mechanical laws—laws of a machine, not of an artist. They hold things together and push them apart; they do not paint a picture, organize a stage, draw a landscape, or create an aura of physical beauty. They push, pull, and emit, but tell no story. Put another way, they are forces of a mechanical world, not of a dream. When we say that the laws of nature caused dead and dumb matter to form the world resting outside your window, we can see that scientists have added some unknown and unnamed force to account for the beauty and order we see all around us.

Modern science nevertheless believes that the creation and present state of the universe can be explained by just these four forces.[310] But they might as well also tell us that to paint the Mona Lisa or compose a Shakespearean sonnet, all they need is a fulcrum and a pulley. Science's forces are those of brute strength, not art.

How did these rudimentary forces assemble lifeless objects of the universe together? Furthermore, how did they also paint rainbows, waterfalls, snowy mountain peaks, the spiral galaxies, the lilies of the field, and the countless wonders of the world? What force explains nature's artistic creations? The answer is none. Science's particles are blind, and so are its forces.

Material science supposes that an independent world exists external to the mind. Therefore, by definition, the mind can give this hypothetical independent world no help in arranging itself into symmetrical patterns. The blind particles are left to themselves to create the beauty of nature. But random particles have no more reason to organize themselves than dust floating in the wind. These particles forming the picture-perfect world outside your window requires the same thing for which scientists criticize religion: a leap of faith. Except with material science we leap to a meaningless world, deceived into believing that we are being scientific as we give up control, and then responsibility, for the world.

Scientists do something here that may escape attention. They take the mind that they have removed from scientific theory and place it among their random particles. Random particles alone do not create the world, but random particles dancing to the tune of the laws of nature do.[311] Scientists replace faith in God with faith in natural law.

Heinz Pagels, in his book *The Dreams of Reason*, expresses this viewpoint clearly:

> Whether God is the message, wrote the message, or whether it wrote itself is unimportant to our lives. We can safely drop the idea of a Demiurge, for there is no scientific evidence for a Creator of the natural world, no evidence for a world with purpose and nothing that goes beyond the laws of nature.[312]

Because material scientists, under their worldview, cannot attribute harmony to a mind or intelligence, they necessarily look to the laws of nature. Religion stops the questioning at God; science stops it at the laws of nature. But science's approach begs the questions: How are the laws of nature possible? Why is it that physics can describe nature by mathematics? Why do key physical values, such as the strength of the four fundamental forces and the speed of light, remain constant? How did these mechanical forces create a world in which only the imagination can measure the depth of its beauty?

Material scientists avoid answering these questions because they have assumed both matter and the laws of nature as given.[313] They find no need to explain what they have assumed. But what do scientists mean by the word "nature"? Do they perhaps mean "mother nature," as in the invisible guiding force to the workings of the world? Is not "mother nature" just another name for mind or intelligence? Without natural law, physicists have only the random particles of wandering gas molecules; with natural law they have order. But rather than attribute this order to God, as do theologians, they attribute it to "nature"—the hidden constant in their materialistic theories. Physicists, in other words, place the mind in nature, rather than in heaven; they are closet pantheists who believe that nature is God.[314] Albert Einstein, notably, is known for having sympathized with the philosophical views of Benedict Spinoza (1632–1677), who equated God with nature.[315]

Now nothing is wrong with equating God with nature; the Real Dream reaches the same result. But because material science simply takes the laws of nature as given, it offers no explanation how its material objects—mindless particles detached from the mind—can ever hope to operate in harmony with each other. To material science, the universe, like any other machine, possesses no spiritual force that makes its moving parts work together. Only forces and objects that can be physically sensed have value in material science. Material scientists no more believe in an invisible spirit who organizes the physical world than they believe in the powers of lucky charms or rabbits' feet.

Instead of positioning ourselves in an assumed world, we need to sit behind the one mind, or behind our body and the space outside our body. When we look out at the world, we must see our body and the world as existing on the same level. This is a simple thought.

In the Real Dream, the mind projects physical objects. We know the mind possesses this power. This dreaming power may admit of no explanation; it is a miracle—but a miracle we know is possible.

Material science asks for two miracles. It knows that the mind is capable of projecting a three-dimensional world. It knows that in lucid dreams and powerful hallucinations this mind-projected world duplicates physical reality. It knows that something can come from nothing in this manner. But dissatisfied with what it perceives as the ephemeral nature of dreams, material science demands that a real world also exist outside of the mind. It wants a near infinite amount of matter and energy to spring out of the void and then assemble itself into a world. But everything its theories cannot explain—matter, order, space, and time—one miracle (the dream) already explains. Does this fact not tell us something about truth?

Chapter Twenty

CREATION AGAINST THE TIDE OF ENTROPY

ANOTHER EXAMPLE OF THE problems created when scientists use purely mechanical rules to account for the universe concerns the Second Law of Thermodynamics and the related law of entropy. The Second Law of Thermodynamics is the law of the engine: heat, generated by a fuel source, cannot be converted completely to work (such as moving the pistons in a car). Some heat or energy is always lost in the process.[316] In an automobile, for example, only about one-third of the energy supplied to the engine moves the car; the rest is wasted as exhaust or lost in the cooling system.[317] This law precludes perpetual motion machines, because some energy must always be added to the system to make up for the unavoidable energy loss.

Using this law, Rudolf Clausius (1822–1888) showed how, for any isolated system, energy in the form of heat moves toward equilibrium.[318] Hot bodies lose heat and become cooler. Cool bodies do not spontaneously become hot because energy would have to be added to the system. Energy systems, by nature, move toward lower energy states. This formulation of the Second Law of Thermodynamics is known as *entropy*, which states that for any closed system, the entropy or heat loss increases.[319] Ludwig Boltzmann added one more piece to the Second Law of Thermodynamics that concerns us more directly here. Boltzmann showed that entropy is related to disorder: as entropy increases so does the disorder of a closed system.[320] As a matter of probability, as heat disperses from a closed system, the gas molecules have more disordered states to assume than ordered states.[321]

As physical systems change, there is a much greater chance that they will move toward a disordered state. For example, leave one hundred children to play unsupervised in Toys"R"Us, and there is a great chance the store will be more disorganized than it began the day; the kids had many more ways to create a mess rather than order.

When modern science applies the Second Law of Thermodynamics to the universe, serious problems develop, particularly for the future of humankind. Modern science considers the universe a great big machine.[322] According to the First Law of Thermodynamics, the total quantity of heat or energy in the universe is conserved.[323] This energy may change form—such as hydrogen into radiation, or motion into heat—but the total quantity of energy cannot change. In other words, material science believes that the universe is a closed system; energy cannot be added to it without violating the First Law of Thermodynamics.

Applying the Second Law of Thermodynamics to the universe, the most gigantic of all engines, yields the result that the stars will eventually cool and their hot gases dissipate, as the universe seeks thermal equilibrium just like any other engine. This prediction is known as the "heat death" of the universe,[324] which dooms distant generations. Under the law of entropy, the ordered universe over time will collapse into total disorder; the stars in spiral galaxies will wander off, and all the heavens, including our planet Earth, will give way to this law of physics and flee toward chaos. Fortunately, physicists put the death of the universe off for several billion years.

Using the Second Law of Thermodynamics, therefore, material science predicts that the ordered universe—our Earth and all life—will someday dissolve into a sea of particles. When we apply the law of entropy to the big bang, however, a question arises: If energy seeks a state of maximum disorder, then should not an event consisting of an explosion of near-infinite energy have produced near-infinite disorder? The big bang was the greatest explosion of matter and energy imaginable. Therefore, it seems, the big bang should have been an entropy-generating event; it should have, according to the laws of thermodynamics, scattered these primeval particles to the four corners of the universe where they could have rested, satisfied to know they had obeyed the laws of physics.

Material science's standard response to this point is that entropy only increases with regard to the whole system; individual segments of the system are allowed to violate the second law of thermodynamics, provided that the entropy for the entire system increases. Therefore, scientists contend, isolated fragments of order in the universe, such as the planet Earth, are the exceptions to the rule; as a whole, the universe is fulfilling the law of entropy. Now, abstractly this may be true, but 14 billion years after the hypothesized big bang, it is indisputable that this wild explosion produced endless order—at least on this planet—rather than chaos. Spiral galaxies and great nebula clouds decorate outer space, and constellations, reminiscent of childlike drawings, sketch the sky. Creation occurred against the tide of entropy. In short, entropy may be the law of engines, but it does not appear to rule the universe.

Brian Greene, in his book *The Fabric of the Cosmos*, reaches a necessary—and noteworthy—conclusion when applying the Second Law of Thermodynamics to the big bang. He observes how it is so much more likely that broken eggs do not miraculously reassemble themselves back into an egg, or that the pages of *War and Peace*, when thrown into the air, do not flutter down to earth in perfect order. But in analyzing the second law of thermodynamics in the context of the big bang, he comes to a startling conclusion: Since entropy must increase with the passage of time, the universe we see today must be extraordinarily less ordered than the universe at the time of the big bang. He concludes,

> *The ultimate source of order, of low entropy, must be the big bang itself.* . . . The egg splatters rather than unsplatters because it is carrying forward the drive toward higher entropy that was initiated by the extraordinarily low entropy state with which the universe began. Incredible order at the beginning is what started it all off, and we have been living through the gradual unfolding toward higher disorder ever since.[325]

If the universe as it existed at the moment of the big bang was more ordered than it is today, then who or what created the order? What force or particle in material science's repertoire can be responsible for ensuring that the universe at creation had more order than it has today?

The common answer is evolution.[326] But this theory, which we will take up in section 3, cannot possibly begin until there is a struggle for existence, for which we will need living things. So we need greater order at the big bang than we see in today's universe, which includes living things. Evolution, even if it operates as Charles Darwin envisioned, does not help explain how the big bang can be the source of order.

An obvious solution presents itself: The big bang never happened. Rather, the big bang is what it has always been: an artist's rendition of a materialistic creation, mindless energy propelling matter and space to the four corners of the newly born universe. But the only possible way for the stuff in the world to reach the heights of mathematical order is for a mind to do the organizing.

Scientists can believe that the big bang actually happened; they can trust their theories and believe deep in their hearts that the stuff they see really exists outside the mind. They can line up all the science professors from all the great universities and proclaim their faith in a materialistic conception of the universe and pledge their allegiance to the big bang. But at the end of the day, they will have mistaken the power and source of this belief, for they are simply reflecting the tail end of the dreaming power. Our mind's infinitely intense desire for *something* has somehow given us an apparent world. Running headlong away from the blackest nothing, we enter the world as beings lost in our own imaginations.

Chapter Twenty-One

MATERIAL SCIENCE'S MATHEMATICAL LAWS

The miracle of the appropriateness of the language of mathematics for the formulation of the laws of physics is a wonderful gift which we neither understand nor deserve.
—Eugene Wigner

SCIENTISTS SUBTRACT MIND FROM matter, leaving only matter. Matter—grains of sand, rocks, and the flames of fire—is by definition dead and dumb. At the same time, material science rests on the notion that the workings of nature can be described by mathematics, from Newton's laws of motion to the charge of an electron. Mathematical order or symmetry represents the limit of physical order. No more perfect four-sided form is possible than a square, and no more perfect round form than a circle. Even complex natural shapes, such as snowflakes, honeycombs, and planetary orbits, possess an internal balance describable by mathematics.

Here then we find two facts in conflict: Material science separates mind from matter, but then proceeds to catalogue the laws by which this mindless matter organized itself to the limit of mathematical order. Matter is dumb but the laws of nature are brilliant. Scientists mathematically describe the orbits of the planets around the sun, and the electron around the atomic nucleus. They mix elements in constant proportions to make chemical molecules; marvel over the universal constancy of the speed of light, the force of gravity, and infinitesimal nuclear forces; and delight in depicting the wonderful intelligence of the DNA molecule. Material science's dead and dumb particles did not just organize themselves; they did so to the limit of mathematical order. But while material science proudly uncovers the symmetries of nature, it forgets that its mindless world has no means to get these particles organized.

As a matter of scientific inquiry, we must find a way for an ordering mechanism to influence the physical world. Of course we know of one way: the mind can always influence its own dream, since it creates both the physical image and the means by which it operates.

We may note that scientists regularly report experiencing religious-like feelings when they uncover one of nature's hidden harmonies, as if the harmony fulfills a secret wish of the soul. Professor Lederman calls these experiences "Eureka!" moments, and Professor Krauss says new scientific discoveries produce a "rush" of excitement. Here, the alien, brute material world appears not just as an object thrown together by irrational random forces. Rather, with harmony found, the universe moves closer to us, as if the mind reunites with its creation. In the Real Dream, we may observe that the universe and our lives represent the limit of the mind's dreaming power; we are pressed to the wall of infinity, and roll through space building upon our own creativity. When one scientist uncovers a harmony in nature, there should be no surprise if excitement accompanies the discovery; she for a moment has reached a stage of inspiration achieved first by the one free mind of God. The conscious mind of the scientific theorist joins with the unconscious mind of God.

One of the best examples concerns Johannes Kepler (1571-1630), who started his career with hopes of becoming a theologian, but had his meeting with God through the study of the stars. Kepler sensed that the planetary system followed a mathematical symmetry, and he spent years studying astronomical data collected by his predecessor, Tycho Brahe, in the hope of finding the secret harmony in the heavens.[327] One day nature's secret came to him. Using Brahe's data, Kepler was able to calculate both the time it took for a planet to orbit the sun (the period of the motion)[328] and the planet's distance from the sun. With these values, Kepler found that when he cubed the radius of a planet's orbit, and squared each planet's period of motion, all the planets in the solar system obeyed the identical mathematical proportion.[329] The simple proportion R^3/T yields the same value for all the planets. Planets move through the heavens as if on key.

The music of the spheres inspired later scientists to search for mathematical harmonies in nature. Indeed, if the planets in the solar system, millions of miles apart and with no means of communication, obeyed the same symmetrical relation, then perhaps other parts of nature did so as well. Today we regularly read about modern science's search for the symmetries of nature, as if science knows they are hidden there.[330]

Kepler's discovery led Newton to deduce his own famous law of gravity: that the attractive force between two bodies varies in proportion to the square of their distance from each other.[331] (Or, for example, the closer a planet is to the sun, the greater the sun's attractive force, and the faster the planet's orbit.) Perhaps as a matter of common sense we are not surprised to find that the gravitational force increases as the distance between two bodies decreases. This fact is what we understand by gravity and the observation that a falling object's acceleration increases the farther it falls and the closer it gets to earth. But what may seem odd is that this gravitational force is universally constant and is expressible in mathematical terms. In a random world of wandering particles, many other possibilities suggest themselves. For example, as Hume might say, no necessity exists that two stellar bodies (sun and earth) millions of miles apart should even attract each other, much less attract each other in a regular manner. Moreover, no logical reason exists why gravity should be proportional to the product of the masses,[332] or why it should vary according to the square of the distance, rather than vary randomly.

Under the material science worldview, it must be considered a curiosity of nature for the other major force of the macroscopic world—electromagnetism—to obey a mathematical formula of the same form as gravity: the strength of the electromagnetic force = a constant times(rest charge a)(rest charge b)/ R^2.[333] In other words, the electrical force between two electrical charges at rest is inversely proportional to the square of their distance, just as with gravity.

Newton's law of gravity tells us that the attractive force of one body (the sun) upon another (the Earth) decreases in proportion to the square of the distance. But why should one physical object stand in such a symmetrical relation to another that it can be expressed by a mathematical formula? Put another way, of all the possible relationships that one object can have to another, why should the relationship be one that can be expressed mathematically and that holds true as universal law? Physicists find the law but then stop when they get to this most important question.

For many of science's formulas to remain valid, certain important values must remain constant—across the entire universe and for all time. These values range from the very large, such as the speed of light, which clocks in at 186,000 miles per second, to the incredibly small, such as the rest mass of the electron, one of materialism's many elementary particles and the carrier of electricity. Its rest mass is .00000000000000000000000000911 grams (9.11 x 10E −27).[334] Another universal constant is the gravitational constant, which is expressed as 6.67 x 10E −8 dyne-cm/gm. Oddly, these values, despite the precision with which scientists have measured them, do not change throughout the universe.

We may now ask again why the force of gravity varies in inverse proportion to the square of the distance between two bodies? Here Kepler told us all we needed to know: if gravity operated otherwise, the planets might not move in harmony. In the Real Dream, that completes the explanation.

Chapter Twenty-Two

THE MELODY CAME FIRST

It is difficult to look out at the world and not marvel over its apparent design and how the parts—the planets, stars, clouds, weather, vegetation, life—all seem to work together to form an interlocking whole. Standing alone on a clear night, peering overhead at the stars, with the Earth balanced in its orbit around the sun, and the strength of the sun's rays adjusted to just the right temperature to allow life to prosper, with drink and food aplenty, and life in harmony with Nature, we might come to realize that we belong here. This is a home made for us; it fits so well that it seems as if the world is an outgrowth of something we need deep inside.

These feelings are often categorized as religious or mystical: the sense of oneness with the world and the transportation of our souls to a spiritual place where we feel we belong.

Looking out at the world, we might well ask ourselves the deep, unavoidable question of whether, even in the God-less, sterile worldview of material science, some force other than the blind laws of science is behind the curtain, directing the action on stage.

We may see without the use of laboratory instruments that the living world fits together: male and female, bird and sky, fish and water. In each climate life abounds and plants yield fruit, vegetables, spices, and treatments for disease. *Here, on our planet Earth, we find a giant garden of life stocked with everything we need for a grand voyage through time.*

The Design of the Universe and the Anthropic Principle

Looking out at the world, we see that events occur with astounding regularity; we measure a year by the time it takes for the Earth to orbit the sun, and a month by the moon's orbit around the Earth, as if we were lowered down into a storybook world. Engineers send rockets to the moon and satellites into orbit in complete reliance upon the fixed strength of gravity; the stars in the sky and the sun seem to burn at a steady pace—no different than giant heat lamps—as gravity and nuclear reactions balance off and provide billions of years of energy.

It may be enough to make us stop and think how it came to be that the physical world, this supposed chance production of random forces, turned out to operate with such fixed regularity. If somehow the exploding particles from the big bang managed to align themselves into a fixed order—like a monkey who randomly happens to play the notes for Beethoven's Fifth Symphony on a keyboard—how did the monkey happen to keep repeating the same song in perfect rhythm for all time? Was the form of the song "in the air" such that once the monkey found the right melody, it became fixed into space? Was the form in the mind like Plato first envisioned, and did those forms implant themselves on the physical world?

As we have seen, the answer that scientists give is that the laws of nature govern the physical world. This response begs the threshold questions: How are the laws of nature possible? What force in material science's arsenal locks the gears of the universe into place and keeps them spinning at a constant rate? It is one thing to believe that the big bang radiated energy evenly across the celestial sphere, but it is something else altogether to believe that this infinite explosion set the clockwork universe into perpetual motion.

And of course the creative ability of the big bang becomes even harder to fathom when we consider the phenomena of life. Even if we accept that a form of evolution occurred, how did life, a self-replicating, embodied fluid in motion, arise from an explosion? What force set the conditions of the universe in just the right alignment to allow life to emerge from a swamp?

That the universe is designed should be apparent to any observer. As we know from the current debate between adherents of intelligent design and Darwinian evolution, however, the question is: How did this apparent design originate? Is a mind necessary for the order and patterns we see, or can the mindless process of natural selection generate a world of such intricate design that observers are misled into looking for an intelligence behind the scenery?[335]

From the study of cosmology, we find a universe resting in a precarious balance of gravity and repulsive force, as if the two contrary powers were programmed to cancel out. We find the cosmos uniform across distinct reaches of the sky, the galaxies arranged overhead as if someone painted them to create a stunning background for the heavens. The sun undergoes a series of synchronized nuclear reactions to provide an almost endless amount of power to distribute heat and light to the Earth.[336] Dark energy, the mysterious background force accelerating the expansion of the cosmos, is precisely the strength required to ensure a balanced universe and, remarkably, 120 orders of magnitude less than quantum theory predicts.

That constants even exist should be a source of profound amazement. The speed of light, 186,000 miles per second; the gravitational force, 6.67×10^{-11}; the mass of an electron, 9.11×10^{-31}; and the charge on a proton, 1.67×10^{-19}, are among the fundamental values that are presumed to hold true throughout the universe.[337]

It is as if creation generated trillions of tiny widgets refined to the smallest degree of tolerance possible, sprayed them across the cosmos, and infused them with instructions to follow precisely choreographed movements. Every electron in the universe weighs the same and has the same electric charge; the tiny gravitational force is assumed to be constant throughout the universe as if it is an embedded property of matter.[338]

Deeper inquiry into the relationship between the constants yields further mysteries. The ratio between the mass of the electron and proton is 1/1836. Another so-called dimensionless constant is the fine structure constant; this number combines the speed of light, the charge on a single electron, Planck's constant, and the vacuum permitivity into another ratio, 1/137. The interesting part of these ratios is that if they were even slightly changed, neither the universe nor living beings could exist.[339] As John Barrow writes,

> If [the fine structure constant] had a different value, all sorts of vital features of the world around us would change. If the value were lower, the density of solid atomic matter would fail ..., molecular bonds would break at lower temperatures ..., and the number of stable elements in the periodic table could increase. If the fine structure constant were too big, small atomic nuclei could not exist, because the electrical repulsion on their protons would overwhelm the strong nuclear force binding them together. A value as big as 0.1 would blow apart carbon.[340]

We thus walk the narrowest of tightropes, balanced on a taut stretch of values and forces that are fixed into the cosmos just so life can exist.

Faced with the obvious fit between humans and the world, some material scientists rely upon what is known as the anthropic principle and the multiverse to explain the fine-tuning of the universe. The anthropic principle recognizes that we cannot help but view the universe from the perspective of life, and therefore, by necessity, the conditions of the universe must allow for the possibility of life.

The question then becomes *how* the universe came to welcome life. Is life a fundamental force of the universe that imposed itself on the possible array of physical constants and laws? Or does the existence of life simply limit the possible arrangements of these physical parameters and require at least one suitable for life?[341]

If the conditions of the physical world *must* allow for life to exist, then we draw closer to the argument from design for the existence of God; specifically, some intelligence would be necessary to fine-tune the physical world and to pave the way for life.

This conclusion, however, which is tantamount to invoking the supernatural, is rejected by the majority of scientists who prefer to seek refuge in the wild supposition that our universe is one of a vast landscape of other universes, the great majority of which are unfit for life: we just happen to find ourselves in the "goldilocks" universe, with physical parameters happily geared to support life.[342]

The multiverse is the last refuge of the die-hard materialist. Once scientists disconnect the physical world from the mind and treat the world as an independent object, they are left to explain the fine-tuning of the world not through tight reasoning and experiments, but by resort to an infinite array of universes they can never know. The multiverse becomes a "cop-out,"[343] "philosophical speculation," but not science.[344]

It should be apparent that the ground-up approach, this attempt to explain the world starting with particles and forces and ending with a three-dimensional world, will never work for the simple reason that there are far more possible configurations that do not lead to a balanced, inhabitable universe. As some theists use "God" to explain every gap in scientific theory (such as how something came from nothing or the source of the laws of nature), so the followers of the multiverse call in their vast array of unknowable universes to explain any troublesome fine-tuning of the cosmos.[345]

From the Outside In

So how do we explain the order we see? Why is it that the smallest particles seem to follow an intricate guidance system and dance to an inner harmony? Why do the tiny parts align so precisely to form the symmetrical shapes decorating the heavens and the earth, from spiral galaxies to the rings of Saturn, to falling snowflakes, and the twinkle in a little girl's eyes?

We begin with the most basic observation: Any possible world must start with something—with stuff—unless there is a thing nothing else follows, including of course life, and the tendency of life's highest form to examine the world about it. If we skip over this question, and simply assume that the world came into existence on its own power, with no help from a mind, we will always be at a loss to explain the order to the material world because we will have no means to connect an organizing force with matter.

The essential feature of this book is that something is possible in only one way: through the mind's dreaming power. What we see outside of the mind—our bodies and Mother Nature—is a mind-projected world; the perfectly formed, infinitely powered dream. This is an apparent world, in the sense that it does not exist on its own power, apart from the mind. But because our bodies, or our most immediate reflections of what we are inside, are also an appearance, the world external to our bodies—nature—exists on the same level; the "apparent" nature of both the body and the outside physical world cancel out, thus bringing us the real world.

With the world connected to us, we should not be surprised if we find in it reflections of ourselves: it is unavoidably true that the world we see and experience does in fact reflect, in a three-dimensional way, the sum total of our conscious and unconscious thoughts, needs, and emotions. A poet in a rush of inspiration spills out his soul on paper, expressing in words an emotion once thought beyond description. The artist paints his vision of a conquering hero riding off to encounter an unknown enemy. The scientist, with formulas and principles buzzing in her head, leaps to a new theory of gravity. At the height of inspiration, the mind loses itself in its creation; there is nothing else—no distraction, no other thought but a laser focus on the single creative act.

Now multiply each element of the creative process by infinity: a mind with unlimited power, left alone in the blackest of nothings. Somehow at the center of being there is a creative force; we will never know where it came from, for it is the greatest miracle imaginable. *That there* is *something will be an object of wonder that we will ponder for the rest of eternity.*

Material scientists, with the independent-world assumption guiding the way, take precisely the opposite approach: they want to explain everything by reductionism: by explaining the large as a result of the small, by reducing the world to its smallest working pieces and then explaining how the world we see resulted from these small pieces. They take the miracle of the world for granted.

The three-dimensional world we see can only have come about as a result of a dream; therefore, we must look to the rules of the mind to assume how it is ordered.

When projecting the world, the mind is not concerned about fixing the constants of nature. Rather it is projecting a homeland for the mind. We wrap ourselves around the rope strapped to a ledge and hold on for dear life; it is all we have. We will have to create the world here—a storybook world, one where the sun always rises on time, the stars shine a steady glow, and we can know that tomorrow will always come.

You need to look no further than your own needs and wants to find the source of constants. They are right inside of us, as the world reflects our deepest need for something to hold onto. The outer physical forms came first, and the inner working parts look up to the whole.

The three-dimensional world we live in is a projected *translation of* internal states. The mind of God is the grand animator, weaving a story acted out on the stage we call the planet Earth, with our hopes, dreams, and fears churning through the creative waterwheel of the mind, spilling out and expressing itself into space.

Material scientists thus have it upside down: the world does not arise naturally from fundamental equations, but rather the equations arise naturally from the forms of the dream world. The melody came first, but scientists since the beginning have instead sought to prove how the notes arose from nothing and organized themselves into a song that keeps repeating and evolving. They are looking through the wrong end of the telescope.

The universe did not create itself from the small bits to the three-dimensional forms of the physical world, but *from the outer forms inward.*

In the Real Dream, humans and the outside world evolve together as two self-reflective forms. The internal parts, by definition, cannot control the dream, any more than manipulating an image on a movie screen will alter the movie projector.

But in this dream, as in any other, when we fool ourselves into thinking that it controls us, this thought becomes programmed into the dreaming mind and we operate following that guide; our dreams always push against the limiting thought, as we strive for immortality, for peace, for heaven in a material world. But the world we believe exists pulls us down. The most positive and healthy attitude is not to give up control;

adopt the no-limit thought of the artist and athlete, and fight against the belief that the world controls you.

We know that the dream must follow the command of the mind, but our day-to-day conscious minds are floating on top of a united, unconscious mind that spins the world out, like a spider its web. The end point to the dream—the edge of the universe, the tip of a rose petal, the end of a rainbow, and sparkle in a child's eye—is a creative expression of the mind. We can explain the laws of nature as the relationships and values necessary to form a three-dimensional storybook world. In running away from nothing, the dark void, we pull hard on the rope and it tightens into a crystalline form; but we pull this rope with an infinite dreaming mind, and leave behind a projected world formed into patterned internal structures.

We exist as survivors, not of a big bang but of an explosion of infinite creativity. We are the result of an infinite mind becoming aware of itself; for a time the wave pulls us along by its own power, but after a while the mind comes to understand itself. It unites and we catch the wave and try to ride it out, mastering it the best we can. Realizing that we sit at the control of creation is the first step of an eternal quest to command the dream. It may never happen—the dream may always race just ahead of us, beyond our farthest grasp—but we have no choice but to chase after it, striving for an endless future.

Chapter Twenty-Three

MATERIAL SCIENCE'S LAST MODEL

Within the mighty fortress of material science theory lies a built-in defect. Material science rests on two great theoretical foundations that stand in direct conflict: quantum theory and the law of gravity. Quantum theory, about which we have more to say shortly, governs the very smallest pieces of nature, with its effects only uncovered at sizes millions of times smaller than a grain of sand. Gravity, which by definition is only an attractive force, operates between particles of all sizes but because it is so weak, its presence is only noticeable with large masses: we know the sun's mass holds the earth in orbit, but we do not consider the gravitational effect that a baseball flying out of the stadium exerts upon the Earth.

The gravitational force operates smoothly and consistently. Its power is proportionate to the mass of an object; the more massive the object, the greater the gravitational force. This smoothness is often represented by the illustration of placing a bowling ball on a stretched rubber surface, or trampoline, to show how the mass of the ball smoothly warps the space—or rubber surface—around it.

Quantum theory holds that we can never have exact knowledge of a particle's location and momentum or energy level at the subatomic level. At the base of the physical world we find not small pieces of stuff, but mathematical equations telling us the probability that we will find a particle at a certain place;[346] the smaller the time scale or distance, the greater the uncertainty.[347]

According to material science theory, at its birth, the entire universe was condensed into a tiny fantastically dense seed; at this size, both gravity and quantum effects need to be considered. This dense seed would have exerted a tremendous gravitational force, but because it exists on the subatomic scale, quantum effects would also have to be considered. But here there is a big problem. As Brian Greene writes, "Calculations that merge the equations of general relativity and those of quantum mechanics typically yield one and the same ridiculous answer: infinity."[348] Now clearly, if you are trying to work out a mathematical equation to prove true a theory about the physical world, and the solution yields an infinite answer, you have to be on the wrong track.

This fundamental incompatibility between two of the bedrock theories of modern science, however, has not stopped the scientific establishment from preaching quantum theory and gravity as gospel truths. Quantum theory and the general theory of relativity have, of course, been extremely successful in describing attributes of the physical world. They are certainly true on at least one level of analysis. But placed within the context of the material science worldview, which speculates that a big bang blew up a tiny, massive seed into the universe, they cannot both be true. Scientists must thus find another theory to explain the entire universe.

Quantum theory and general relativity are what the explanations always have been: descriptions of the workings of an apparent physical world. If scientists want to create a conflict between quantum theory and gravitational theory, such as by imagining the inner workings of a black hole, nothing can stop them; the conflict will only show that it will forever be impossible to use a materialistic-based theory to explain a dream world. Material scientists can use theory to describe what happens in the physical world, but no complete explanation will be possible without recourse to the world-projecting power of the united mind.

Devising a complete explanation for the physical world was always Einstein's dream and the reason he rejected quantum theory, but as he himself said, "No problem can be solved from the same level of consciousness that created it." *We must rise beyond the misperception that the physical world has an existence independent of the mind in order to achieve a unified theory of the cosmos.* This rise in consciousness is the one we must make to understand the world, an upward movement that Einstein, given the nature of the times, was unable to make. The world waits for us to understand.

As one way out of the intractable conflict between quantum theory and gravity, some theorists have placed their bets on string theory. This theory holds that the fundamental constituents of matter are not point particles, but vibrating strings, infinitesimal reverberations lying within what we perceive to be particles; different vibrations of the strings create the effects of the elementary particles. For this theory to work, however, theorists must have access to up to seven additional dimensions: three-dimensional space and time are simply not enough for string theory to work.[349]

String theory can be viewed as humankind's last attempt to provide a mathematically consistent *physical* description of a dream world. No physical theory, or one that assumes the independent existence of the material world, can ever precisely replicate the workings of a dream world, but models no doubt serve a purpose. The challenge, however, is not to get fooled into thinking that the *model* is reality.[350]

This is painfully true for string theory, as it is hard to believe that the chaos of the big bang spun out a cosmic orchestra of vibrating strings tuned to such a precise harmony that their quiverings gave rise to the elementary particles, and then to the picturesque beauty of the natural world. A fatal flaw of string theory is that, as Lee Smolin notes in *The Trouble with Physics*, the theory is simply a "web of conjectures" that "no experiment will ever be able to prove true."[351] Smolin quotes Nobel laureate David Gross, a strong advocate of string theory, who ended a string theory conference by saying,

> We don't know what we are talking about. . . . The state of physics today is like it was when we were mystified by radioactivity. . . . They were missing something absolutely fundamental. We are missing perhaps something as profound as they were back then.

The harmony that modern physicists attempt to capture through string theory is the reflection of the outer harmony of a dream racing just ahead of any theory. We can be confident that the mind took the simplest route to creation: it desired something, and then through a miracle that we will spend the rest of eternity pondering, light flashed, then flashed again.

SECTION 2

QUANTUM THEORY AS THE PHYSICAL SCIENCE TO A DREAM WORLD

Chapter Twenty-Four

ATOMISM REDEFINED

Today there is a wide measure of agreement, which on the physical side of science approaches almost to unanimity, that the stream of knowledge is heading towards a non-mechanical reality; the universe begins to look more like a great thought than a great machine.
—Sir James Jeans, from *The Mysterious Universe*

THE SCIENTIFIC METHOD should lead us to understand what makes up the world. Evidence gathered through experimentation and analysis should reveal the inner workings of physical reality. It is this evidence, not our preconceived notions, that should guide the search for scientific truth.

If we live in a machine-shop world of tiny ball bearings, then penetrating into the interior of the machine should reveal its smallest working parts, the ultimate pieces to the machine.

If, however, we live in a mind-projected world, then peering into the stuff of the world should reveal the essence of nothing: we might see pulsating images, waves, or shadows, but no *things*. In such a world, the mind builds the bridge between nothing and something. It spans the distance using a stream of infinite desire, an expanse made of bottomless willpower and strength. By our experience of night dreams, day fantasies, hallucinations, and mirages, we know a mind-projected world is possible.

In contrast, material science, highlighted by the big bang theory, has been unable to bridge the infinite gap between the dark void—the beginning of it all—and the singularity that supposedly existed at the time of the big bang. It cannot connect something with nothing other than by *imagining* through highly speculative theories that something burst from the void at the moment of creation. Certainly, if we can replace the *assumption* of a material world with an *explanation* for that world, we will have made a significant advance toward a better science.

The difference in these viewpoints is that in the Real Dream, the imagination, together with infinite desire, creates the appearance of an external world; we are connected to the world because the world *is* mind. The world is a direct and real product of the united imagination.

From Naïve Realism to Atomism

Using the naïve realist assumption, it is a natural step to believe that by breaking down the stuff of the world we will find the ultimate working parts to the machine. For thousands of years, materialists have searched for the ultimate particle, the most elementary building block to the universe. In the course of this investigation, material scientists have held onto their assumption: they search for an elementary particle of matter created external to the mind—some particle with no constituent parts, the smallest ball bearing in a ball-bearing world.

But before reviewing how this investigation has gone, we may ask this question: If there really were such a tiny indestructible ball bearing, where exactly would this particle come from?

Does not science's quest for the ultimate indestructible particle conflict with its need to show how something came from nothing? If such an indestructible particle actually existed, would this not show a leap from nothing to something that could never be executed? And, does this quest not in fact reveal that science is not interested in showing how something came from nothing? But how can science ever hope to offer a complete explanation for the world if it avoids the ultimate question? The answer is, it cannot. This fundamental and erroneous assumption of material science corrupts the rest of its theories, including, in particular, Darwinian evolution.

In the next few chapters we review science's search for the ultimate particle. As we will see, when scientists peer into the heart of matter and complete all of their experiments and thought exercises, they reach a surprising result: they disprove materialism and show that the world must be mind-created. At the bottom of the mind shaft of the physical world is not a ball bearing, an indestructible thing, but a pulsating image, a probability wave, a shadow of something, a quantum world of uncertainty and mystery—exactly what one would expect to find if he chose to break apart a dream.

Chapter Twenty-Five

FREEZING A PHANTOM WORLD

The stuff of the world is mind-stuff.
—Sir Arthur Eddington

We are such stuff as dreams are made on
—William Shakespeare

THE GREEK PHILOSOPHER Thales (circa 585 B.C.) was the first to view ultimate reality in materialistic terms; he thought water made up everything.[352] Other Greek philosophers chose different elements as matter's most fundamental constituent. Anaximenes (circa 528 B.C.) thought everything was made of air;[353] Heraclitus (circa 500 B.C.) picked fire,[354] and Empedocles (circa 445 B.C.), earth, air, fire, and water.[355] Democritus (circa 400 B.C.) looked deeper and believed that small imperceptible things called atoms made up the visible world.[356]

Each of these early philosophers reasoned along the same lines: the smallest and most fundamental constituent of nature must be something out in the world, embedded in the physical things we see with our eyes. Implicit in atomistic philosophy is the belief that beneath the diversity of nature lies a simple structure.

Although the atomistic form of materialism now controls our worldview, it has not always held such a dominant position. It was not until the time of Gassendi (1592–1655), Robert Boyle (1627–1691),[357] and Isaac

Newton (1642–1727) that atomism showed advantages in describing the workings of nature.[358] In the early nineteenth century, when atomism was still far from a widely accepted worldview, the English chemist John Dalton published a book in which he presented new evidence for the atomic theory. Dalton's work followed up on that done by Joseph Louis Proust (1754–1826). Proust found that compounds, such as salt and water, are made of elements combined in fixed ratios.[359] Nature fixes the proportion of elements necessary to form a compound. Like other constants of nature, once nature sets this proportion, it does not change. Because of his work, Proust is credited with discovering what is known as the *law of constant proportions*.[360]

Dalton deepened the understanding of Proust's law by explaining it in terms of atoms. Dalton reasoned that to account for the law of constant proportions, one could view natural compounds such as air and water as being made of more basic elements called *atoms*. Atoms represent the smallest unit of measurement for an element. For example, the smallest unit of the element oxygen is an atom. Broken down below the level of the atom, the substance ceases having the properties of oxygen. Different proportions of these basic ingredients (atoms) combine to form compounds in nature. Thus, for example, eight units of oxygen when combined with three units of carbon form the gas carbon dioxide. Dalton thought that this proportion was fixed in nature because the carbon atom was three-eighths as heavy as the oxygen atom. He thought that combining one unit of carbon with one of oxygen yielded the compound carbon dioxide, a molecule. Later discoveries proved Dalton's conjecture regarding the weight of individual atoms wrong; more than one atom of an element might form a compound.[361] Nevertheless, his atomic theory greatly advanced the field of chemistry and raised the stature of the atomistic worldview.[362]

Scientists have found no variations to the law of constant proportions. Dalton attributed this constancy to the stability of the atom, as if some force supplies chemists with preset measuring cups to work with nature's ingredients, a point that did not escape Proust: "We must recognize an invisible hand which holds the balance in the formation of compounds. A compound is a substance to which nature assigns fixed ratios, it is, in short, a being which Nature never creates other than balance in hand."[363]

The book of nature contains fixed recipes for combining atoms into molecules. Nature's elements, such as hydrogen and oxygen, can be mixed in any ratio, but to form a new substance they must be mixed according to a ratio established by nature. Two hydrogen atoms plus one oxygen atom makes water.[364] Three hydrogen atoms plus one oxygen atom makes no new substance but simply a mixture, like oil and water. Today science works with eighty-three different elements[365] or ingredients that combine in prescribed ways to form molecules and all the substances we encounter in the external world.

Democritus, it turns out, was right: the ultimate ingredients to matter are not water, fire, or air but things called atoms. It seems that water, fire, and air did not give nature enough flexibility to make all the things it desired. Dalton's findings show that matter can be explained in terms of atoms, and the atomic theory helps us work with nature because it underlies recipes for all of the things in the world.

But once again material scientists gloss over the central question: How did mindless residue from the big bang manage to organize itself into a set of eighty-three fundamental ingredients (atoms) that never change their properties and that when mixed in fixed proportions always form the same substances? Why should these atoms bind together in whole numbers? Of course this fact makes the elements much easier to work with, but why should the proportions remain constant?

The law of constant proportions, like the laws of gravity and the speed of light, are held up as proof for the atomic worldview, but they actually work against it. Mathematical constants are repeating fixed patterns, reflecting the highest form of organization achievable by an intelligence. If there were no intelligence to marvel over the structure of mathematical constants, they would mean nothing. That such patterns exist strongly suggests a connection between the inquiring mind and the source of the constants, and the history of science can then be viewed as a single scientific mind (or part of the whole) marveling over a creation of the united mind. Indeed, we understand the world when we understand the mind of God.[366]

But in studying the world, material scientists have assumed that what they see is what is real. They then define what is real as something independent of the mind. They have confused the working pieces to nature as its fundamental elements; they look out on the movie screen for the secret to the ordered parade of images they see, ignoring the role of the projector and the movie producers.

In the mind-independent world of material science, scientists freeze into place a phantasm of the mind; they give it solidity in their minds, and assume it is hard, solid and firm with no contribution from the mind. Taking their pickaxes, scientists then strike the frozen figure and find that it crumbles, fades, and then disappears; it was nothing after all.

Mendelev's Classroom

Nature did not stop with the law of constant proportions. It also saw fit to arrange the elements into an organized table. Scientists first organized the elements of nature according to atomic weight.[367] They found hydrogen was the lightest element and gave it an atomic weight of "1." Scientists gave additional elements atomic weights based upon multiples of hydrogen's weight. Thus, the carbon atom has an atomic weight of 12 because it is twelve times heavier than hydrogen.

Of the many scientists who organized nature's elements, the work of Dmitri Mendelev (1834–1907) stands out. Instead of simply listing the elements by atomic weight, Mendelev sought to organize them by common properties. The story goes that Mendelev[368] put all the elements on cards and shuffled them until he discerned a pattern. He placed elements with similar properties in vertical rows. For example, the common elements fluorine, chlorine, bromine, and iodine belong to the halogen family and fall in the same column on his table.[369] To keep the families of elements together he found he needed eight columns.

With some exceptions, Mendelev found that common properties repeated according to a regular pattern on the table. This pattern is the basis for the periodic law. Put another way, the periodic law is not so much a property of nature as it is a feature of Mendelev's table. The law states that if the elements are arranged in order of increasing atomic weight, those with similar properties will appear at regular intervals or periods on the table; as if to make it easy for us to grasp, related chemicals fall in the same column.[370]

But Mendelev encountered a problem as he set out to organize the known elements by weight and chemical properties. He found that in some instances, the next heavier element did not fit on his chart because it did not share the properties of the chemical family with the next open spot. Instead of disrupting the harmony of his table he chose to leave the spot open and place the element where it fit better. He went on to predict that elements properly fitting into the spots left open on his table would someday be found. Three of those predictions, for gallium, scandium, and germanium, later proved true.[371]

Why was Mendelev successful? Why does nature allow her elements to be organized nicely on a table? Does the periodic law say something about one's ability to organize the random pieces of nature, or does it show humans discovering a harmony that the mind put there for itself to find? Did the mind create the internal order (system of atoms) and external order (mathematical forms of nature) all at once for later scientists (dreamers) to uncover, or do scientific theorists—as thought leaders of the mind—create the order as a work in process? In other words, are we in a constant state of creating the world and therefore simply observing the inner structure of matter conform to the latest theories, or did the mind establish the order in the beginning?

Perhaps we will forever ponder the question of whether the atomic structure of matter existed in the beginning of the dream, or whether the mind of God, in the form of the great scientists in history, has continued the creation by imposing a logical internal structure upon the core of matter to make the scientific enterprise possible. As we peer with ever more powerful microscopes into the pieces of our dream, perhaps our minds drill order into the picture, like an artist giving a conception of something he does not know exists.

As the atomic structure of matter shows the inner components to the dream looking up to the whole, so Mendelev's table shows that when boundless creativity is applied to the phenomenon of life, the end result is a story. The periodic table shows the organization of the elements becoming real for us, as students of nature sitting in chemistry class, trying to understand our world.

Chapter Twenty-Six

TO THE CENTER OF THE ATOM HYPOTHESIS

For the smallest units of matter are, in fact, not physical objects in the ordinary sense of the word; they are forms, structures or—in Plato's sense—Ideas, which can be unambiguously spoken of only in the language of mathematics.
—Werner Heisenberg

THE FINDINGS OF DALTON and others supported the notion that atoms make up matter. With this fact now written in their textbooks, material scientists consider the atomistic worldview established, leaving for future research the small detail of discovering what lies within the atom. Of course these material scientists also have glossed over the other detail of how these microscopic things can exist in the first place. Like a child captivated by the reality of an imagined play world, material science never stops to ask how it happened that the world it so fervently desires stands before it.

In our mind we picture an atom. We see a tiny billiard ball. To make a molecule of water, we picture two red balls for hydrogen, one white ball for oxygen, and link them together. We envision these molecules of atoms as hard and massy. In the late 1800s, material scientists took this mental picture and chased it out into the world.

Reductionism tells a simple story: Scientists first assumed that the world was made of things with defined locations and velocities; they were hard, massy, and solid, exactly like little ball bearings. As scientists penetrated into the material world, however, they encountered a microscopic world that looked less and less like the world their theories told them should be there. One hundred years ago scientists stopped finding things; instead, they began encountering a reality that still avoids description: wave-particles, probability functions, and quantum waves—all words describing nothing.

J. J. Thompson (1856–1940) struck the first blow against the atom. Thompson discovered that under the right conditions, cathode rays[372] easily penetrated thin sheets of metal.[373] If all substances in the world consisted of indestructible atoms, these cathode rays should have bounced off the metal sheets, not penetrated through them.[374] Researchers found these penetrating cathode rays consisted of negatively charged particles one two-thousandth as massive as the lightest known atom. This finding meant that atoms were not the most fundamental constituents of matter. Scientists had found something smaller—the electron. The atom was not indestructible after all. Because of data strongly suggesting that atoms had an electrical character, scientists quickly categorized electrons as elementary parts of an atom.[375]

Atom Model Building

From Thompson's findings, researchers knew that the electron's mass was about one two-thousandth that of the atom. Atoms are electrically neutral and thus must contain a positive particle roughly two thousand times as massive as the electron.[376] With these facts, scientists attempted to create a conceptual model of the atom.

Two models dominated scientific theory in the early 1900s. The first model, formulated by William Thomson Lord Kelvin (1824–1907) and J. J. Thompson, became known as the "plum pudding" model because electrons were viewed as "raisins" placed in a "cake" holding the positive charge.[377] The second model, proposed by Ernest Rutherford (1871–1937), pictured the atom as a miniature solar system, where the electron orbited the heavier atomic nucleus that held the positive charge.[378]

Researchers found that Rutherford's model gave a better picture of reality. Experiments performed in Rutherford's laboratory[379] showed that most of the atomic mass had to be concentrated in the nucleus, in the same way that most of the mass of the solar system is concentrated in the sun.[380]

The year is 1920 and science has a model of the atom reflecting the planetary system on a scale 10^{21} times[381] as small. Electrons were pictured as microscopic planets orbiting the nucleus-sun. Although, as we will see, the atomic model changes, scientists still use the solar system model today.[382]

The Atom of Air

Rutherford's model of the atom greatly influenced both modern physics and the formation of our worldview. It began the process of uprooting the deep belief that hard, massy things comprise the objects in the universe. Rutherford's data showed that the mass of the atom had to be concentrated in a sphere with a radius of about 10^{-12} cm; electrons were spread over an area of about 10^{-8} cm from the center.[383] These numbers mean that the atom—that hard, indestructible billiard ball sitting at the core of matter—consisted of mostly nothing. In the Rutherford model, the electron stands as far away from the nucleus as the earth is from the sun.[384] These facts led physicist Sir Arthur Eddington (1882–1944) to make a famous comparison between his study table and the new table built by scientific theory:

> My scientific table is mostly emptiness. Sparsely scattered in that emptiness are numerous electric charges rushing about with great speed; but their combined bulk amounts to less than a billionth of the bulk of the table itself.
>
> There is nothing substantial about my second table. It is nearly all empty space—space pervaded, it is true, by fields of force, but these are assigned to the category of "influences," not of "things." . . . In dissecting matter into electric charges we have traveled far from that picture of it which first gave rise to the conception of substance, and the meaning of that conception—if it ever had any—has been lost by the way. . . .

The external world of physics has thus become a world of shadows. In removing our illusions we have removed the substance, for indeed we have seen that substance is one of our greatest illusions.[385]

Science, armed with modern technology, had just begun its search for the atom, and already the picture was becoming cloudy. Science was uncovering a world of shadows, not of substance. With Rutherford's atom model, physical science began a gradual but inexorable slide away from materialism, and toward a world of the mind.

Chapter Twenty-Seven

THE VOYAGE STOPS AT THE QUANTUM

It will remain remarkable, in whatever way our future concepts may develop, that the very study of the external world led to the conclusion that the content of consciousness is an ultimate reality.
—Eugene Wigner

RUTHERFORD'S ATOM MODEL showed a negatively charged electron orbiting a positively charged nucleus. Electricity held the electron in its orbit around the nucleus, as gravity holds the planets in their orbits around the sun.

But this picture admits of a fatal flaw. Under the laws of physics, the orbiting electron must lose energy as it moves; if the electron acted as other physical objects known to science, it should, in less than one one-millionth of a second,[386] dive into the nucleus[387] like a ball dropping onto a roulette wheel.

We know that electrons do not spiral into the nucleus and collapse matter into a point. If they did, all the matter in the universe would have long ago disintegrated. Furthermore, if the electrons behaved according to Newtonian physics, electrons would emit a continuous spectrum of light as they dove into the nucleus. Experimenters, however, witnessed only discrete spectral lines coming from individual atoms.[388] These elementary particles seemed to obey some strange rule not found in existing science textbooks.

Nature's Rainbow Meter

Common sense suggests that things come in bits, and energy in waves. Crushing a rock makes dust; thrown into the wind the dust creates a cloud of fine particles. Particles never disappear into nothing or join together to form a wave; breaking a particle into pieces may make the pieces smaller, but it does not destroy the concept of a discrete unit. The bits are microscopic, but they remain distinct and do not merge together into the continuous flowing pattern common to waves.

Energy seems different. A dimmer switch on a lamp turns smoothly, reflecting a continuous flow of energy. We tend to think that energy comes in streams, like the sweeping of an artist's brush across the canvas.

At the end of the nineteenth century, scientists discovered that at its most fundamental level, energy is discontinuous, just like a cloud of dust particles. To explain a phenomenon known as "black-body" radiation,[389] physicist Max Planck (1858–1947) introduced the "quantum of action," which effectively puts notches on nature's energy meter. Working backward from experimental results, Planck reasoned that light had to be emitted in small packets called quanta. Between a 0 reading and the first quantum, nature is silent; it does nothing. Only when it reaches the quantum, expressed as 6.6×10^{-27} erg/sec.,[390] does nature speak, though quietly. Nature emits energy in discrete units. Each packet is so small, however, that energy, such as light, nonetheless appears continuous in the same way a motion picture appears continuous even though the film is made of still picture frames. When we slow down a film and view it frame by frame, we see that the motion picture is actually discontinuous. In a similar way, only at atomic dimensions can we notice that energy is also discontinuous, or broken up into "frames."

Planck's constant enables nature to exhibit an important feature. Modern science relates the color of light to wavelength. The color spectrum, from violet and blue to green, yellow, orange, and red, corresponds to light waves with increasingly longer wavelengths.[391] The speed of light in any color is constant. Therefore, the frequency of light—the number of wavelengths that passes a given point per second—depends only on the wavelength. As an illustration, a train with short rail cars will have more cars pass a given point than a train with long rail cars, provided that both trains travel at the same speed.

Planck's formula[392] states that the higher the frequency (and hence the shorter the wavelength), the more energy will be required to produce that color of light. Thus, light of shorter wavelengths (for example, in the violet end of the spectrum) requires more energy to produce than yellow or red light. If there were no notches on nature's energy meter, a given amount of energy would be distributed over all possible wavelengths.[393] This result would either mean that no light at all is emitted or light only in the ultraviolet region.[394] Planck's constant guarantees that a heated body such as an oven or a star will change colors as its temperature increases, and as more energy is applied to produce light of higher frequency. Planck's constant thus ensures all the colors in the rainbow are represented in nature, and that the sun glows a brilliant yellow.

Planck's constant shows that when material scientists attempt to use mindless particles to account for the harmonies and symmetries of the universe they encounter intractable problems. They must first find a way for the particles to assemble themselves so precisely that they form mathematically fixed patterns. They then must explain how it came to be that these patterns became associated with a harmony in the outer world—how, for example, atomic structures produce spectral lines.

From the dream perspective, the explanation comes much more easily: the quantum is not a mere happenstance resulting from big bang residue but is, rather, a consequence of the outer harmony of the physical world. The melody, or the dream, came first, and the internal, quantum structure trails behind. The quantum is the physical image of the internal workings of an infinite dream. From this perspective, quantum theory is the physical science of a dream world.

Bohr's Rescue

With the Rutherford atom model, material science had a problem on its hands. Experimental evidence had produced an atom model that concentrated most of the atomic mass in the positively charged nucleus, around which circled the negatively charged electron. But science does not allow for perpetual motion machines; under the laws of physics, the orbiting electron had to lose energy and could not remain in its orbit. The scientific method had led to an atom model that violated the laws of physics. One of them had to go—the model or the laws of physics; science chose to keep the model and change the laws of physics.

In much the same way that Planck worked backward from the experimental results of black-body radiation to derive the quantum of action, so Niels Bohr used experimental data to arrive at a new model of the atom. This model would not obey the laws of Newton, or what common sense would expect to lie at the base of matter. Science discarded its billiard-ball pictures. Physics no longer would explain nature according to how atomists had pictured reality; rather, physics would now explain nature according to what the experiments showed.

If the orbiting electrons conformed to the classical laws of physics, then the model collapsed; therefore, Bohr theorized that the electrons did not obey those laws. According to his new theory, as long as the electron stayed in one of certain preassigned tracks around the nucleus, the electron lost no energy; it would just orbit forever with no questions asked about how it started moving or why it seemed to violate the Second Law of Thermodynamics in the process. Bohr said only that certain tracks around the nucleus were allowed; only when the electron changed tracks did it radiate energy.[395]

The Rutherford-Bohr atom moves us from a picture of hard, massy clumps of ball bearings to gyroscope-like atoms, tiny spinning tops with electrons humming around the nucleus at unheard-of speeds, fixed for all time in orbits possessing a faint but steady harmony.

Chapter Twenty-Eight

FROM MATTER TO WAVES AND BACK AGAIN

The world we live in is but thickened light.
—Ralph Waldo Emerson

FOLLOWING BOHR, MATERIAL SCIENCE began to bury the notion that solid, self-supporting things rest at the heart of matter. French nobleman Louis DeBroglie (1892–1987) reasoned that if a light wave could be considered a particle, then perhaps a particle could be a wave. In his 1923 doctoral thesis, he proposed replacing Bohr's electrons with standing waves[396] wrapped around the nucleus. Experimenters soon proved his thesis correct in the laboratory.[397] Science no longer held the view that electron-things jumped from orbit to orbit as they sought different energy levels. Instead, the electron-wave went in and out of focus as the standing wave undertook different ways to envelop the nucleus.

Theory had replaced the image of a thing with a wave, a vibrating shadow, an invisible guitar string tuned to a perfect note around the nucleus. But this wave hung on no string. Theorists believed that the electron carried an associated wave as a sort of tail. But waves are only patterns, forms in a medium; waves are not supposed to be material things.[398] What then is this thing? Nothing?

Following DeBroglie's findings, Erwin Schrodinger (1887–1961) found that Newton's laws of motion were no longer practical for predicting the behavior of nature's most elementary particles. Newton's laws are for simple everyday particles like baseballs and rockets. The electron is no simple particle, but something that exhibits the features of both a wave and a particle. We now needed Schrodinger's wave equation to describe how atoms behaved. By definition, waves are not localized in one place, but are spread out over an area like a water wave. Solutions to Newton's laws of motion yielded clear pictures of rockets shooting through the air and landing at the intended destination. In contrast, solutions to Schrodinger's equation yielded clouds, blurred images purporting to show the distribution of the wave.[399]

Simple pictures of hard massy objects locked together in a tight configuration did not work in describing the physical world. Materialism, using the scientific method, tunneled into this thing it called matter but came upon the stuff of which dreams are made.

DeBroglie and Schrodinger helped replace the clear idea of a "thing" with the idea of a "wave-thing" as the ultimate constituent of matter. Of course, when we look at a chair we do not see it waving in the wind, as might be depicted in an animated film. We instead see a hard, firm chair. Only when the scientist penetrates into the core of matter, only when she attempts to connect her mind with an assumed, independent object, do these problems arise. And in our world—in fact, in any possible world— we should not be surprised that no definable, discrete thing exists at the core of matter. Only the knowing mind can understand the world, and only the dreaming mind can create a world.

The Wave–Particle Reveals Itself

In 1789 Thomas Young conducted a famous experiment proving light was a wave.[400] By passing light through two holes in a screen and noting the patterns formed on a photographic plate, Young showed that light exhibited the telltale sign of a wave: interference patterns.[401] These patterns consisted of alternating light and dark streaks. The dark streaks showed where the colliding light waves had canceled each other out, and the light steaks showed where they had combined.[402] Faced with these interference patterns, no one could now dispute the notion that light was a wave.[403]

That light is a wave can hardly be considered a surprising revelation, except that in 1921 the Nobel Committee awarded its prize in physics to

Einstein for showing that light is a particle.[404] So J. J. Thomson proved the electron was a particle and DeBroglie showed it also was a wave; Young proved light was a wave, and Einstein showed it was a particle. Scientific experiments carried out by leaders in the field showed that at the heart of nature is some strange substance resting in the borderland between a wave and a thing.

Physicists also used Young's double-slit experiment to show that particles act like waves.[405] Instead of shining light on the pierced screen, they fired electrons.[406] Behind the screen was placed a device, such as a TV picture tube, to record the arrival of the electrons. The purpose of the experiment was to uncover the real nature of the electron—is it a particle or a wave? Waves form interference patterns on the detection device; particles do not.

As an illustration, imagine a pitcher throwing baseballs at a screen with two holes. Clearly, each baseball thrown must go through one of the two holes (assuming, of course, a very accurate thrower); one ball cannot go through two holes at the same time, any more than a person can enter a building from both the front and back doors simultaneously. If a net is placed behind the screen to catch the baseballs, such as might be found at an arcade, we obtain the expected result. Individual balls go through either one hole or the other, and stack in the net accordingly.

Now replace the baseballs with water waves. By definition, the wave is spread out and not localized in one place. As the wave approaches the screen it will go through both holes at once (assuming the wavelength is longer than the area between the two holes). As the wave forces itself through the holes, two separate wave patterns form that spread out on the other side of the screen. As they spread, the two waves collide and form interference patterns on the detection screen. Where crests of the two waves collide, constructive interference occurs; where crest meets trough, destructive interference occurs.

Now use electrons. Electron after electron is fired at the double-slit screen. The electron, which surely is a particle, must go through either hole one or hole two, and strike the screen just like a baseball. And indeed that is what the electron does.

But after all the electrons are fired, and the detection screen examined, it is found that the electrons formed an interference pattern just like a wave. An individual electron struck the screen as if it went through one hole at a time, but formed an interference pattern as if it also went through both holes simultaneously and interfered with itself. As one writer describes the results of the double-slit experiment, "It is as if the electrons start as particles at the electron gun, and finish as particles when they arrive at the detector, but the arrival pattern of electrons observed at the detector is as if they traveled like waves in between!"[407]

We then turn to the leading architect of our current worldview, material science, for an answer to this simple question. Its answer is that an electron is both a wave and a particle, although not at the same time.[408] The electron is a "wavicle"[409] or a "lave," but not the sort of thing we encounter on a beach or at a pool table.

A host of scientists have made note of the conundrum these results pose for the realist view of material science. Jim Al-Khalili, in *Quantum: Guide for the Perplexed*, writes,

> I should come clean at this point and state that no one really knows what the wave function actually is. Most physicists regard it as an abstract mathematical entity that can be used to extract information about nature. Others assign it to its own, very strange, independent reality.[410]

Countless books have been written about the ephemeral nature of what we call matter; how matter is a "myth,"[411] which does not consist of "things" or objects,[412] does not exist independently of consciousness,[413] and actually consists of "waves of nothing"[414] or "potentialities."[415] "The doctrine that the world is made up of objects whose existence is independent of human consciousness turns out to be in conflict with quantum mechanics and with facts established by experiment."[416] "The basis of quantum theory is more revolutionary yet: it asserts that perfect objective knowledge of the world cannot be had because there is no objective world."[417] "It will remain remarkable, in whatever way our future concepts may develop, that the very study of the external world led to the conclusion that the content of the conscious is an ultimate reality."[418]

As Professor Richard Conn Henry writes in the prestigious science magazine *Nature*, "In the place of 'underlying stuff' there have been serious attempts to preserve a material world—but they produce no physics, and serve only to preserve an illusion. . . . The Universe is entirely mental."[419]

This is the same "matter," by the way, upon which our leading thinkers have built the towering edifice of modern science, a system of belief based upon the notion that little billiard balls exist outside of the mind. As may be apparent at this point, modern, materialistic science is moving steadily away from Democritus, away from the conception that ultimate reality is a hard, cutless thing, and toward the position of Bishop Berkeley: "matter," in the end, is a concept, an idea, a figment of the imagination that has no reality without a mind.

The modern scientific mind is thus at the point of no return. Scientists know that the classical world of Newton—this hard, massy, ball-bearing world—does not exist. They know that quantum theory reveals a fundamental link between consciousness and the physical world. They know, "There is no way to interpret quantum theory without encountering consciousness."[420] It's as if scientists know the truth, but they just don't want to acknowledge it. We don't want to live in a world of illusion, so we reject this thought, not understanding that we are part of the same illusion. And so we gradually rise to the realization that together we dream the world, gathering the awareness and the courage to understand there can be no other world.

Science believes that it needs an independent world to practice science, but on this point science is simply wrong. True science must deal with the real world, not a phantasm of the scientific imagination. Here, scientists are being mystical, for they have conjured out of their own minds the notion of a free-standing independent world, and then imagined that it is real even though their own experiences show the notion to be false.

In the end, the source of material science's quandary is that it is our own united mind that is projecting reality. When scientists try to study the external world as an independent entity torn apart from the mind, they cut off the source of the world, as they tunnel into an abstraction they have imagined can exist without the dream-projecting mind.

It may be fine to imagine that this world can support itself without the mind; perhaps this is the type of world we all want. But this desire, the strongest force known, is at the source of the controls. We cannot imagine the world without a mind any more than we can imagine a mind without a mind. As Descartes concluded long ago, the mind is capable of doubting anything but its own existence; only the process of thinking cannot be doubted.

As a young mind, we have failed to grasp that the external world *is* the mind in motion: a three-dimensional real-life drama showing the mind's awareness of itself. When the mind tries to prove the independent origin of the external world, it finally discovers that such a world is impossible. The mind is here attempting to prove that its very own dream has an independent reality.

Boring into the core of matter does not turn up an ultimate particle; instead it runs science head-on into the fundamental limitation of scientific theory. No matter how badly the scientific mind demands an independent material world, the mind can never break the link between itself and the world. This demand for an independent world is more than a theory; it instead reflects the deepest wish of the dreaming mind of God.

Chapter Twenty-Nine

THE MANY-WORLDS INTERPRETATION

*All matter originates and exists only by virtue of a force. . . . We must
assume behind this force the existence of a conscious and intelligent
Mind. This Mind is the matrix of all matter.*
—Max Planck

THE SCIENTIFIC METHOD tells us that theories must be tested by real-world experiments. Any opinion not supported by facts must be discarded. Theories must be capable of being proven either right or wrong.[421] "Science is the attempt to explain the world without miracles."[422] Only what can be sensed or demonstrated has a place in scientific theory, or so we have been taught.

By these standards, the many-worlds interpretation of quantum physics shows just how unscientific some scientists become when they attempt to transform quantum theory into a worldview. The quantum theory states that a wave function best describes the fundamental elements of matter. These elements are not things with a definable location and momentum; rather, they are probability clouds showing where particles might be.

But when we look at electrons we do not see "probability waves"; rather, the observation of the wave is said to "collapse the wave function,"[423] or the measurement of the electron-wave causes a particle to come into focus. A shotgun blast of electrons turns into one pellet when we observe the blast.[424]

What is supposed to exist is a "wave-thing" corresponding to Schrodinger's equation. But of course we see neither a mathematical formula nor a wave; we see only normal, everyday things representing the collapse of the wave function. As one writer notes, "How does the unique world of our experience emerge from the multiplicity of alternatives available in the superimposed quantum world?"[425]

Controversy in physics has arisen over whether the quantum wave actually exists out in the world, or whether it is a mere mathematical formulation used to measure an independent material world we can never know. In confronting this issue, some physicists take what they term a realist[426] approach and suppose that this wave packet actually exists out in the world, *independent of the mind*. Clearly, however, we do not live in a wave-packet world; we are not amoebas swimming in the sea. We live in a hard, material world composed of solid things like trees, stones, and earth. So how do we reconcile the solidity of our world with the wave packets that are supposed to really exist?

If the physical world is a countless mixture of quantum waves, then why do we not see quantum waves? Are we too a quantum wave living in one of the parallel universes represented by one possible position of an electron?

In the so-called Copenhagen interpretation of quantum physics, theorists imagine that the scientist, as observer, lives in Newton's classic world; a defined figure, existing in one state and location. The observer occupies a privileged state of a real, unified, solid entity, peering at this lowly, fuzzy world of quantum shadows.

Hugh Everett, the originator of the many-worlds interpretation of quantum physics, asked, "Why do we here accord the observer a different status than the world outside the body?" He wrote:

> The Copenhagen interpretation is hopelessly incomplete because of its a priori reliance on classical physics . . . as well as a philosophical monstrosity with a "reality" concept for the macroscopic world and denial of the same for the microcosm.[427]

Hugh Everett concluded, therefore, that for any of the trillion possible states of the electron, there must be a parallel universe occupied by an observer.

According to this many-worlds interpretation of quantum physics, the real particles we experience represent one of the many possible states of real wave packets. All nature is composed of these elementary particles. Scientists believe that these particles have an existence all their own, apart from the mind. Therefore, we live in a world representing one of the many possible states of the electrons making up the wave. As Paul Davies writes,

> When the universe splits, our minds split with it, one copy going off to populate each world. Each copy thinks it is unique. . . . The splitting is repeated again and again as every atom, and all the subatomic particles cavort about. Countless times each second, the universe is replicated.[428]

Each electron in the wave represents a different world, which, it may be noted, we have never experienced. How many different, imperceptible worlds are there? Oh, about 10^{100} or so.[429]

This error in perspective, it should be noted, results simply from assuming that the external world is independent of the mind. As one writer observes, the splitting of the physical world into a multiplicity of states "happens regardless of whether a human being is present."[430]

Mistaking the external world as an independent reality leads scientists to view the world as a foreign object. Blasting this world apart, they find it consists of electron clouds, not hard-and-fast things. But we do not see clouds. Holding this blurry image of the world in their minds, some material scientists then opine that we too must exist in a superimposed state, since there is no principled basis to attribute a classical presence to the observer, but a quantum-state presence to what is observed.

In different words, in the many-worlds interpretation, scientists let their assumption of an independent world, which they have now found to be actually a world of shadows, to reflect back into their view of the world and distort the lens through which they observe it. They reason that (1) the external world is an independent object, (2) this independent object is actually a whizzing blur of probability waves, (3) we do not see waves, and (4) thus, we must be connected to one of the trillions of alternate universes, which seem solid and real to us.

The chief designer of our current worldview, material science, tells us that theory should be based only on observation and measurement. No hidden assumptions should enter scientific theory—no unprovable mystical force, no psychokinesis, clairvoyance, mind-reading, and certainly no God either. Instead of grasping onto these mystical forces, many scientists[431] are more comfortable postulating the existence of trillions of other worlds we cannot see, touch, hear,[432] or even imagine, just to be faithful to what they believe is a realist interpretation of quantum mechanics.

The many-worlds interpretation is just one more strange consequence of the material science worldview, and the attempt to devise a mind-independent mechanical model for a mind-projected reality. Once we correct this error in perception, we no longer find ourselves trapped by the paradox of formulating a consistent worldview from quantum theory. We simply remove the distorting glass lens from our viewfinder. Once we remove the source of distortion, we can see the world clearly for what it is: a mind-projected reality.

The shadowy waves that quantum theorists find at the core of matter are in fact the ultimate constituents of dream-stuff—nothing at all. We are supposed to ignore the infinitesimal blurriness at the center of the dream-stuff in the same way we today ignore the findings of quantum theory when looking at a rock, a tree, the sky, or other people. We experience only hard, solid things because we too are made of dream-stuff, and thus dwell in a world as real as we are.

Chapter Thirty

THE WORLD'S MOST ACCURATE THEORY

MOST MATERIAL SCIENTISTS SHOW little hesitation in admitting that quantum theory is weird,[433] astonishing,[434] or even "cockeyed."[435] According to material science, the ultimate makeup of the universe consists of something transcending what we think of as particles or waves. Material science theory describes particles that exist in two places at once, revealing particle features at one moment, but wave features the next. What Democritus envisioned as irreducible, machine parts turns out to be a blurry, unpredictable sea of wave functions.

Faced with this bewildering picture of ultimate reality, modern physics falls back upon its last line of defense: quantum mechanics works. In fact, the theory of "quantum electrodynamics (QED), which describes how light interacts with matter through force fields, is the "jewel of physics—our most prized possession."[436] QED is the "most accurate and successful theory in the history of science."[437] QED's accuracy is truly astounding, with theory matching experimental results in some instances to one part in a trillion.[438] Armed with this incredibly accurate theory, physicists are ready to take on anyone who disputes the validity of quantum theory. Let's see you do better, they say.

Once again, however, material scientists have missed the point. The question is not whether the theory works, but how it is possible for it to work, particularly to the claimed level of accuracy?

Under the material science worldview, we may recall, mind cannot operate on matter. Nerve impulses within the brain cannot touch or affect the world outside the body; no visible connection exists between brain and nature.

In material science's picture of reality, the theorizing mind is locked within Plato's darkened cavern;[439] it stares at shadows on the wall as it tries to match mental theories with independently occurring physical events. Scientists press their faces against the television screen separating their mind from nature, hoping to guess how she operates. How is it, we then ask, that a purely mental theory locked within the head of a scientist can describe the workings of an external world to an accuracy of one part in a billion? How can theory be so closely synchronized with a completely detached world? Are these scientists really so good at guessing that they can predict how a photon, one quantum of light, will interact with a particle having a mass of 1 one billion-billion-billion-billionth of a gram? Does not the accuracy of QED suggest that scientists knew the answer before they took the test?

How does the scientist know that the independent material world will obey the theory, much less to the claimed level of accuracy? If the world was actually detached from our mind, we would have no basis for the faith and belief that the physical world tomorrow would act the same as it does today, or whatever faith we had would be misplaced. It would be no different than picking lottery numbers with millions of possible outcomes but having confidence that the balls will align perfectly in order.

On this point, detaching the mind from an assumed independent world leads to two serious problems: How can a mind-independent world, operating on its own power, lock into mathematical patterns accurate to one part in a billion? Second, how can our mind, detached from the assumed independent world, predict with any confidence that this precision-tuned world will continue following the same pattern the next second? These questions have puzzled philosophers of science for centuries, but have been largely ignored by the scientific mainstream, which seems content to measure and record the regularities of nature but not wonder too much about why their instruments or theories work.

The answer is self-evident: scientific theories work because they are conceptual models for mind-created phenomena. Mind and external world are the same thing. QED works because the scientific mind uncovers a harmony of the dream created as a consequence of the dreaming, infinite mind of God.

The sequence works as follows: the unconscious mind projects a three-dimensional form, which leaves behind a trail of internal parts that look up to the whole. The pieces stand in the same relation to the dreamed forms as mechanical components stand in relation to a man-made machine. Instead, however, the inventor is not a team of engineers working in an office building in downtown Detroit but the unlimited creative mind of God. Thus, the dream-pieces are a bit more intricate, interwoven, and complex—as we see, for example, in the atomic structure of matter and the DNA molecule.

The scientific mind searches for symmetry that it believes must exist in the world.[440] In a random world of ricocheting, chaotic particles, this quest may seem quixotic. Why should there be symmetry in the material world? Why should it obey mathematical formulas? What makes scientists so devoted in their belief that beneath the stunning complexity of the world beats a steady rhythm? Science, the cataloguing of laws and regularities, would not be possible without order. But what is the source of the order? It can only be the mind's infinitely free, unencumbered demand for order, as propelled by the rise in the self-consciousness of being in the world. Material scientists stand in awe at the symmetries woven into the fabric of nature, but in their wonderment they forget that only the mind can weave this dream into the interlocking, mathematically precise patterns we see out in the world.

Chapter Thirty-One

THE PARTICLE ZOO

MATERIAL SCIENCE, FOLLOWING THE dream of Democritus, believes that all physical reality—from sunsets and rainbows, to forests, grassy plains, planets, stars, and living things—can ultimately be reduced to fundamental particles. Simple, undifferentiated things combine in infinitely complex ways to create the world we experience.

But, as argued above, Democritus—and material science—are both wrong. The mind-created dream world, this three-dimensional apparent world of spirit, cannot be reduced to material particles; there will always be a gap, which might as well be an infinite chasm, between the smallest particle and nothing. In the end, only our mind can connect something with nothing.

Our reality cannot be broken down into tiny ball bearings. Rather, at the furthest reaches of scientific theory, we can at best create a physical model that closely aligns with the workings of ultimate reality; we can never capture its true essence through materialistic reductionism. There will always be categories of phenomena outside of material science's reach because a physical model cannot precisely align with a mind-created world. The universe sings in its own voice. One must experience the song in the original form, in the same sense that Muslims believe the Qur'an cannot be truly experienced when translated out of the original Arabic through which Muhammad first uttered the words of God. The physical models can mimic, to an extremely fine degree, the flow of the dream-reality, but the models can never quite capture the original form.

In daily life, we are seldom concerned with what lies at the inner depth of matter. Material science conducts this search because it is looking for God—or Truth—inside a particle. Rather, when it comes to the workings of the physical world, we are more interested in knowing at what speed to launch a satellite into orbit, how strong to build bridge supports, or how deep to drill the foundation of a skyscraper.

The scientific models of material science no doubt work to a precision that more than satisfies our needs in daily life. But we should not mistake the physical model for the fluid reality that moves beneath the surface; this world is not made of rocks strewn from the violent eruption of the big bang, but by the hardened resolve of our inner drive for something firm on which to stand.

The scientific mind peers at the world and believes it exists naturally as an independent physical thing. The mind forms an image of matter and then penetrates into this substance, hoping to find the smallest pieces to what lurks deeply within. But the will constantly changes the mental image, shuffles the parts, and replaces the pieces to find the best arrangements to reflect the outer movements of the physical world.[441]

The Standard Model

This view of the world, where material scientists futilely strive to find a model of physical reality using theories based solely on particles in motion, helps explain both the complexity and success of what is known as the Standard Model of particle physics.

The Standard Model,[442] according to material science, is "the most successful theory of nature in history."[443] It predicts, to an astonishing degree of accuracy, the interaction of particles and forces at the base of the material world. The most fundamental particles, less than 10^{-19} meters in size, are found to obey strict mathematical rules, interacting with precise charges, forces, and "color." "Force carrier particles" bounce back and forth between "matter particles" trillions of time per second, holding the particles together at just the right distance and with just the right constancy to form the chemical elements; the residual forces (electromagnetism and the strong force) then bind atoms into molecules and molecules into chemical structures.

As the Real Dream worldview begins with one Mind, so material science begins with one Particle. Both worldviews conclude that the universe began as a simple place. This is a logically necessary starting point with any world theory. By definition, the greater the complexity imagined to exist at the beginning of time, the more improbable the creation theory. As others have noted,[444] a complex beginning, such as a universe with the laws of nature and the periodic table of elements already established, implies an intelligence behind the "original" design that will itself have to be explained. (This is the same problem confronting a creation theory based on the book of Genesis. If God created the universe in a prefabricated state, then what created this all-powerful, designer God?)

The Standard Model of material science is the latest form of Democritus's original idea that all the matter in the universe can be reduced to fundamental, universal things. But where Democritus began with the idea of a cutless piece of matter—a tiny, indestructible billiard ball—modern science finds itself in a particle zoo.[445]

In 1930, only three elementary particles existed in the model of the atom—the electron, proton, and neutron. But as modern science continued to use increasingly powerful particle accelerators to explore the atom, more and more particles began turning up. Peeling away the shell to the atomic nucleus revealed ever smaller things.[446] Soon the number of elementary particles had increased by a hundredfold, most of which are called hadrons.[447] Scientists began classifying the particles by electrical charge, mass, spin,[448] and whether they are subject to the strong force.

Professor Murray Gell-Mann, now of the California Institute of Technology, proposed in the 1960s that hadrons were composed of still smaller particles that he named "quarks."[449] Part of the motivating force for the quark theory is that a hundred or so elementary particles is aesthetically displeasing.[450] Because atomic theory is based on the principle that the wide diversity of nature can be reduced to an underlying simplicity, physicists consider unacceptable a system containing hundreds of elementary particles.

Today, with the Standard Model, scientists arrange nature into sixty-one elementary particles consisting of forty-eight "matter and anti-matter particles" (fermions) and thirteen force-carrier particles (bosons).[451]

With regard to normal, everyday matter, such as rocks, dirt, and trees, science only needs six total particles: the electron, the up and down quarks, the gluon (which holds the quarks together), the photon, and the Higgs particle, also known as the God Particle.[452] The other particles explain more "esoteric phenomena"[453] studied by particle physicists in cosmic rays and their billion-dollar particle accelerators.[454]

Again, the question of how material science's big bang managed to spray the exploding debris neatly into the sixty-one "fundamental" particles of the Standard Model goes unanswered. Nor is it an easy task to find simplicity in this model. If the world of material science began with one particle, then how did this thing separate itself into an array of smaller particles that work together in harmony? What force split the primordial atom into a symphony of coordinating parts?

But it gets worse. Since the time of Newton in the seventeenth century, scientists have been troubled by the notion that forces can act at a distance between material bodies.[455] If considered as lifeless accumulations of matter, how indeed can one massive body (such as the Earth) act upon another body (the moon) across empty space with no strings attached? How does the electron stay in orbit around the nucleus, the neutron and proton within the nucleus, or quarks within protons?

To say that one body *feels* the presence of the other body has an aura of mysticism unacceptable in the material science worldview. Material science holds that there must be some way to account for action at a distance using materialistic concepts.

Science thinks it has found the answer. Rather than picture one physical object, whether the Earth or an electron, as exerting a force across empty space, scientists theorize that tiny messenger particles travel between the electron and the nucleus, Earth and sun, and in fact all objects in the universe, carrying the necessary force to hold them together.[456]

For example, in the model of the atom, the electron carries a negative charge as it circles the nucleus, which holds the positive charge. Quantum mechanics allows this electron to go on orbiting forever. But space exists between the electron and the nucleus. To keep this electron in orbit, science says that a photon, a massless particle of light, hops back and forth between the electron and the nucleus, like a radio signal telling the two particles to stay together. The photon travels at the speed of light, making roughly a billion round trips per second between the electron and the nucleus. That's one photon commuting between one electron and one nucleus. Considering that roughly 10^{78} atoms populate the universe, at this moment trillions upon trillions of invisible particles are dashing between electrons and neutrons, cementing matter together.

Particles called *gluons* carry the strong (or "color") force between quarks. The residual strength of the gluons holds protons and neutrons together in the atomic nucleus. Three other force-carrying particles transmit the weak force. The weak force is responsible for the decay of certain elementary particles, and causes up quarks to change into down quarks, and electrons into neutrinos. It is also responsible for radioactive beta decay,[457] and is "involved in the formation of the chemical elements."[458] The three force-carrying particles are called the W−, the W+, and the Z°.[459] These weak force particles are massive by subatomic standards, one hundred times heavier than the proton.[460]

If we look inside the atom or out in space for these messenger particles, we will not find any. In fact, by definition they cannot be directly detected.[461] A good reason exists that they cannot be detected. The law of energy conservation states that energy or matter cannot be created from nothing.[462] If a photon or gluon suddenly sprang out of thin air and started commuting between the nucleus and the electron, energy would be created out of nothing. So these particles cannot exist in the manner of normal particles that make up the stuff of the world.

Here, the Heisenberg uncertainty principle comes into play. This principle is named after German physicist Werner Heisenberg (1901–1976), winner of the 1937 Nobel Prize in physics. In simple terms, the uncertainty principle is a law of nature stating that we cannot have absolute knowledge of both the position and the momentum of a particle.[463] Nature, in a sense, imposes a blackout period upon the scientific investigation of the ultimate substratum to matter. The uncertainty principle states that nature does not show itself on a continuous film that can be slowed down to infinity. Instead, nature reveals itself just like the motion picture films: in picture frames, but ones measured according to Planck's constant. When breaking down the film of nature, science finds individual picture frames but cannot see what lies between the frames.

Particle physicists turn this blackout period into a realm where anything can occur, even events violating science's conservation laws. First, scientists convert the uncertainty principle into functions of time and energy. Framed in this manner, science finds a fundamental uncertainty in ascertaining both the exact energy of a system and the time over which the system operates. The uncertainty in a particle's energy multiplied by the uncertainty in the energy's operating period must at least equal Planck's constant.[464]

Now a negative principle of nature telling us what we cannot know or observe[465] becomes a principle saying that what can occur must occur. According to the uncertainty principle, an energy imbalance may arise in a system if it does not last too long. Science thus interprets the uncertainty principle as allowing the creation of energy out of nothing as long as it quickly disappears and no one notices it.[466] As Professor Georgi explains, "The uncertainty principle does not invalidate the conservation laws of energy and of momentum, but it does allow a violation of the laws to go unnoticed if it is rectified quickly enough."[467]

Material science takes advantage of nature's blackout period and builds a new particle-world in the space between picture frames. Because the existence of each messenger particle violates the conservation of energy, the particles must come and go quickly. The greater the energy they carry, the shorter their allowed life span; conversely, the smaller their mass, the longer they can live.[468] For example, the photon has a rest mass of 0, thus allowing it to travel an infinite distance to carry electromagnetic energy.[469] Because these particles do not exist in the sense of sand pebbles and raindrops, they are called "virtual particles."[470]

What Heisenberg's uncertainty principle allows is now guaranteed.[471] Refusing to accept the notion that objects can act on each other across empty space, science inserts a theory expressed in the language of materialism. Space between bodies is not in fact empty; rather, it is filled with an endless sea of invisible virtual particles transmitting forces between physical masses.[472]

Problems with the Standard Model

Despite the success of the Standard Model in organizing the particles and forces of nature, the model is by its structure limited and incomplete. Among its chief limitations is that it cannot explain the force we are most accustomed with: gravity.[473] As we have seen, Newton thought that material bodies attract each other according to their distance and mass; Einstein believed that massive bodies, such as stars and planets, warp the space around them, creating curved paths upon which surrounding bodies can travel. In the quantum theory of gravity, where messenger particles rule, the graviton is supposed to carry the news between massive bodies that they should attract each other.[474]

Scientists, however, have never detected one graviton.[475] Gravity operates across the universe, so the range of the graviton must be infinite and its mass zero.[476] But to create the force necessary to explain the operation of gravity among the 10^{20} or so stellar bodies, outer space must literally be flooded with these virtual gravitons.[477] If space is flooded, then each fleeting graviton must contribute a small gravitational force on space. The cumulative effect of this ocean of gravitons would warp space according to Einstein's theory. But we do not see space warped. Nor does the Standard Model account for dark matter or dark energy. Thus, the Standard Model of particle physics, this materialistic mapping of physical reality, is necessarily incomplete.

So scientists replace the concept of action at a distance with a theory based on an endless rush hour of invisible particles commuting throughout the universe. But then the question becomes: How did the big bang spin off 10^{80} little particles programmed to talk with each other in perfect harmony? How did they all get the same message? Did these infinitesimally small bits of something all come off the same assembly line? What organizing power in the chaos of the big bang infused these particles with directions to hum a perfect note?

Material science, of course, assumes the laws of nature as given. So it catalogs the regularities and symmetries of the Standard Model, proclaiming that the model must be true because all of their mathematical calculations work. But this purely descriptive theory does not explain how the chaos of the big bang could have produced trillions upon trillions of particles all performing on key.

The Standard Model of particle physics is exactly that: a particle-based model of a physical reality that material science has assumed. This material-based model can map creation, but it can never capture its true essence for the simple reason that the world we live in arose not from one particle, but from one Mind.

Chapter Thirty-Two

THE GOD PARTICLE

*The experiment therefore ought to be made, whether we should not suc-
ceed better with the problems of metaphysics, by assuming that the objects
must conform to our mode of cognition, for this would better agree with
the demanded possibility of an a priori knowledge of them, which is to settle
something about objects, before they are given to us.*
—Immanuel Kant

ONE GLARING SIGN THAT material science is on the wrong track is the
complexity of its theories. Common sense—and the core of our beings—
tell us the world is a simple place. Material science itself wants the universe
to be so simple that scientists can write the final theory on a T-shirt,[478]
but they are far removed from this lofty goal.

Pick up any book on modern particle physics or cosmology, and
we'll find not simplicity but a torrential downpour of confounding,
unsettled, and obtuse theories.[479] But this is the result when material
science's "dream of a final theory" is a mental image of a mechanical
contraption gone mad. Despite the profusion of elementary particles and
forces, material scientists still believe that they all arose from the same
source; in the beginning all was one. All particles were the same and all
forces emerged from one power at the moment of the big bang. But then
incredible temperatures and thermonuclear reactions destroyed the symmetry of the early universe; a rough wind of force fields blew through
the early universe, shattering the perfect symmetry—the perfect particle
oneness—creating the disparate particles and forces we see today.

Here then is a dilemma for any world theory: the universe in the beginning must have been a simple place—undifferentiated, united, one. But today we do not experience an undifferentiated, united world, at least in appearances. Rather, physicists count sixty-one elementary particles, trillions of stars fill the sky, millions of plant and animal species populate all corners of the globe, and billions of people inhabit the Earth.

How does any science get from the logically necessary One to the apparent Many? How does it get from the big bang singularity or other creation event to the diverse universe we now experience?

In the Real Dream, the answer is straightforward: we began as one mind and we are still one mind. As we discuss more fully below, the one Mind—*our mind*—created the world so that it would not be the only one: this diverse, endlessly varied, densely populated place is a product of the Mind's ocean-wave desire for companionship, the highest form of which is friends and family. This may seem too simple, but it is a theory that explains *this* world far better than the mechanistic theories of material science: an all-powerful Mind, somehow blessed with the miraculous ability of projecting a real-seeming world, saw the power work and then bootstrapped its way to what is now the world of our dreams.

We can be divided *in appearance* but there is nothing that can ever divide us completely because we necessarily come from the same source. We are attached at the root of Being.

Material science too must journey from the One, its big bang singularity, to the diverse world we now experience.

But the oneness of material science is a bit of lifeless matter and energy—an emotionless bit of nothing, a spray gun of particles shot from a common cannon. Material scientists know that its current array of particles and forces cannot have existed in the beginning; how could creation have exploded itself into this intricate assembly of interlocking parts? No, the particles and forces must have started as one—a perfect symmetry that divided itself along the way. According to material science, in the beginning there must have been one bit of unified something, an energy packet, a common particle, that somehow grew into the diverse world we now see.[480]

Material science, however, needs a force to break the perfect symmetry that existed at the beginning of time. This force, it is theorized, is now hidden among the stars in the sky because conditions today are much different than they were at the time of the big bang. At that moment, infinite energy was condensed in a tiny seed and the temperatures beyond anything experienced in our world or achievable by modern technology. So this force at the big bang divided the one particle, split it into many, and as the universe cooled, the symmetry-breaking force got lost in the crowd.

The chief candidate to perform this symmetry-breaking is known as the Higgs field. This new force again shows how astray material science has gone in its attempt to cobble together a workable mechanistic picture of the physical world.

The Higgs Field Made Easy

The role that the Higgs field plays in modern physics takes a little explaining, but it is important to an understanding of where material science is taking us on the quest to understand our world.

A subject that puzzles material science is why its elementary particles have different masses. As measured by scientists, the masses of these particles differ by roughly thirteen orders of magnitude, from the electron neutrino, with a mass of 10^{-11} electron volts (eV),[481] to the top quark, with a mass of 10^2 giga-electron volts.[482] The puzzles exists because *the mathematics of the Standard Model of particle physics requires that all force carrier particles be massless.* If these particles are not massless, the equations underlying the Standard Model produce nonsensical results, such as probabilities greater than 1, something that by definition is impossible.[483]

The Higgs field comes into the picture at this point. The particle (or "boson") associated with the Higgs field has been named the "God Particle,"[484] and it is essential to the validity of the Standard Model of particle physics.[485] The Higgs boson "is introduced explicitly and solely as a mechanism to improve the mathematical consistency of the standard model." Simply put, the Higgs field determines the mass of elementary particles; the masses are not inherent in the particles.

The thinking is that, in fact, all the particles have a common source; they are identical in their true being, and the Higgs field gives them differing mass. Professor Gordon Kane writes, "Particles that interact with the Higgs field behave as if they have mass, proportional to the strength of the field times the strength of the interaction." In other words, when these symmetrical particles travel through the Higgs field they pick up mass, like a kickoff returner in football attracts tacklers.[486]

The important point here is that material science's mathematical equations do not work unless theorists invent another field. But in inventing yet another field they simultaneously increase both the complexity of theory and the odds *against* this miraculously finely tuned infrastructure (the Higgs field) arising from the void.

Among the unusual and counterintuitive features of the Higgs field is that it has a nonzero rest energy. It started as *something*; it was more than nothing. This something[487] then injects mass into elementary particles to make them appear different. Thus the Higgs field hides the true symmetry of the universe.[488]

But, as Professor Veltman observes, the Higgs field replaces a mystery over how particles acquired differing mass with the mystery over why the hypothetical Higgs field possesses a nonzero energy value.[489] And this is a special-case field, as theorists have imbued it with just the right values to produce the observed masses of the particles in the Standard Model.

So when all particles in the universe were born, they had the same mass; they were identical. It's as if tiny orbs ejected from the void moved through a magic filter that transformed them into the diversity of particles and forces we see today. The field plays the role of God, and the ejected quanta are the field's raw material.

On July 4, 2012, a team of scientists at Europe's Large Hadron Collider, the world's most advanced particle accelerator, announced that they had discovered a particle that looked like the long-sought-after Higgs boson, and in March 2013, investigators announced the the particle they found really is the Higgs boson. These announcements then led to the award of the Nobel prize in physics to the discoverers of the Higgs particle, Peter W. Higgs and Francois Englert, in October 2013.

Now what did the scientists actually see? For one, they did not see a Higgs boson, for this particle cannot be observed directly.[490] Rather, they observed decay patterns of billions of particle collisions and, after analyzing the data, they found patterns consistent with the Standard Model prediction for the Higgs particle.[491] From these decay patterns in a particle accelerator, some theorists are ready to conclude that an "ethereal fluid"[492] permeates the universe and gives the sixty-one particles of the Standard Model their masses.

The Higgs particle shows material science barreling headlong down the wrong road to find truth. It uncovers quarks, leptons, pions, mesons, virtual particles, and particles with life spans of a billionth of a second; exploding bits of antimatter; and whizzing particles following precise mathematical equations. But something does not make sense within one of material science's theories, so it invents more particles and fields, and then convinces governments to spend billions of dollars tracking down the missing values to their equations.[493]

Is the Higgs Particle Real?

With the announcement of the finding of the Higgs particle, the question arises whether the particle is "real" and not just a mathematical construct. This question, of course, is related to the one raised earlier in this book regarding the world at large: Does it exist independently of the mind or is it a projection of the mind?

Here we reach another juncture in the road forcing us to decide whether the world is a creation of the big bang or of the mind.

Suppose that—despite the findings of quantum theory, the reality of dreams, hallucinations, the paranormal, and the logic behind idealism—there really is a world independent of human consciousness; in other words, Newton's mechanical universe really does exist. If so, then how did this independent, mindless world *not only conform to mathematics but also reflect the theoretical musings of the human mind*? The greater the number of mathematical symmetries, force fields, and constants scientists find "out in the world," the less likely that this mathematical world arose from the chaos of the big bang. If a Higgs field really does permeate all space, then how did it get there? Did it just so happen to spring from the big bang and spread itself out with just the right properties to give particles the masses they needed to form the universe standing before us?

In fact, the Higgs field really does perform the role of God as it gives order to the faceless world of mindless, massless particles that existed – somehow—in the beginning.

This line of reasoning again shows that modern scientists are more interested in supporting their current model and platform than asking the big question of how this theoretical structure can possibly exist in the real world.

So now let's look at the same picture from a different perspective. Let's suppose that the unconscious, united mind of humankind projects the world as in a dream.

From this perspective, a rational explanation is much more readily available. As participants in the evolving dream of God, we are slowly rising to the realization that we dream the world, or that it comes from us. Material scientists then represent an evolutionary stage of humankind as they climb the mountain of awareness to realize that the world they envision "out there" is a reflection of the world "in here."

Not understanding this truth, material scientists devise mathematical theories of the physical world, not realizing that the world follows mathematical equations because the mind imposed the order before the theorizing began. And since we are in a continual state of creation (as we would be God), we will create images of a world determined by the thought leaders of science. Does this sound radical? It may be, but it is also true, and the prime reason we must overthrow scientific materialism.

Material scientists are like a coxswain on a boat, shouting out orders for the oarsmen (i.e., us) to follow. Materialism controls the dream and determines the route we take. As long as materialists are in control of the scientific enterprise, they will continue having us look for God in the decay patterns of billion-dollar particle colliders, oblivious to the fact that whatever they find is simply a shadow image of a misguided scientific theory.

The Solution to the Hierarchy Problem

Although there have been many breathless reports about how the Higgs discovery answers the question of why particles have mass,[494] any such Higgs particle does not answer the much deeper question of why the particles of the Standard Model have the masses they do. The masses of the numerous elementary particles in the Standard Model span eleven orders of magnitude, from the electron-neutrino to the top quark.[495]

The Standard Model does not account for the masses of these particles, which are put in by hand to make the model work. Instead of asking why elementary particles have the masses they do, the question becomes, Why does the Higgs field couple to these faceless, massless particles in the manner it does?

This problem may not seem too significant, except that scientists desire a *natural* explanation for the wide divergence in masses; they want the masses to come naturally out of the equations and not be inserted on an ad hoc basis.[496] Leading scientists view the hierarchy problem among the most serious enigmas of the Standard Model.

But there is another way to account for the masses of elementary particles without the need for a $6 billion particle accelerator. This explanation simply requires a change in perspective rather than another subatomic particle, force field, the multiverse, or multiple dimensions. It requires that instead of looking at the world from the standpoint of particles and forces (or matter), we look at the world from the standpoint of the mind *toward* the particles and forces.

A Return to the Dream Perspective

If the mind creates reality, then it will necessarily *project the three-dimensional form first and the interior parts will align in accordance with the outer form.* Or the outer harmony determines the inner harmony of the physical form.

Modern science thus makes an error of perspective: because it believes the ultimate substance to the universe is a *thing or matter*, modern science attempts to explain why these things have the properties they do without recourse to a mind or intelligence. But once we eliminate this unnecessary prejudice from scientific theory, the answer becomes apparent. When we peer into the interior of physical forms we are actually looking into a *dream image*. This approach also recognizes the findings of quantum theory, which, as discussed earlier, shows that at the heart of matter are not things, but waves of energy. These statements are all factually true because they describe the inner workings of a dream world.

This approach takes quantum theory to its logical conclusion and articulates a result that is appearing increasingly obvious: consciousness truly does create reality because somewhere inside of us is the power of the dream.

Is this science? If the goal of science is to describe the world we live in rather than a world we once presumed to exist, then of course this is science, and the only true science. Materialism must be discarded so that the true practice of science can begin.[497]

Ignoring the unavoidable role of consciousness in forming our world, some material scientists have come to label the universe absurd because they cannot make sense of it.[498] The universe may be mysterious, beguiling, even at times strange; but it is not absurd. Rather, it should be evident that the theoretical foundation of material science is absurd. The exalted assumption that a grand material world arose from the void and spun itself into a world of three-dimensional beauty, all on its own power, is what does not make sense. The world is after all a simple place: a projection, an expression, a feeling of the mind, a wish come true. We dwell in a place and at a time to experience once-buried dreams that now stand in glory before us.

Chapter Thirty-Three

THE UNIVERSE THAT APPEARED BETWEEN PICTURE FRAMES

I regard consciousness as fundamental. I regard
matter as derivative from consciousness.
—Max Planck

DESPITE THE ENORMITY of its assumptions, material science today has few competitors when it comes to explaining the world. No one presents a serious challenge to material science's grip on our worldview. Bursting with confidence, some scientists are ready to take the final step. Though the big bang theory rests upon an assumption of preexisting infinite energy, some scientists want to go back to the moment of creation and explain how something came from nothing within the material science worldview. Merging quantum physics with cosmology, these scientists propose that the universe originated as a "quantum fluctuation, starting from absolutely nothing."[499]

Now what exactly is a quantum fluctuation? The same principle by which quantum physics allows virtual particles to appear out of nowhere is used to account for the creation of the universe out of nothing.[500] Stephen Hawking explains,

> What we think of as "empty space" cannot be completely empty because that would mean that all fields, such as the

gravitational and electromagnetic fields, would have to be exactly zero. However, the value of a field and its rate of change with time are like the position and velocity of a particle: the uncertainty principle implies that the more accurately one knows one of these quantities, the less accurately one can know the other. So in empty space the field cannot be fixed at exactly zero, because then it would have both a precise value (zero) and a precise rate of change (also zero). There must be a certain minimum amount of uncertainty, or quantum fluctuations, in the value of the field.[501]

In his book, *A Universe from Nothing*,[502] Lawrence Krauss attempts to explain how the universe outside our windows "could have" come from nothing. But this is simple high-order speculation showing the consequences of a theorist separating his own mind from a universe that comes from the mind.

As we saw with virtual particles, using the uncertainty principle as a positive rule, "nothing" no longer means "nothing." Rather, the nothing of material science is a vacuum bursting with energy. According to some theorists, in the blink of the eye, out of the space between the picture frames of reality, a virtual universe emerged from the void.

Heisenberg's uncertainty principle tells us that we can never measure the exact location and velocity of an elementary particle. There will always be an uncertainty in the measurement. Applying this principle to the dark void, scientists reason that we cannot know for certain that what appears to be empty is really empty because we would then know the absolute value of the field, a measurement deemed off-limits by the uncertainty principle. This uncertainty leads to the supposition that what is really nothing is actually filled with "virtual particles" that operate between the picture frames of our perception of the world. Virtual particles, however, are by definition not real. They can only be said to exist as a matter of mathematical theory, because their appearance in reality would violate the first law of thermodynamics, which prohibits the creation of energy from nothing.

This description is no doubt an oversimplification.[503] But what it shows is the mind of the scientific theorist implanting a mathematical theory upon the physical world as if the theory is a property of the world, not of the mind. Heisenberg's uncertainty principle necessarily assumes both an observer and a physical world; only by observing an assumed external physical world does one reach the conclusion that the interaction of a photon with an elementary particle creates an uncertainty in the motion of particles. Heisenberg set up a *model* of the world and then thought through the consequences. But his model is wrong. The body and the external particle-world are both images of the mind. The uncertainty principle is better explained as the bottom depth of the dreaming mind's ability to conjure something from nothing; only the imagination can ultimately join the dark void with the first particle.

But even within the material science worldview, several problems exist with the quantum-fluctuation creation theory, and adherents are in the minority. As noted earlier in the discussion on antimatter, virtual particles are created in pairs of particles and antiparticles.[504] If both were created in the blink of an eye, they would destroy each other, and we would be left again with nothing. Some force must separate the virtual particle from the virtual antiparticle and "promote it into reality."[505]

To supply the necessary push, some scientists speculate that what we thought was nothing is really a false nothing.[506] This false nothing met up with a real nothing and created the necessary energy to promote the virtual particle into reality. Then, under the inflationary universe hypothesis, a few more minor steps occur before this quantum fluctuation "evolves to become stars, plants, human beings, and so forth."[507] See how simple this all is? A false vacuum collides with a real vacuum causing an outburst of energy; the energy is just enough to separate a virtual particle from a virtual antiparticle. The virtual particle then inflates 10^{80} times in a fraction of a second to produce stars, plants, human beings, and so forth. And, may we ask, why is there a universe? Well, according to the originator of this fairytale creation story, "Our Universe is simply one of those things which happen from time to time."[508] That may be, but thank God it did not arise from a quantum fluctuation.

One fact about this creation theory is indisputable: the theory originated in the mind. More than three hundred years ago, Descartes established another fact never seriously disputed: we have greater certainty about our own mind than about the independent reality of the external world. That external world, said Descartes, might well be a dream. But carrying a deep belief in God, Descartes refused to conclude that God would deceive him into thinking that the world existed on its own unless it really did.

Since the time of Descartes, the mind of man, led by material science, has ignored the possibility that the world might be a dream; this science wants a metallic, rigid workshop within which to do its job. In creating a real world, we have rejected the thought that it is a dream. In rejecting this thought, however, perhaps we have helped contribute to the reality of the world, for we have imbued it with the clockwork precision and solidity of Newtonian mechanics.

Through the history of philosophy and science, humans have been unable to disprove Descartes. We have greater certainty over our own mind than over any other fact in the universe. We also know, through our dreams at night, that the mind is capable of projecting a three-dimensional world that fools the dreamer into believing he is not dreaming. But we deeply want the world to be more than a dream, and material science represents the greatest endeavor of the mind to fulfill that want. To carry out its goal, material science has assumed an independent world and sought to build a body of knowledge upon its assumption. But in doing so, scientists have been forced to assume a universe of matter, separate that world from our control, and remove us from taking responsibility for it. To fulfill our wish for something more than a dream, material science has delivered to us a mechanical world that operates beyond our control and according to its own schedule—and that, in the end, alienates us from our own creation.

Heisenberg's uncertainty principle tells us that the job of creation is over. We have drilled down far enough; we have made the most solid of possible worlds. But still gripping onto its material world, scientists apply the creativity of the mind and use this period of uncertainty to account for the very universe the mind has already given them.

Material science separates the mind from matter in its theories, but it cannot separate the scientist from her mind when the theorizing begins. Looking at this universe bursting with energy, material science overlooks the creativity of the mind as it uses the same mind to solve the problem of creation. In the end, its theories fail because the mind is not only a theorist, but also the creator of this world. The mind's dreaming power, the original but forgotten force in the cosmos, must be the missing element that will unify the laws of physics.

SECTION 3

LIFE AS THE BATTLE AGAINST NOTHING

Chapter Thirty-Four

WHERE DID THE STRUGGLE BEGIN?

Parts of speech are metaphors, because the whole of
nature is a metaphor of the human mind.
—Ralph Waldo Emerson, *Nature*

MATERIAL SCIENCE CURRENTLY FACES only one competitor in the contest to explain how life arose on earth: religion.[509]

Although their belief systems vary, religions share a similar view of God's relation to humanity and to nature. Most Western religions believe that God dwells in some far-off realm separate from the human world. The Hubble telescope will not detect this God. Religious followers find God through faith and belief; their God cannot be studied and measured like a planet passing across the night sky.

In a similar way, many Eastern religions believe God rests at the base of the One Self—some deeply internal state of being underlying the world. Again, however, the bridge between people and God is made invisibly beneath the heart; modern science's X-ray machines do not detect Brahman.

Science opposes the religious worldview because science claims to take nothing on faith alone. Science, by definition,[510] uses only "natural" explanations to account for the physical world; science's rejection of so-called supernatural explanations (such as resorting to a heavenly God to explain creation) sharply distinguishes science from religion.[511]

But buried within science's conception of the "natural world" (or a "natural explanation"), is the great assumption of material science. As the late Harvard biologist Ernst Mayr explained, scientists, like theologians, bring a set of assumptions with them when studying the world. The key assumption of material science is that "there is a real world independent of human perceptions."[512]

As noted earlier, the great intellectual flaw of material science is that its adherents believe they cannot practice science without making the independent-world assumption, or without abstracting the physical world from its source—namely, the mind. But it must be taken as a sign of a failed worldview to accept a false assumption as a condition for practicing an intellectual discipline aimed to discover truth. The investigation to find truth must be assumption-free.

Science must redefine the concept of "natural explanation." The term "natural" is commonly used to mean something real or physical, as opposed to a spiritual, imaginary, or supernatural realm. But projecting a three-dimensional world is natural to born dreamers, which is what we are. We are, in fact, *supernatural* creatures living in a *supernatural* world. The worldview of modern science has limited us to playing the role of machines in a confining, mechanistic world; it is now time to break through this mental prison and explore our true potential.

We are dreamers to the core of our beings. It is natural for us to dream, to project a world. Deep inside something gave us this power, and we know we have it; to us it is natural. We are engaged in a waterfall of creativity—dreamers in the beginning and dreamers now. How can one explain the natural world without recourse to our natural abilities? Thus, when we speak of a natural explanation in *this world*, we must include the dream-creating ability of the mind. Adding this force to those of science, as we are beginning to see, unlocks the secret to understanding the world and why we are here, which is to write the story of God on the stage we call Earth.

Science progresses by the testing of hypotheses through experiment and reasoning. But material scientists want to go out into the field to test their theories about the material world without critically examining whether the independent-world assumption is true in the first place.

If we simply take for granted the great assumption of material science and fail to critically examine it, we are not practicing science, but rather advancing a system of belief. In the Real Dream, when we are done cataloguing the regularities of nature, we wind up turning back on ourselves. We must ultimately focus on the source of the dream—our relationship with other people and our attitude toward the world—to bring about positive change, the true aim of science.

The Scientific Method Works

The great advantage of science is the scientific method. Science is a testing ground for ideas about the world. It is based upon the notion that facts which withstand logical criticism and experimentation have a deeper validity than facts held together only by a spiritual faith.

Religions adopt the opposite standpoint: they believe that God reveals truth, not the scientific method.[513] Religious followers take no time to determine whether these revealed truths also withstand the scientific method; they accept the Word without questioning either its internal logic or empirical validity. Here, it may be said, the failure to question checks the thought process; inquiry stops, the mind closes.[514] If it were really the truth that God delivered, should not that truth stand up to questioning and testing?

The constant reappraisal of existing theories is the lifeblood of science.[515] But when we learn of this feature of science from a material scientist, he sounds like a member of a political party: he will question everything except his own platform. Material science's greatest assumption—that a physical world of matter exists outside of the mind—is untouchable under its theories, even though quantum theory shows the assumption to be wrong. This situation must change.

In the same way that most people are not born into a political party, however, none of us are born followers of material science. Nothing stops us from questioning the assumption that we are nothing but particles in motion, part of a material world detached from any intelligence force. If the great assumption is true, it also should withstand questioning.

We need not go far to find something that in fact withstands questioning: our own ability to think or the questioning ability itself. This truth Descartes firmly established. Looking inside ourselves, however, we also find something else. Mixed together with what we call the "mind" or the "seat of the soul" is an inner drive, a steady drumbeat of the heart, a quiet, incessant striving; the elusive quality pushing us on; the urge to get everything out of our time on Earth, to look adversity in the face and surge ahead; the fight for awareness and for knowledge. In the material science worldview, however, no matter how hard our inner spirit strives, the great wall of matter constrains and limits us. Sooner or later we come upon a mountain too high to climb. We struggle to live, but our bodies repel the urge; they wrinkle and die.

Material science disregards this inner urge for survival as the source of physical life-forms. Instead, science takes the opposite approach: it maintains that the life-urge evolved from lifeless bits of dust. To materialists, life becomes a complex interplay of the same particles that make up rocks and stardust.[516] When asked how these mindless particles happened to arrange themselves into the order and diversity we know as life, material scientists give a common answer: through a combination of blind chance and natural law.[517] According to material science, life arose from dead matter through happenstance, and varies randomly across time and space, but is ordered according to natural selection.[518]

Charles Darwin, the founding father of material evolution, recognized that because individuals multiply at a faster rate than food supplies, they will "struggle for existence."[519] In the ensuing struggle, "Any variation, however slight and from whatever cause proceeding, if it be in any degree profitable to an individual of any species, in its infinitely complex relations to other organic beings and to external nature, will tend to the preservation of that individual, and will generally be inherited by its offspring."[520] This process Darwin called natural selection.[521]

To Darwinian evolutionists, therefore, the "struggle for existence" is the mechanism pushing living things onward; they compete for limited food supplies under a given set of environmental conditions.[522] This mechanism, however, is not some invisible urge, but can be explained in materialistic terms.[523] Though we examine the concept of natural

selection in more detail below, we can here make the following observation here. Darwinian evolutionists assume that living things struggle
for life, but they say little sabout why these creatures are bothering to
struggle. Where did the struggle begin? Why do we all fight for life? Is life
a complicated chemical reaction and nothing more?

As physicists take matter and the laws of nature for granted, so biologists take the struggle for existence for granted. Their theories assume
that dead bits of matter will miraculously decide to struggle for life, as if
the life-urge is a property of the utterly dead.

With the physical world pictured as a projection of the mind, or a
great dream, we take the opposite perspective on the problem. In this
world, there must always be a subject and object—"I and Thou," actor
and stage. Evolution, or forward change, occurs reflectively, as the dreaming source becomes inspired by its own creation.

The sky above, the trees, hills, plains, streets, and everything else
we see represents the background scenery against which to live; physical
bodies are three-dimensional beings swimming through the sea of creation. We are out in the world, in the midst of the dream.

In a dream world, nothing actually exists apart from the mind. But
because we are accustomed to viewing the mind as synonymous with the
"brain," we tend to think of the mind as a physical entity locked within
our heads. This is the wrong perspective. Creation is flowing from us: *The
mind is the world.*

Perhaps in today's materialistic worldview, this perspective may seem
all too odd and far-out. But once we realize it is more probable that the
world is a great dream rather than a collection of mindless residue rocketing away from the big bang, we must be scientific and apply this new
viewpoint consistently to the world we experience.

Contrary to the material science worldview, we do not hypothesize
that bits of dust decided to struggle for existence. Rather, taking what
we know is true—the mind's ability to dream—we surmise that a noth-
ing-creature, given the power of the dream, will seek to escape from the
darkness. Imagine this situation: a mind suddenly discovers, through
a miracle impossible to understand, that it has a magical power it had
always attributed to a God overhead, or the "laws of nature." The power

is the ability to project a real-seeming world from the depths of the soul, and this power is wild, unlimited in scope. One day the mind awakens to discover itself in a perfect garden, and it wonders how this came to be. The awareness propels the mind to flee the darkness, to hide, run off in the opposite direction to higher ground, leaving behind the relics of its journey—also known as archaeology and the recorded history of human civilization.

By taking the mind's soul-deep struggle for granted, scientists overlook the highest achievement of the mind: a three-dimensional flowing movement of such complexity and variety that the mind loses itself in its creation and comes to believe it is something, and that is the point—for at bottom we are nothing. *Life is the battle against nothing*, an army sent out on a mission to conquer a perpetual nightfall. When material scientists take life for granted, the world indeed may look like the empty, meaningless place they tell us it is—but only because these scientists have separated their hearts and minds from a creation that flows steadily only from those hearts and minds.

Chapter Thirty-Five

AN IMPERFECT DARWINIAN WORLD

But speak the truth, and all nature and all spirits help you with unexpected furtherance.
Speak the truth, and all things alive or brute are vouchers, and the very roots of the
grass underground there seem to stir and move to bear you witness.
—Ralph Waldo Emerson, *The Divinity School Address*

In *The Origin of the Species*, Charles Darwin offers an explanation of life on Earth directly opposed to the biblical worldview. Where a literal reading of the Bible suggests that God created the universe and all life over a six-day period roughly six thousand years ago,[524] Darwin theorized that life gradually evolved over several hundred millions of years.[525] Where the Bible suggested that creation occurred as the sudden act of an omnipotent, farsighted God, Darwin said that life evolved in slow, groping steps following natural processes.[526] Where the Bible said God created each plant and animal specie as unique forms, Darwin said all species evolve from a common earthly organism.[527] Where the Bible said creation was planned and life fulfilled God's program,[528] Darwin said strictly natural forces—without foresight, plan, purpose, or goal[529]—guided the course of evolution. God knew where life was going; natural selection has no idea.[530]

Natural selection wanders from environmental setting to environmental setting, with only the number of survivors—or reproductive success[531]—determining the winners and the losers. Finally, where God made man and woman in God's image as the centerpieces of creation,[532] Darwin placed humankind in the "stream of animal evolution."[533] Humans hang as a branch on the same tree as the rest of the animal kingdom;[534] people may possess a host of qualities different from the rest of the living world, but they are subject to the same laws of evolution as bacteria: random inheritance of physical traits ordered by natural selection.[535]

In the perfect Darwinian world, all the 500 million[536] species that once roamed Earth could be traced to a single one-celled organism[537] that sprang from a hot chemical mixture 3.5 billion years ago.[538] This simple organism arose from Newton's dead particles.[539] No mind assembled life in Darwin's world.

But this simple one-celled organism possesses a special quality; it struggles for life. In the ensuing struggle, the cell multiplies through reproduction. Sometimes reproduction fails to exactly copy the parent, and a mutation arises. The environmental setting usually rejects this mutant organism, but now and then a favorable one survives. Step-by-step, Nature[540] selects the favorable mutations until more complex organisms develop. Some organisms become separated from their parents and evolve with small groups where large populations do not dilute mutations, and new species form. Eventually, some simple organisms develop the ability to reproduce sexually, allowing blueprints for separate individuals to mix and produce more varied offspring upon which natural selection can do its work.

And so Darwin's common ancestor spread from a single birthplace and populated the globe with millions of species. From this single birthplace, developing species rode newly formed continents that drifted away from an original land mass; other species were blown with the wind, sailed on mangrove rafts,[541] or were carried in the beaks of birds to new regions of the Earth. Three and one-half billion years later, here we are, one of 10 million living species, each possessing an intricate design—each arising from a primitive organism that happened to mutate in its struggle for life, a product of reshuffled blueprints and haphazard environmental conditions, descended not from the mind of God but from bacteria.

Though some material scientists say we must be insane not to believe in evolution,[542] many people, unremarkably, find it absurd to believe that we were born in slime or share a common ancestor with apes. These people disagree with the Darwinian viewpoint for good reason: We were not born in slime, and we are not descended from the apes.

Charles Darwin broke the intellectual hold on irrational explanations of life's origins arising from overly literal readings of the Bible. It was as if human beings had reached the stage of evolution where they could throw down the crutch of religion and explain the world on their own, without recourse to a truth handed down from heaven. The popularity of Darwinism in the scientific community does not result from the absence of flaws in the theory, but rather because it offers a credible explanation for the diversity of life using the mind's inherent reasoning ability. As we have seen with the big bang theory, any *scientific* theory—or theory using reason and experiment—appears superior to the hand-me-down belief systems of religion. Again, at least scientists use their minds. If the beliefs of religion are true, such as God handing Moses the Ten Commandments on Mount Sinai, then those beliefs should stand up to critical examination.

Darwin holds an exalted place among the modern science community[543] because he offered a rational explanation for the rise of life on Earth and the divergence of species from a common source. God did not lower the living world down from the sky as a preformed stage setting bustling with characters. Rather, life evolved from a common ancestor following the slow, groping steps of natural selection.

Darwin's theory, however, must necessarily be wrong.

Darwin's theory fails because it is a product of material science's wrongheaded outlook toward the world. Darwinians, like material scientists generally, believe that truth lies locked inside elementary particles existing wholly separate from the mind. They then must speculate how these particles formed themselves into living things that reproduce and pass on traits to their offspring and then compete for survival, as if life is nature's version of a grand, three-dimensional, flowing art competition. In aggressively advancing the Darwinian position, modern biologists wind up injecting intelligence and an organizing force into their mindless particles and Nature herself. Having taken God down from the sky, they instead place this intelligence within the DNA molecule and cell nucleus and watch as these amazing particles generate data and body-building parts to construct the living world.

The Real Dream perspective tells us we should not position ourselves inside these imagined particles, but instead we should view life from behind the mind. From this vantage point we can see that the urge to survive reaches as far as the physical world. The struggle for life floods nature and radiates throughout the physical world. Yes, evolution occurs, but not in the mindless style Darwin envisioned.

Contrary to the Darwinian blind watchmaker, this mind—our mind—knows where it wants to go. In the next several chapters we analyze key components of Darwin's theory of evolution and show that the Real Dream better explains the living world. We focus on only the key elements of Darwin's theory: (1) the theory that all living things derive from a common organism, (2) the theory that evolution occurs gradually and not in leaps and bounds, and (3) the theory that natural selection is responsible for the order and beauty in the living world. We will see that viewing the world as a dream provides a fuller and deeper explanation to the living world than Darwin's theory.

Chapter Thirty-Six

DARWIN'S COMMON ANCESTOR

DARWIN BELIEVED THAT "probably all the organic beings which have ever lived on this earth have descended from some one primordial form, into which life was first breathed."[544] Today, biologists are more confident. According to Professor Mayr, "There is probably no biologist left today who would question that all organisms now found on earth have descended from a single origin of life."[545]

Material scientists take the same approach to explaining the origin of life as they took in explaining the origin of the universe. They first assume that the big bang worked according to theory,[546] and that matter came before mind. They then believe that by dissecting mindless bits of matter, the "secret to life"[547] will be found. Working again like nature's mechanic, material science takes apart a living thing and finds its smallest working part.[548] Then, having reduced life to its simplest components, scientists attempt to explain how this simple thing arose from dead particles left over by the big bang.[549]

The Cell—The Smallest Unit of Life

When taking apart the atom, material science found constancy and order at the most fundamental levels of matter. When material science takes apart the smallest living thing—the cell—it finds not only deeply rooted order, but also properties of a special kind.

As the smallest unit of life, cells possess an organized complexity rivaling man-made machines but on a scale billions of times smaller. According to one biology textbook, the "living cell is a chemical industry in miniature, where thousands of reactions occur within a microscopic space."[550] Cells store an immense amount of body-building (genetic) information. One human cell, for example, stores the equivalent amount of information as an entire set of the *Encyclopedia Britannica*.[551] Cells also possess features that modern technology cannot match. All cells have the ability to maintain themselves through a process called *metabolism*, where energy (such as sunlight in photosynthesis) is converted through multiple chemical processes that allow living things to grow, develop, and reproduce.[552] Two other features of the cell interest us here. Cells duplicate and also store and transfer cell-construction information to daughter cells.[553] The first process is known as *reproduction*, and the second, *inheritance*.[554] Self-reproduction and the transfer of genetic information (construction blueprints) to offspring distinguish life from nonlife.[555]

Scientists examine a cell with a high-powered microscope and expect to find how it works. They expect to find how this tiny machine reproduces itself and transfers building instructions to new generations of cells that are not randomly produced but are instead exact copies of their parents.

In the everyday world, we understand the role of instructions in assembling a machine. A factory may make a million sets of the same bicycle parts for customer assembly. Building instructions accompany the shipping box and come in a language the consumer understands. As in all languages, certain written symbols correspond to physical objects (the wheels, handlebars, and seat) and others provide directions on how to put the parts together (insert screw A in hole B). Try as we might, it is hard to imagine a better or simpler method to ensure that consumers build the million different bicycles the same way; one set of instructions (or blueprints), parts corresponding to the instructions, and a worker (the consumer) who understands the instructions and carries them out.

When scientists penetrate into the cell, they find an information transfer system modeled after those found in our everyday world. In the cell, scientists find that worker molecules (enzymes) translate coded messages (the genetic code) into the language of the body (proteins). This body-building machinery is found within every living cell, but on a scale millions of times smaller than the machines we make.

The information system of the cell has been compared to a library,[556] a computer disc,[557] a tape recorder,[558] and toolbox subroutines in software programs.[559] These comparisons are not mere metaphors. Close similarities do exist between the cell's information transfer system and those that humans have devised.

DNA—The World's Smartest Particle

To understand better Darwin's common ancestor, we need to take a closer look at the cell's information transfer system. This system is the lowest common denominator to all life-forms, and Darwin's first organism, therefore, must have possessed at least the early rudiments of it.[560] In the early 1950s two scientists, Francis Crick and James Watson, found the secret to the cell's information network in a molecule located in the cell's nucleus. This molecule is known as DNA, short for deoxyribonucleic acid. DNA is no simple piece of matter.[561] Crick and Watson found that through some unknown process, the structure of the DNA molecule acts as a code containing instructions for building living bodies.

The DNA molecule is shaped like a double-helix, or twisted rope ladder.[562] Sugar and phosphate molecules, both of which provide structural support for the molecule, make up the two ropes (or strands). DNA's key feature is how the ladder rungs hook together between the two ropes.

Running down each parallel strand of the double-helix is a sequence of four chemical base molecules: adenine (A), thymine (T), cytosine (C), and guanine (G).[563] Each base can be visualized as half a ladder rung extending out from the inner edge of the rope. Watson and Crick found that the same base-pairs always line up across from each other on parallel DNA strands to form a single rung. Adenine (A) always pairs with thymine (T), and cytosine (C) always pairs with guanine (G).

DNA's most fascinating feature is that the base molecules (A, C, G, and T) act as letters of a true alphabet.[564] All words in this alphabet are made of three bases or letters arranged in a series (called *triplets* or *codons*). Most DNA words code for one of the twenty amino acids found in all living things; other words direct worker molecules (enzymes)[565] when to stop and when to start building amino acid chains.[566] Amino acids form protein molecules; proteins, in turn, determine physical characteristics and direct bodily processes.[567] Thus, the order of bases determines the sequence of amino acids, which in turn decides the specific proteins synthesized, which in turn regulate the development of all plants and animals.

Thousands of DNA molecules, each with their own sequence of bases (or sentences), are laid down along thin strands called chromosomes found in the cell's nucleus. The number of chromosomes in living things varies widely: a mosquito has 6, slime mold, 12, humans, 46, the red viscacha rat, 102, and the Adders-tongue fern the most, 1260.[568]

If, in the translation from the DNA code to proteins, the amino acid step is skipped, it can be seen that longer segments of DNA messages generally code for individual proteins; these segments are known as *genes*.[569] Because proteins are the building blocks to living bodies, genes are considered the unit of inheritance.[570] As Professor Dobzhansky explains, "It can be said that heredity is 'coded' in the genes, or in the DNA of the chromosomes, in a manner similar to a message written in Morse code or in some secret code used by diplomats, generals, or spies."[571] In other words, material science believes that the simple arrangement of dead, mindless particles linked together along chromosomes contain hidden instructions to build the millions of plant and animal species populating the earth.

The DNA molecule may be viewed as nature's idea of a dictionary for life. Chemical bases along the backbone of DNA code for the production of amino acids, which in turn line up to form the proteins necessary for a cell to grow into the parts of a body. But how a mindless particle manages to contain instructions for building living things must be counted as one of the great mysteries in the material science worldview.

The actual process of how the cellular machinery translates the DNA code into protein is something to behold. First, worker polymers, or enzymes, unzip the DNA polymer along the length of the nucleotide, dividing the complementary base pairings; then another polymer—messenger RNA (or simply mRNA)—comes along and matches up with the exposed DNA bases to make an image of the instructions, much like a photocopy machine taking an image of an original. The RNA molecule, rather than copy the exact sequences of bases, aligns the complementary base pairs according to the base pair rules: A with C, U with A, G with C.

The transfer RNA (tRNA) then meets up with one of twenty enzymes, called amino acid activating enzymes,[572] which somehow hitch up the right amino acid to correspond to the anticodon (a "word" of three bases spelling an amino acid) at one end of the transfer RNA. As one textbook writer puts it, "The tRNA molecule is like a flashcard with a nucleic acid 'word' (anticodon) on one side and a protein 'word' on the other."[573]

The tRNA, now with an anticodon word on one end and the amino acid bonded on the other end, slides its way through the ribosome, with each new tRNA picking up another three-code word, adding another amino acid to the growing polypeptide chain, also known as protein.

To summarize, RNA picks up the triplet codes from the DNA molecule, the source of the genetic code. The mRNA then takes the coded instructions through the nucleus membrane where it hooks up with another molecule, known as tRNA, which translates the delivered message into the language of proteins: amino acids.

This incredibly complex and lightning-fast[574] RNA transcription and protein synthesis, however, does not occur without errors. Perhaps the wrong triplet (codon) is substituted for its complementary base, or the RNA hooks up the wrong amino acid for a codon. These errors, if not corrected, may lead to mutations in the organism. But the cell also comes equipped with its own repair enzymes to fix the errors.

Working like a quality control team in an automobile plant, special enzymes detect mismatched triplet pairs, remove the wrong codon (word), and replace it with the right one. Biochemists have found over fifty different worker particles that repair damaged strands of DNA.[575] Even apart from DNA replication, an entirely different set of enzymes regularly scan the DNA strands for mistakes; when any are detected, a different team of enzymes comes to the rescue to correct the errors, substituting the correct words for the wrong ones.

After the exacting replication and transcription process is completed—DNA replicated, instructions delivered by the messenger RNA, amino acid chain assembled, and proofreading and repair enzymes finish their work—some mistakes still get through, and a mutation arises. These mistakes form much of the raw material for evolution to do its work.

So, peering deep inside the cell, material scientists believe that they have found the working parts to living things: a library of instructions for building living things, as well as a method for transferring the building instructions to workers who read the instructions and then take the right part off the shelf to build proteins, the stuff of life.[576]

Material scientists are so spellbound by the workings of the DNA molecule, however, that most of them have not considered how such a smart particle made its way into their mindless world. It may be said that if a group of engineers were to devise a system for a cell to store and transfer information necessary to build the infinite diversity of living things, they might very well have designed a system similar to the DNA molecule.

Where Did DNA Get Its Intelligence?

The design of the DNA molecule and the rest of the cellular machinery presents a problem for material science. In its worldview, mind did not create life. Therefore, material science must account for the generation from dead matter of an information storage and transfer system rivaling any that the mind of man created, without recourse to the creativity of a mind. Having eliminated mind, God, and intelligence from their worldview, material scientists are left to rely upon dumb luck to create the original molecule that carried the genetic code.[577]

We can now perhaps better understand one reason that Darwin evolutionists believe that all living things descended from a common ancestor: they need only explain how life arose from the dead once. As Professor Mayr observes,

> The problem of the origin of life, that is the reconstruction of the steps from simple molecules to the first functioning organism, is one that poses a keen challenge to the students of molecular evolution. A full realization of the near impossibility of an origin of life brings home the point how improbable

this event was. This is why so many biologists believe that the origin of life was a unique event. The chances that this improbable phenomenon could have occurred several times is exceedingly small, no matter how many millions of planets in the universe.[578]

This first simple organism, as we have seen, was not very simple. Darwin's original ancestor must not only possess the peculiar ability (at least for a dead particle) of converting energy to fuel bodily processes, but it also must reproduce itself and transfer body-building information to new generations. This information transfer system, moreover, appears fully integrated. The language of the genetic code, by which base triplets translate into specific amino acids, appears established in the first living thing. Even if it is conjectured that a nonsense code predated the ordered genetic code, it is nonetheless true that according to material science, a completely nonrandom, ordered language appeared by chance.

And so grows the dilemma of accepting the material science world-view as true: making an ingenious world from nothing and mindless little particles bursting from a hypothetical big bang which now decide to write codes for building living things and to engage in a synchronized dance to carry out the instructions.

As we note again later, Darwin firmly believed that nature "cannot make a leap."[579] Darwin believed that nature did nothing suddenly; species were not instant creations of an all-powerful force; they were not made whole. Insects did not sprout wings in one generation, nor fish legs. And surely, God did not create the earth in six short days. Darwin's world is a gradual world, a world of slow changes. Richard Dawkins writes,

> We have seen that living things are too improbable and too beautifully "designed" to have come into existence by chance. How, then, did they come into existence? Darwin's answer is by gradual, step-by-step transformations from simple beginnings, from primordial entities sufficiently simple to have come into existence by chance.[580]

Slow changes fit in better with material evolution. If an organism took a sudden leap to a favorable feature, such as an eye, it would strongly imply that either the organism or nature had "something in mind," or that God planned creation.[581] But material science outlaws the concepts "mind," "plan," and "purpose."[582] Only God makes plans; natural selection has "no long-term goal."[583]

If this is true, how then did a dead particle *gradually* acquire the intelligence that the DNA molecule exhibits? How did the dead particle make the leap to the intricate arrangement of chemicals that form even the simplest living thing? Does not the slow struggle toward the DNA molecule suggest either that the lifeless bits of dust knew where they were going, or that perhaps we are looking at these molecules from the wrong perspective?

Chapter Thirty-Seven

HOW MATERIAL SCIENCE BELIEVES LIFE BEGAN

IN ONE WAY, THE problem of explaining the origin of matter is simple compared to the origin of life. Scientists will take any type of thing—hydrogen atom, neutrino, cosmic ray—to begin creation; they just need one thing to pop out of nothing.[584] Scientists investigating the origin of life, however, need the matter left over from the big bang to do something special: they need it to arrange into highly intricate molecules possessing the ability to absorb energy, pass on coded messages to their offspring, and copy themselves. They need tiny pieces of matter to form notes and then for the notes to become a song—with no songwriter.

Material scientists, having rejected so-called supernatural explanations to the origin of life, opt for the only explanation that appears scientific: particles combined into a simple living thing that grew in complexity over 3 billion years to form humans. These scientists have rejected the role of mind or God in creation and must live with the alternative, no matter how long the odds. Despite the vast improbabilities of living particles rising from the dead, scientists are willing to accept the odds because they believe there is no other rational alternative. As we will see, this is an unnecessary, if not foolhardy, decision.

In considering science's failed attempts to explain how life arose from the dust, we can see the source of the difficulty. Science has defined the DNA molecule as the basis of life. Looking deep inside this molecule, science finds the "brains" for living things. The task then becomes explaining how mindless particles came together to form the epitome of intelligence on a molecular level. Working backward from this most intelligent of all particles, scientists must speculate how dust assembled itself into a molecule they can call alive.

But one source of their difficulty is that creation and evolution occurred *forward* in time. Instead, they first assume the existence of the DNA molecule and then, working *backward*, imagine how dead particles flowed toward the structure of DNA, or at least a replicating molecule.[585] The DNA molecule becomes a *given* for biologists; DNA plays the role of a powerful magnet set off in the future that draws the helpless big bang residue toward DNA's double-helix form. Material scientists want, or perhaps need, to believe that the road from mindless particles to a world bursting with life is downhill all the way.[586]

Because most biologists are also adherents of the material science worldview, the impossibility of life arising from dead matter has no effect on their theories or opinions. It is either creationism or Darwin. As Professor Mayr writes, "The truth of the matter is that unless a person is still an adherent of creationism and believes in the literal truth of every word in the Bible, every modern thinker—any modern person who has a worldview—is in the last analysis a Darwinian."[587] Not much of a choice. Either we close our mind and blindly accept the teachings of creationism, or we put our credulity to the side and believe that the universe exploded from the dark void and then painted itself into a picture of endless beauty—all without the use of a mind.

And given the choice, the "great majority of biologists subscribe to the hypothesis that life developed on Earth from nonliving material that became ordered into molecular aggregates that were capable of self-reproduction and metabolism."[588] By "nonliving material," biologists mean a so-called prebiotic soup that just happened to contain the ingredients found in the simplest living molecules.[589]

In other words, because modern biologists have convinced themselves that life must have emerged from dead particles, they let their imaginations roam free to find a way for these particles to become filled with the pulsating vibrancy that characterizes life. But none of their theories work. A review of material science's origin-of-life theories illustrates the problem.

The Prebiotic Soup

The standard theory, like many others in evolutionary biology, has its source with Darwin. Although Darwin was wary of proposing a scientific explanation for the origin of life, he ventured a guess in a famous letter to a friend:

> But if (and oh! What a big if!) we could conceive in some warm little pond, with all sorts of ammonia and phosphoric salts, lights, heat, electricity, etc., present, that a protein compound was chemically formed ready to undergo still more complex changes, at the present day such matter would be instantly absorbed, which would not have been the case before living creatures were found.[590]

In other words, a primordial chemical stew contained all the ingredients to make living molecules, and through some improbable sequence of mixing, shuffling, and reacting, these ingredients decided to join together and harden into a life-form.

This initial speculation, however, is flawed at its inception, as it assumes the essence of life is an ordered molecule, a thing. Once biologists take for granted that life began as a self-perpetuating particle, the belief takes hold that they simply have to wait for the right mixture of chemicals to join together and form what would later be known as the DNA molecule. But even if these particles are somehow randomly drawn to the right shape, where is life? Where is the beating heart? The struggle to survive? The inner, indescribable feeling of watching a mother give birth? The home team coming from behind to win? A poet's inspiration? The all-fulfilling sense of a higher power resting at the core of nature? Where among science's periodic table will we find what life is?

We sit and wait for this mysterious thing called life to emerge, like a hovering spirit, out of the dirt. But nothing appears.

Even when scientists assume a materialistic origin to life, they still confront insurmountable obstacles to articulating a credible theory. Origin-of-life researchers come face-to-face with barriers so dense that they should be perceived as dead ends; something is sending them a message, but they are not reading it. The message says, try another route.

For example, after assuming that the soup contained the right ingredients, scientists then assume that the environmental conditions on the young Earth favored the generation of organic molecules or simple bacteria. A condition generally considered critical to the formation of the first organism is that the atmosphere contains "little or no free oxygen."[591] Apparently, a strongly oxidizing atmosphere, such as the one we live in, could poison primitive bacteria.[592] Although some scientists are "certain"[593] that these conditions existed, other scientists contest even this basic assumption.[594]

So far we have a soup of the necessary ingredients and a favorable atmosphere. Next, according to the textbook version of the origin of life, a form of energy such as lightning or volcanic ash[595] zaps the soup, forming organic molecules in the process.[596] According to the standard teaching, these molecules are the "building blocks of life."[597] Support for this viewpoint is found in a classic laboratory experiment that Stanley Miller and Harold Urey performed at the University of Chicago in 1953. In a flask, Miller placed various chemicals believed to have been present on the young Earth and subjected the mixture to an electrical charge intended to mimic a thunderstorm. The experiment produced various organic chemicals, including some of the twenty amino acids common to all life-forms. This experiment is usually offered as support for the notion that life, or at least its building blocks, can arise from dead matter.[598]

In his helpful book, *Origins: A Skeptic's Guide to the Creation of Life on Earth*, Robert Shapiro places the Miller-Urey experiment into perspective. He explains that about 90 percent of the dry weight of a typical bacterium consists of proteins, nucleic acids, polysaccharides, and lipids.[599] The Miller-Urey experiment produced none of these molecules.[600] With regard to the subparts of these building blocks, the Miller-Urey experiment produced no component of nucleic acids, polysaccharides, or lipids.[601] Only two of the twenty amino acids were present in significant concentrations.[602] Furthermore, the experiment produced many amino acids of no relevance to life.[603] Thus, as Shapiro explains, only about 4 percent of the subparts to the building blocks of life were formed.[604] He concludes,

> The very best Miller-Urey chemistry . . . does not take us very far along the path to a living organism. A mixture of simple chemicals, even one enriched in a few amino acids, no more resembles a bacterium than a small pile of real and nonsense words, each written on an individual scrap of paper, resembles the complete works of Shakespeare.[605]

Since the original Miller-Urey experiment, investigators have produced additional building blocks to living things.[606] But no experiment has produced all of them, and their generation on the young Earth remains a matter of speculation and debate within the scientific community.[607]

Even if scientists were able to synthesize in a test tube all the molecules necessary to build the simplest organism, several serious problems still confront them. It is not just necessary for the chemical soup to contain the building blocks to the complex living molecules, but these substances must come together in the right proportions and then stay linked together. As Professor Robert Hazen writes,

> The prebiotic ocean was an extremely dilute solution of many thousands of different organic molecules, most of which play no known role in life. By what emergent processes were just the right molecules selected and organized?[608]

Professor Hazen, among others, is searching for this "emergent" process. But it should be evident that the use of the term "emergence" is simply a placeholder concept to mask material science's ignorance over how life came from dead particles.

Indeed, the problem in the material science worldview is how to get these ingredients to agree on forming a self-replicating organism. Harold Morowitz of Yale University proposed an experiment to calculate the chances that these ingredients would come together to form a bacterium. In the experiment, a living bacterium is placed in a test tube, which is then heated, causing the bacteria to dissemble into its component molecules. The necessary ingredients to form a simple living thing are now all in one place. We have only to wait for them to reassemble. What are the chances the ingredients will decide to re-form into a bacterium? Morowitz says one chance in $10^{100,000,000,000}$,[609] roughly the odds of winning the lottery every day in a row for 40 million years.[610]

But perhaps we do not need to have a whole bacterium form at once to prove that life can spring from the earth. Another option is to consider the production of smaller parts of organisms, such as protein molecules. One protein molecule common to all life is the enzyme cytochrome c.[611] Like other proteins in living things, this enzyme is made of twenty different amino acids. Cytochrome c is made of those twenty amino acids arranged in a 104-link chain. Or, if considered as letters in an alphabet, cytochrome c would be a sentence consisting of 104 letters. Assuming these twenty amino acids are all present in one place, the odds against this particular "sentence" forming through chance have been estimated at one in 10^{130}.[612]

Similar calculations have been performed on the chances that other necessary combinations of particles randomly came together in the form of a molecule necessary for life. These odds are more than mind-boggling; they are impossible. The impossibility, however, results from the same weakness of the material science world: the lack of a force to organize the independent material world. Remember, in order to study the mind, material science has detached the external world from it—the greatest of all specimens. Thus, scientists leave out of the explanation the only intelligent force in the cosmos of which we have direct knowledge: our own mind.

The Birth of RNA

Most unique to life is the process of self-replication,[613] the creation of new life nearly identical to the parent. With the DNA molecule, scientists believe that they found the mechanism for reproduction. The double-helix splits down the middle, and specialized molecules within the cell's nucleus reconstruct a new DNA molecule from materials available in the cell.

Some scientists have looked at the odds against the simplest possible replicating atom assembling itself through chance processes. For these calculations, scientists chose RNA over DNA; they consider RNA simpler because it consists of only one strand, though it also carries the genetic code. DNA is just too complicated to arise by chance. Paul Davies summarizes the predicament:

> There is no reason whatever to suppose that, left to itself, [the prebiotic soup] would spontaneously generate life, even after millions of years, merely by exploring every combination of chemical arrangements. Simple statistics soon reveal that the probability of the spontaneous assembly of DNA—the complex molecule that carries the genetic code—as a result of random concatenations of the soup molecules is ludicrously— almost unthinkably—small. There are so many combinations of molecules possible that the chance of the right one cropping up by blind chance is virtually zero.[614]

So scientists turn to the simpler RNA molecule as the first living particle. But this molecule is hardly what one would call simple. Robert Shapiro reports that the simplest RNA molecule would have about twenty nucleotides, or "rungs." This simple structure is composed of roughly six hundred atoms laid out in a specific sequence. Depending on the number of different atoms assumed available on the young Earth, the odds against even this simplest of RNA strand forming through sheer chance ranges from 10^{600} to one (for a ten-atom alphabet) to 10^{992} (for a forty-five-atom alphabet).[615]

Because material scientists have written mind and God out of life's script, they again encounter insurmountable problems explaining how even the simplest RNA molecule formed itself. These scientists seem to think that if chance can be appealed to just once to arrange the necessary molecules in the right order, this magical particle will start struggling for existence and continuously replicate itself, all so that Darwinian natural selection can begin.[616] Blind luck builds the bridge to the ordering mechanism[617] of natural selection. If these molecules would start replicating, theorists hope, the particles would compete for survival and the best replicating system would win.[618]

Where Darwin envisioned iguanas and finches competing for survival on Galapagos Island, modern evolutionists line up RNA molecules in a replication race. Manfred Eigen writes,

> Prebiotic [before life] RNA chemistry provided an environment for Darwinian evolution: populations of self-replicating species (RNA strands with different sequences) competed for the available supply of "food" (energy-rich monomers). The continuous generation of mutant sequences, some of them having advantageous properties, forced evolutionary reevaluation of the fittest species.[619]

Several problems exist with this picture. The investigators assume RNA evolved from the prebiotic soup because RNA was the favored structure for transferring genetic information.[620] This is a fine theory, but what drove this dead and dumb particle—several million of which can fit on the head of a pin—to undertake the role of an efficient replicating machine? Why should molecules bother competing in the first place? If through some wild streak of luck the right molecules joined together to make an RNA strand, what kept them from falling apart? If conditions on the young earth did not destroy this fragile molecule, as some speculate,[621] what force held it together and protected it from the elements? Do molecules have an urge to survive? Physicists gave particles minds of their own; biologists now give them life. In the same way physicists attribute the order their minds' demand to mindless particles, so biologists attribute their own life-urge to dead particles.

Researchers, working against impossible odds, nonetheless continue the effort to build a replicating molecule in a test tube. Recent attempts focus on finding a molecule that not only can store and transfer information, but that also undertakes the role of worker molecules (enzymes). This line of research is important because of a chicken-and-egg dilemma created by considering RNA the first living thing.[622] RNA is considered an informational source; RNA tells enzymes what amino acids to link together to form the necessary proteins. Enzymes carry out the instructions coded in the RNA molecule. But enzymes are themselves proteins. Therefore, the first RNA molecule would have had no worker (enzyme) to carry out its order to replicate itself or to build protein. In existing cells, reproduction takes place along an assembly line. DNA, RNA, enzymes, and other proteins all have their roles. Labor is divided in an efficient production system, but the whole assembly line is too complicated to have formed through chance. Unless researchers are bold enough to speculate that both the RNA molecule and the necessary enzymes arose by chance together (which, because of the mind-boggling odds, is not a popular theory) they must imagine an RNA strand, unlike any known to exist today in living creatures, that could also function as an enzyme.[623] They need an RNA molecule to play the role of designer, mechanic, and parts shop.[624] But once having formed on the young Earth, this all-purpose molecule departed and gave way to a more efficient system that divided labor among distinct particles.

Recent investigators have been able to manufacture some RNA strands in the laboratory that perform the most simple enzyme functions; they can chop themselves apart and reassemble some nucleotide pieces into a strand.[625] But these laboratory creations fall well short of what a living cell does; the man-made creations are slow, clumsy, and sloppy, while the real thing is lightning-fast and seldom makes a copying error.[626] Nevertheless, researchers continue to shake their test tubes and experiment with different additives in the "hope that a handful of the possible trillions of new combinations will turn out to be more efficient enzymes."[627]

Here we see the peculiar picture of a living, breathing scientist, a representative of the most intelligent life-form on earth, mixing up dead particles in a test tube in the hope that a living thing will crawl out. Scientists who are followers of this worldview push to the side both the mind and the will to live, the two inner powers we know best, as they seek out signs of life among particles floating aimlessly in test tubes.

It Came from Outer Space

Not all material scientists believe that life crawled out of a swamp on the young Earth. Some of them, recognizing the enormous improbability that such a miraculous event actually occurred, turn to other theories.

One theory, called *panspermia*, looks to outer space as the source for the necessary organic molecules to create Darwin's common ancestor.[628] This theory notes that because the universe is billions of years older than the Earth, life had more time to crawl out of some other planet's swamp.[629] Once conceived on an alien planet, comets, meteorites[630] or even unmanned spaceships[631] then delivered these extraterrestrial seeds of life to earth.

That such a theory finds its way into a college biology textbook reflects the desperate nature of origin-of-life research.[632] Examining alternative scientific theories is no doubt a healthy practice. But transporting the origin-of-life problem to outer space appears to be passing the buck on a large scale. For now we must ask, How did life originate on the alien planet?

Recently, a group of leading scientists has suggested that when considering the existence of life on other planets, we should expand the search to encompass chemical forms and structures foreign to the planet Earth.[633] These new life-forms, according to this scientific panel, might not be based on DNA, water, or carbon, although they still assume these new forms will know how to engage in a Darwinian struggle for existence.

Or It Grew from Clay

Another origin-of-life theory is that life-formed not from some premixed hot soup but from ordinary clay.[634] This theory recognizes that life's most unique property is self-reproduction. Rather than speculate how a self-replicating molecule arose from a hot soup, the theory uses inorganic materials that perform a crude form of replication—clay crystals. According to A. G. Cairns-Smith, the originator of this theory, "Life began in crystals which had the ability to reproduce themselves."[635] By "reproduction," Cairns-Smith means that clay crystals, formed by the forces of wind and rain, broke into two pieces; the crystals did not lay eggs or bear offspring.

The theory takes advantage of one feature of clay crystals—none is perfect. These defects, according to the theory, act as the beginning for an early "genetic code." If every crystal looked the same and broke into identical pieces, there would be no individuality and, hence, no message other than silence. The defects become the early scratches on a rock, the first rough code. But where this "pet rock" got a brain to write an intelligent message for future generations remains unexplained.

Where Manfred Eigen applies Darwinian natural selection to an RNA molecule, Cairns-Smith applies it to clay. According to the clay theory, defective clay crystals better adapted to the environment beat out competing crystals by wedging into rock formations or river beds. Gradually, as a means of furthering survival, the clay crystals acquired organic ingredients, such as RNA and proteins, which presumably just happened to be in the area. These organic molecules proved more successful at adapting to the environment than the lifeless clay crystals and mounted a "genetic takeover."[636] Clay provided a "naked gene" or copying device; the organic molecules filled in the necessary blueprints and building equipment. The organic molecules proved more adept at competing in the struggle for life, and that is why we are no longer clay creatures.

It is testimony to the weakness of the "RNA world" hypothesis that scientists sign up to the Cairns-Smith theory.[637] Of course no one has ever seen a "genetic takeover," nor is much said about why ordinary clay, on its own power, should decide to become a bacterium or a human. More importantly, little is said about how this rock gained the education to write building instructions for a living thing. These scientists, neck-deep in the material science worldview, seem to assume that in the beginning of time, nature, as a bonus, programmed dead particles complete with the laws of physics and Darwinian evolution.

Chapter Thirty-Eight

THE MELODY CAME FIRST: THE ORIGIN OF LIFE

The Origin of Life

Unlike the origin of matter, which material scientists concede entails mostly wild speculation, the question of how life began has spawned a vast literature.[638]

While cosmologists are acknowledging that the origin of mind-independent matter is beyond the realm of science,[639] Darwinians stand at podiums proclaiming that Darwinian evolution is a fact, if not ultimate truth, and that anyone who disagrees with them is uninformed if not crazy.[640] How did a purely hypothetical big bang for cosmology become a fact of nature for biology?

Darwinians believe the physical universe can ultimately be explained as a combination of mindless particles following natural laws.[641] These are the same particles that biologists assume were left over by the big bang; but, of course, if there were no big bang and if the appearance of matter instead occurred through a projection of our internal states, then every subtheory that material science advances based on the workings of these mindless particles—including Darwinian evolution—collapses. For this core reason, Darwinism cannot be true: it depends upon the truth of the big bang—the creation out of nothing of a mind-independent world that operates according to the mathematically precise laws of nature. Darwinians not only assume the truth of the big bang, they also assume that life—the majestic flowing movement streaming from nothing— arose from the utterly dead residue of the big bang.

Because some readers may assume that this line of argument is some roundabout way to promote creationism or intelligent design, let me quickly eliminate that notion. The flaw in any religious-based explanation, whether titled "creationism," "intelligent design," or something else, is that the rational inquiry to find the truth, or the true explanation of how we got here, stops at pronouncements made in old religious texts (such as the Bible or Qur'an) or at a picture of "God" inferred by others from these texts.

The problem with stopping the search for truth at the pages of religious texts should be self-evident: if these texts are true, then they should be able to be explained within a larger theory of the world. (This topic is also addressed in the final part of this book.) Taking the words of old religious texts as the unchangeable ultimate truth assumes that the mind, God, or thought has never evolved to a higher understanding of the world or itself over thousands of years of history. This makes no logical sense. If God is or has a mind, will not this Mind gain in knowledge through time? And, if the words of the Bible, Qur'an, or other religious text are true or accurate, then should they not withstand logical scrutiny? Indeed, if we analyze the words within the framework of the Real Dream we can place them in the stream of the history to the dream and give them deeper meaning.

The second problem, also addressed in the last part, is that certain influential readers of these texts project an image of God framed within the scientific worldview of the time. Note that both material science and Western religions picture God as existing in some far-off realm wholly distinct from the material world. Now if we do not assume the truth of the material science worldview, but instead picture "God" as the substratum of the world, or the united mind, then we can make sense of both science and religion. The new science becomes an evolution of material science where the matter assumption is replaced with complete certainty that the mind projects the world, and we gain this certainty through real-world experience and open, rational inquiry. The Mind or God is not just part of nature, but the source of nature. We call it Mother Nature, an apt name.

This book penetrates through the matter assumption of science and the God-picture of religion. The result is to combine the two into a united outlook, where both science and religion find God, but from different angles. In sum, if you choose to relegate the arguments in this book to the category of intelligent design or creationism, you are not reading closely enough. I believe creationism is indeed a "science stopper."[642]

But material science is wrong for a different reason. As noted, by "supernatural," science means any force not apparent in their assumed mindless universe, specifically God or Mind. Biology builds upon cosmology, physics, and chemistry and takes the material science worldview as given. Several times removed from the intractable problem of explaining the origin of matter and natural laws, biologists can happily assume the big bang myth is true.

Thus, Darwinians, like all material scientists, must assume that something came from nothing outside the control of the mind. They must assume that modern science has crossed the infinite divide and found a credible way for something to come from nothing without the assistance of the dreaming mind.[643]

But here again we find the great error of material science at work: Through its dispassionate stance toward the world, science takes the observer out of the picture as a creative force and then studies the regularities of that world; this approach leads to profound puzzlement over the origin of the very regularities they study. No problem is more acute for material scientists than the origin of life.

Life did not arise from particles—atoms and molecules—to the physical form of a dog, tree, or woman, but emerged from the fiery intensity of the mind. The form-projecting power of the mind created the melody before the notes. The song came first. When we pretend material science is the true science and that material particles are the source for the world, we find ourselves looking under the hood of the dream world and getting a glimpse of the software program to an infinite dream. We are peeking at the most complicated machine imaginable, a machine born in the fire of an infinite dreamer, radiating images of a world with boundless creativity.

As we watch scientists attempt to explain how material particles joined together on their own initiative to form the physical world, we are in truth observing the trail of a comet. Chemicals did not evolve to form the physical world or life; rather, the internal chemical composition of all physical things, including living organisms, is a reflection of the workings of the whole. If you disagree with this conclusion, then you must overcome the six great mysteries of the material science worldview:

- How something came from nothing

- How these mindless particles became infused with the laws of nature

- How these laws are constant throughout the universe

- How dead particles spontaneously became alive

- How the intricate, integrated coding system of the DNA molecule formed itself from mindless particles

- How the mind could ever know about this mind-independent world

In short, the Real Dream worldview has a decisive advantage over the worldview advanced by material science: the Real Dream deals with a *possible* world.

Chapter Thirty-Nine

DARWIN'S COMMON ANCESTOR POPULATES THE GLOBE

To ACCOUNT FOR THE countless galaxies in the sky, material science assumes that all the necessary star matter was present at the moment of the big bang, though condensed into a point. To account for the countless life-forms flooding the Earth, material science takes it for granted that life arose on Earth from this same barren star matter. With no other explanation available, material science concludes that because life must have come from dead matter, therefore it did.[644] This line of thought is more wishful thinking than scientific reasoning.

Nevertheless, we now go along with Darwin and assume that through an incredible run of luck, dead, mindless matter turned into a living thing programmed with the early words of the genetic code. Through another series of fortuitous events, this fragile microcell stayed in one piece long enough to somehow convert energy from the environment to allow it to survive and then reproduce. With this first organism assumed, we next consider further evidence that scientists believe supports Darwin's theory of common descent.

The Common Ancestor Disperses

Darwin's common ancestor necessarily arose at a single place on Earth. As Darwin said, "It is also obvious that the individuals of the same species, though now inhabiting distant and isolated regions, must have proceeded from one spot, where their parents were first produced; for it is incredible that individuals identically the same should ever have been produced through natural selection from parents specifically distinct."[645] In other words, to conclude that the same species arose at more than one place on Earth at the same time not only makes a materialistic explanation to the origin of life even more improbable, it also invokes the "agency of a miracle."[646]

In contrast, under the creationist account, God quickly populated the Earth with life, like a director ordering actors to take their positions on stage, or a theater operator switching on a movie projector. To conclude that the same species arose at multiple places on the Earth implies a mystical, supernatural connection between living things. Plants and animals are undoubtedly intricately built, complex things. To suppose that the same living thing, such as a sunflower, developed independently in separate regions of the Earth demands a coincidence too far-fetched for Darwin's theory. Darwin said that if numerous species . . . have really started into life all at once, the fact would be fatal to the theory of descent with slow modification through natural selection. For the development of a group of forms, all of which have descended from some one progenitor, must have been an extremely slow process; and the progenitors must have lived long ages before their modification.[647]

In Darwin's theory, an organism's "infinitely complex relations to other organic beings and to external nature"[648] determine which variations nature selects.[649] No two sets of "infinitely complex relations" are identical. Therefore, under Darwin's theory, if the same specie turns up in isolated areas it must be because they both derived from a common ancestor and migrated to those regions.[650]

Darwinians typically use the geographical distribution of species as support for Darwin's theory of common descent.[651] Darwin observed, as had others, that similar environmental settings on the Earth do not produce similar species.[652] For example, climates and physical conditions in certain areas of North America and Europe are nearly identical. Yet, Darwin noted, organisms living in those regions were "widely different."[653] Rather, species are more closely related to those in adjacent geographical areas than to those living in similar environmental settings.[654]

To illustrate, suppose a duplicate of the Galapagos Islands (a group of islands in the Pacific Ocean off the coast of South America where Darwin made many of his observations) is placed at exactly the same latitude off the coast of Africa. Animals and plants on Galapagos II are more likely to resemble those on the African mainland than those on Galapagos I.

This observation led Darwin to conclude that today's variety of existing species spread from the same birthplace. Species are then more likely to resemble those in close geographical proximity than those in similar but isolated environmental settings. We see a picture of the primordial ancestor radiating descendants, branching[655] throughout the globe like a vine; some variations in offspring better adapt to the newly encountered environmental conditions, resulting in a spectrum of diversity. Periodically, a specie will come upon an impassable barrier, such as a water body or mountain range, and migration will stop.[656] The population may become isolated and evolve unique characteristics, such as the marsupials (pouched animals) in Australia.[657] Darwin's theory of common descent thus attempts to explain the geographical distribution of plants and animals throughout the globe.

Comparative Anatomy

Darwin's theory of common descent also helps explain other observed facts. Darwin noted that apparently diverse animal species share similar anatomical (bodily structure) features. For example, common skeletal components comprise the forelimbs of cats, bats, whales, humans, and other mammals.[658] But the same bodily structure often serves different functions. The same skeletal system, for example, forms the wing of a bat and the flipper of a whale.[659]

This similarity in bone structures among widely diverse species argues for Darwinian evolution and against creationism. As one textbook explains, "Such anatomical peculiarities make no sense if the structures are uniquely engineered and unrelated. It is more logical . . . that the basic similarity of these forelimbs is the consequence of descent of all mammals from a common ancestor."[660] The same skeletal pattern is used for widely different functions. If these two species were separately created, one might think that the bat wing and whale flipper would be uniquely designed.

Comparative Embryology

Comparative embryology provides additional support for Darwin's theory of common descent.[661] Diverse species, such as fish, frogs, snakes, birds, and humans, go through similar stages of development in an egg or uterus. For example, embryos with backbones (vertebrates) pass through a developmental stage where two holes called gill slits appear in the throat area.[662] As the different animal embryos develop, the gill slits grow into diverse bodily parts. In fish, the gill slits become gills; in land vertebrates, the gill slits develop into other parts, such as tubes that link the throat with the middle ear in humans.[663]

Common Genetic Code

As pointed out above, the same sequence of base molecules in the DNA molecule code form the same amino acids in all living things. The genetic code has the same meaning in all living things, suggesting that nature wrote the code once for the original organism and its ancestors simply copied the same language.[664]

Leaving aside the threshold question of how this first living thing arose from dead matter, these observations indeed seem to support the theory of common descent. Descendants of this universal parent migrated throughout the globe, halting only where impassable barriers impeded their progress.[665] This first living thing established a series of common patterns upon which its descendants were modeled; something programmed a universal genetic code into the first RNA molecule, which then copied itself throughout the history of life. A common bone structure varied over the centuries to fit different uses, but never diverged from the original pattern. Embryonic development suggests that a common seed gave birth to all life. The combination of these facts led Professor

Mayr to conclude, "There is probably no biologist left today who would question that all organisms now found on the earth have descended from a single ancestor."[666]

Darwin's Misplaced Heritage

But the facts are not as perfect as Darwin would have hoped. According to his theory, similar species had to migrate smoothly over the Earth, like a slowly advancing wave. Perfect Darwinian migration would be continuous. Similar species could not suddenly appear simultaneously in isolated regions. This event would suggest special creation, which all Darwinians oppose.[667]

As Darwin recognized, however, there are indeed numerous instances where the same species are found in geographically isolated regions of the Earth, and where the means of dispersal from a common source are hard to explain. For example, Darwin noted that plant species found in the White Mountains of the United States are the same as those found in Labrador, Newfoundland, and the highest mountains of Europe.[668] Other common species he noted were found in such widely separated areas as Australia, India, Japan, and Borneo, but not in the intervening areas. Others were found in such isolated regions as the Kerguelan Islands (a group of islands in the South Indian Ocean) and Tierra del Fuego (a group of islands near the tip of South America).[669] Darwin also noted that New Zealand crustacea were related more closely to those found in far-off Great Britain than to those in any other part of the world.[670] Ernst Mayr cites the example of the blue magpie, which is found in eastern Asia as well as in isolated regions of Spain and Portugal.[671] Richard Dawkins mentions the mystery of how, millions of years ago, monkeys and rodents made their way across the ocean from Africa to South America, and lemurs from Africa to faraway Madagascar.[672]

Darwin candidly confronted the problem that these examples created for his theory: "There are many and grave difficulties in understanding how several inhabitants of the more remote islands, whether still retained in the same specific form or modified since their arrival, could have reached their present home."[673]

In facing the problem of how common species dispersed to widely separated regions of the Earth while leaving no traces of descendants in the intervening regions, Darwinian evolutionists are constrained by their own material science worldview. For Darwin to have supposed that the exact same species arose independently on mountains in Australia and Japan was considered surrendering to creationism, and that would be unscientific. Darwin and other material scientists have defined *science* as a body of knowledge that first assumes the independent existence of the material world,[674] and then applies the scientific method. Central to material science is that no connection exists between either mind or matter, or between living things. For the same reason that material scientists reject anything appearing supernatural or paranormal, they cannot accept a theory of evolution in which isolated members of the same species seem to stay in touch across time and space as they evolve along precisely the same course.

Consequently, to address the mystery of how identical species dispersed to remote islands or isolated mountain peaks, Darwinian evolutionists have devised a variety of mechanical means for descendants of the common ancestor to have made their way to the hills of Brazil and the mountains of Europe. These methods include prehistoric land bridges between continents,[675] conveniently constructed for animals to walk over; dispersal of plant seeds in the feet and mouth of birds, or on the backs of ducks;[676] glacial activity that divided a once-continuous population and placed the animals on isolated mountain peaks;[677] dispersal of plant seeds and small animals by wind;[678] flotation by mangrove rafts;[679] and perhaps the most popular theory—continental drift, under which the existing continents once comprised one primordial land mass that has since broken apart.[680]

Disproving these theories is not a simple task, and that is not the purpose here. Rather, we may observe that Darwinians who attempt to support the theory of common descent are like physicists seeking to explain spiral galaxies using only the four fundamental forces. To fill in gaps, they just add more assumptions. Physicists look to dark matter and the inflationary universe hypothesis, while Darwinians look to continental drift and the dispersal powers of the wind, the sea, and happenstance.

In the Real Dream, no such assumptions are needed. If the universe is viewed as an evolving dream, instead of a mindless machine, it is not difficult to see how the same species could appear at widely separated regions of the Earth. Dream-based evolution is still subject to a succession of events, or time. The world still grows from a simple place to a complex place filled with diversity. But the world evolves in the manner of a dream, which means as a united whole. Living things grow up with the world, as the mind searches for the best physical form to engage in the process of life. The world evolves as a motion picture changes scenery and actors, overflowing from one image into another. But it is the entire scene that changes, not isolated parts working on their own power. Living things represent the infinitely creative mind in a flight from nothing, not embodied chemical mixtures budding from a single, primordial pond.

We also can see that not only the origin of life but also the universality of the genetic code, comparative anatomy, and comparative embryology are all better explained in the Real Dream than they are in Darwinian evolution. Living things are modeled after the same pattern because they were all created by the same mind. The internal composition, or anatomy, of living things reflects the outer form of the three-dimensional dream-projection. One 3-D form, one internal composition. The genetic code, as discussed above, stands in the same relation to a living organism as a gold atom stands to gold. The genetic code reflects the internal composition of life, the notes to a song; the more complex the song, the more intricate the arrangement. Comparative embryology reveals a common seed, but one born in the Mind, not a prebiotic soup.

Darwin, in short, had the right idea but the wrong common ancestor. We did not evolve from a common bacterium, but from a common mind. The Real Dream offers a wider and deeper explanation of the facts, as we will again see below with respect to the fossil record. Based only upon our will to live and the inherent power to dream, the Real Dream worldview uses what we know best to explain life, rather than what we can never know or explain—the independent existence of a self-operating material world.

Chapter Forty

DARWIN'S GRADUAL LEAPS

THE PRESENCE OF A physical world outside our windows is powerful evidence that the world is mind-created. We know that individual minds—or components of the united mind—are capable of conjuring up the appearance of an external world. Through night dreams, hallucinations, and mirages, we know this is possible. Therefore, it should not be surprising for events in this mind-created world to exhibit features of a mind at work.

One such feature is that the growth and evolution of the Real Dream occurs down a path built from ideas, leaping from thought to thought, form to form, model to model. Powering the movement through the dream are two fundamental forces: the will to live and infinite creativity. The combination of these two mysterious powers brings us the world.

The history of the world is the history of the dream. It is a mind coming to understand itself and its powers. It carries out its growth in the pure light of day, with soul exposed . . . working through forms, ideas . . . overcoming mistakes, moving on.

One of the best signs of the mind's travels through time is the fossil record, the historic evidence of how life-forms changed over time toward the human form. In Real Dream evolution (or *reflective evolution*), the fossil record represents the physical relics of a mind building a home for itself.

In this chapter we focus on a fundamental difference between evolution in a dream and evolution in Darwin's machine-world: the mind, by definition, produces everything that makes up a dream, and it works by leaping from idea to idea. An abstract image of physical form, such as the design of a remodeled basement, comes into the mind first; the mind then puts this abstract form into pictures and builds it in the physical world. A transition occurs from an abstract feeling up through the continuum to construction in the external world. It would be hard to think of a creative process dissimilar to this one—a plan for a party, the idea for a painting, the shape of a basketball shot or a soccer kick: the mind plots out what it wants to do and then attempts to execute the plan in the real world.

A mind knows where it wants to go; Darwin's evolution has no clue. It is mindless, directionless, and without purpose. Darwinian evolution can make no leap from form to form—from species to species, cat to dog; horse to zebra, lion to tiger. In Darwin's world, every living thing shades into the next; variations at the molecular level slowly and erratically become translated into physical bodies.

To give the appearance of motion in an animated film, artists draw thousands of discrete still pictures showing small differences in the positioning of the parts. Streaming these still pictures together gives the illusion of motion. Darwinian evolution also works by infinitesimal steps, but with one big distinction: the generator of the steps is mindless and without foresight. The construction of a coherent form, such as a human body, requires countless hit-and-miss steps, sorted out by the process of natural selection, as discussed in the next chapter.

In Darwin's world nothing happens suddenly; nature makes no leaps either across space or time. Species migrate slowly across geographical regions and evolve gradually through history.[681] Though Darwinians need to explain how a one-celled creature evolved into the trillion-celled human being, they believe they have a few billion years to work with.

The Importance of Time to Darwin's Theory

Time is critical to the validity of Darwin's theory, as it is to material science theory in general. Mindless particles, it seems, need a lot of time to create a world of endless order. George Wald, in a 1954 article titled "The Origin of Life," explained how immense time frames support the credibility of materialistic explanations:

> Time is in fact the hero of the plot. The time with which we have to deal is of the order of two billion years. What we regard as impossible on the basis of human experience is meaningless here. Given so much time, the "impossible" becomes possible, the possible probable, and the probable virtually certain. One has only to wait: time itself performs the miracles.[682]

After first allowing themselves two miracles—the creation of matter and the programming of this matter by natural laws—scientists summon the powers of time to provide for the miracle of life. In Darwin's version of evolution, immense time frames are necessary for the primordial single-celled organism to transform itself into the infinite diversity now present on the Earth. Darwin believed that it "cannot be objected that there has not been time sufficient for any amount of organic change; for the lapse of time has been so great as to be utterly inappreciable by the human intellect."[683] Professor Mayr notes that in Darwin's time, the "researches of the geologists . . . left no doubt of the immense age of the earth, thus providing all the time needed for abundant organic evolution."[684] Modern science places the age of the Earth at about 4.5 billion years,[685] with life appearing 1 billion years later.[686] Clearly this is a long time.

Time's importance to Darwin's evolution reduces to this: we are supposed to accept more easily the incredible improbability that mindless particles assembled themselves into living forms if we know that these particles had billions of years to perform the miracle. Therefore, Darwinians believe that evolution can work slowly without making leaps and bounds.

But how do we know that scientists are looking at time from the right perspective? Before considering how Darwinians use immense time frames to support materialistic evolution, let us consider the following scenario.

The alarm clock reads 11:05 p.m., and you doze off to sleep. Reading all those Stephen Jay Gould essays made you carry the thought of paleontology to bed with you. Soon you begin to dream. In the dream, you are a scientist out to discover the age of the Earth. As a location for your research you pick the Grand Canyon. A mule takes you to the bottom. There, using the modern technique of radioactive dating, you determine that rocks at the floor are 2 billion years old.[687] Excited with this discovery, you anxiously mount the mule and ride up to the surface. On the way up you think about the article you will write for *Scientific American* in which you will disprove once and for all the creationist theory that the earth is only a paltry six thousand years old.

Suddenly a car alarm goes off outside your window and you wake up startled; you look at the clock, which reads 11:25 p.m.

Question: How long have you been dreaming? Two billion years or twenty minutes? Clearly the answer is twenty minutes. No one sleeps or dreams for 2 billion years. This example illustrates one point. In a dream, it is inappropriate to base the age of the imagined world from the perspective of a material object in that world. Rather, the story's age is calculated through the eyes of the author, or the source of the imaginary world. During a dream, the dreamer is necessarily fooled into thinking that the object of the dream—here the Grand Canyon—exists independently of the mind. That is the point of dreaming. When the dreamer takes out his modern instrument to measure the age of the canyon rocks, he continues the dream; he continues to believe that both the rocks and the dating device exist external to the mind and were created by forces other than the mind.

But clearly, at least in the example above, the dreamer is imaging both the canyon and the dating device. These objects were placed there as reflections of the internal states of the dreamer; they were put there immediately and created from the imagination. Basing the age of a dream upon a dreamed object simply means that the dreamer continues to be fooled by the apparent independent reality of the imagined world. Once the dreamer realizes that he is the source of the dream—once he wakes up—he may discover that it is senseless to base the age of a dream upon something in the dream. The age of a dream is determined from the perspective of the mind, not the objects in the dream. Even children are capable of dreaming about rocks, dinosaurs, and stars.

However radical it may sound, these same principles apply to our world. We should not be fooled into basing the age of a dream world upon a material object. These are objects of the dream and therefore necessarily stem from the mind. But that is exactly how material science dates the ages of the universe and the earth. It first assumes that the external world has an existence independent of the mind and then takes out its instruments, conducts its measurements, and informs us that our world is billions of years old. Put another way, material scientists seek to explain the evolution of the Earth from the wrong standpoint: once they assume an independent material world, they are led into dating the age of the Earth from the perspective of dead matter. Believing that this is the correct standpoint for dating the age of a dream, they continue the illusion by believing that the age of rocks provides their dead particles ample time to form into a universe.

Well, then, how does one determine the age of a dream world? Among the possible methods are to consider how long it might take to develop a civilization of common dreamers, with language being perhaps the best benchmark. Through the miracle of the dreaming power, we may be able to project an external world, but only raw experience in that world can bring civilization, culture, and modes of communication.[688]

In a dream, time is the forward movement of creativity—rolling inspiration. It is an invisible, three-dimensional coordinate system that locks beings into the same moment. Without agreement on time, we could never relate to other people because they would not be in sync with us; the message, "I will meet you at the corner of Washington and Dearborn at noon," would have no meaning if the other person were not on the same coordinate system. When we turn to talk to another person, their "now" would not be our "now."

We would have the same problem with the natural world. We coordinate our activities—getting out of bed, going to work, planting crops—based upon the regularity of physical events, such as the rising of the sun. If we could not coordinate our lives with events in the outside world, all would be chaos. We would be like falling leaves from a tree, taking our independent paths to the ground, living separate lives.

Our need for regularity fixes a constant moment between us and other people and the natural world. In the same way that three-dimensional space is necessary for experience to occur, so time is necessary for relating to a different person and for living in a world.

Time, thus, is further proof of the world's unity. We dwell in the same moment, acting out the same script, linked together for all time.

Packed into the center of the mind—our mind—is an infinitely deep need to escape nothing, to burst from the void. When this wish is answered in the miracle we know as the physical world, the inspiration that activated the dream continues working, with the throttle wide open. Then, like a young poet inspired by a few lines of verse to write a sonnet, the mind continues building the dream.

Time is only a forward change; the future builds upon the past. Though we sometimes think that time causes things to age, age is also simply change in a forward direction. We have no certainty in a dream world that time necessarily leads to deterioration. Rather, it seems, if the dreamers unite to control the dream, then there is no reason that time may not lead to endless improvement. After all, is that not what it means to dream?

Creationism takes precisely the opposite stance to Darwin's theory of gradualism; under the former view, creation occurred almost overnight.[689] According to creationism, the 10 million existing species did not evolve over millions of generations, but were simply placed on the preexisting planet Earth.[690] Darwin, in contrast, noting the remarkable fit between an organism and its environment,[691] reasoning that new species arise from preexisting ones through natural processes and not through the hand of God.[692]

No material scientist believes that an animal, such as a dog, appeared out of nowhere in one day because there is no natural process that can account for such an event. Darwin wrote, "Natural selection can act only by taking advantage of slight successive variations; she can never take a leap, but must advance by the shortest and slowest steps."[693] Gradualism is critical to Darwin's theory.[694] In his view, new plants or animals cannot appear suddenly upon the Earth, and neither can new organs. As he said, "If it could be demonstrated that any complex organ existed, which could not possibly have been formed by numerous, successive, slight modifications, my theory would absolutely break down."[695] He could not find any,[696] and neither can most of his followers.[697]

Darwin saw that to suppose nature created a feature such as the human eye in one act implies some invisible force at work in the world. But to appeal to such a supernatural force is tantamount to invoking a miracle, and therefore off-limits to science.

Darwinian evolution stands in opposition to what some call essentialism.[698] Darwinian evolution is premised on the view that natural forces[699] caused the original common ancestor to transform[700] itself gradually over time into the 10 million existing species. Darwin's species do in fact shade into each other,[701] and transitions necessarily must exist between either living species or their now-extinct ancestors.

In other words, Darwin's world does not operate according to laws of the mind; it does not jump from essence to essence, or from idea (triangle) to idea (square).[702] Rather, it moves from parent to offspring in what Darwin called "infinitesimally small" steps.[703] Instead of leaping from one animal design to another, Darwin's species change smoothly[704] over time and space. "Natural selection acts," he said, "by accumulating slight, successive favorable variations; it can produce no great or sudden modification; it can act only by very short and slow steps."[705] As Professor Mayr explains, "A true theory of evolution must postulate a gradual transformation of one specie into another."[706] One animal, of course, does not undertake new forms throughout history. Rather, Darwinians speculate that great populations of species gradually change over immense time frames as environmental conditions favor certain variations and preserve them.[707] Consequently, at many points in the transition from a one-celled organism to humankind, there must be, under Darwin's theory, numerous representatives of the transitional period.

Darwin's theory of evolution demands many transitional forms for one chief reason: in his theory, no mind or intelligence directs the course of evolution. In Darwin's world, no connection exists between an animal and nature; variations, such as thicker fur on a bear, are not produced in response to an environment that grows steadily colder. Nor is the variation generated in response to the animal's "struggle for existence"; there is no mind within the DNA molecule that thinks, "It looks like it is growing colder. Better increase the production of fur proteins." Variations, in Darwin's world, are scattershot and directionless; they meet neither the needs of the organism[708] nor the demands of the environment.[709] Some happen to hit the mark and respond to a need; most do not and are discarded. Because variations are wild shots in the dark, a vast number must be generated for one to hit the target.

As an illustration, let us consider what evolutionists call the phylogenetic tree, or "tree of life."[710] These trees purport to show the lines of descent from a common ancestor for a single specie,[711] or group of species.[712] The tree trunk represents the common root of descent, and the branches show lines of divergence and variation. Modern-day species usually are placed at the tips of the branches, while their ancestors appear on lower branches.[713]

Virtually all of these trees show abrupt transitions between separate branches, and the node and tip of a single branch. For example, one well-known tree shows animals such as a frog, kangaroo, rabbit, whale, penguin, and human at branch tips.[714] At branch nodes are one-celled organisms, insects, fish, and birds, leading up to the mammals, and finally to apes and people.[715] (The exact placement of the biologically correct ancestors is not essential for the present point.) The branch length can be divided into many segments, each of which might represent an evolutionary step. The smaller the branch segment, the greater the number of intermediate steps. Remembering that nature makes no leaps in Darwin's world, we must be sure that these steps are very small. Using similar reasoning, Darwin described the number of connecting links with the terms "infinitude,"[716] "interminable,"[717] "inconceivably great,"[718] and "truly enormous."[719] Thus, Darwin realized that if nature made no leaps between species, and species did in fact shade into their common ancestors, the number of transitional species must be much greater than the number of fixed and distinct species, in the same way that most of a tree branch's length lies between its two ends.

How many more transitional types there must be is not known. In modern terms, we learn that one triplet of base pairs along a DNA molecule codes for one amino acid, and that many amino acids link together into a protein molecule. We know that a general correlation exists between segments of DNA (genes) and individual proteins. We also know, as we discuss in more detail below, that modern Darwinians believe that variations in organisms result from errors made at the microscopic level of the DNA molecule. These facts indicate that indeed the transitional steps are "infinitesimally small," as Darwin had supposed, because variations may exist only at the level of the protein molecule, of which there are millions in a living organism. As a rough estimate, if there are in fact 10 million existing species, let's say there must be at least ten times as many transitional species.

And here we see that by rejecting gradual leaps, Darwin painted himself into a corner.[720] The more infinitesimally small the transition between species, the smaller the leap, and hence, the less the need for an appeal to God or a miracle to save the theory. But conversely, the smaller the leap, the more transitional species there should be either in the living world or in the fossil record. Neither source, however, provides evidence supporting Darwin's theory of gradual descent.

Where Are the Transitions in the Living World?

Looking out at the world for ourselves we note the absence of transitional species. Where is the smooth, infinitesimally small transition between a giraffe and anything else? Or an elephant, rhinoceros, ostrich, platypus, penguin, eagle, dragonfly, human being, and anything else? In fact, we can list the entire animal kingdom and what we would find are not transitional species, but their nearly complete absence. If the number of transitions is "truly enormous," then where are they?

The lack of living transitional types, though hardly supporting Darwin's theory of gradual evolution, is not fatal. It can be argued that natural selection rejected the transitional varieties over 3.5 billion years of evolution, and selected those that today appear distinct. As Darwin stated,

Why do we not see these linking forms all around us? Why are not all organic beings blended together in an inextricable chaos? With respect to existing forms, we should remember that we have no right to expect (excepting in rare cases) to discover *directly* connecting links between them, but only between each and some extinct and supplanted form.[721]

Thus, it may be that the transitional types became extinct and we have only to look at the fossil record to find them. But Darwin could not find them there,[722] and neither can modern-day scientists.

The Fossil Record

The fossil record, like the living world, reveals almost the complete absence of transitional forms. To Darwin, this fact meant one thing: the fossil record is imperfect.[723] He knew his theory of gradual evolution was predicated upon the extinction of an "infinitude of connecting links,"[724] and admitted that the lack of any evidence of transitional forms in the fossil record is the "most obvious and forcible of the many objections which may be raised against my theory."[725] "He who rejects these views on the nature of the geological record will rightly reject my whole theory. For he may ask in vain where are the numberless transitional links which must formerly have connected the closely allied or representative species found in the several stages of the same great formation."[726]

Numerous other reasons exist to reject Darwin's theory of gradual descent, but we will rightly reject it on this basis as well. Although creationists[727] and Darwinian evolutionists[728] disagree sharply on the interpretation of the fossil record, everyone who looks at the facts reaches the same conclusion: transitional forms are almost nowhere to be found. For example, David M. Raup, former chairman of the department of geophysical science at the University of Chicago, observes,

Darwin predicted that the fossil record would show a reasonably smooth continuum of ancestor-descendant pairs with a satisfactory number of intermediates between major groups. . . . Such smooth transitions were not found in Darwin's time, and he explained this in part on the basis of an incomplete geologic record and in part on the lack of study of that record. We are now more than a hundred years after Darwin and the situation is little changed. Since Darwin, a tremendous expansion of paleontological knowledge has taken place, and we know much more about the fossil record than was known in his time, but the basic situation is not much different. We actually may have fewer examples of smooth transition than we had in Darwin's time because some of the old examples have turned out to be invalid when studied in more detail. To be sure, some new intermediate or transitional forms have been found, particularly among land vertebrates. But if Darwin were writing today, he would probably still have to cite a disturbing lack of missing links or transitional forms between the major groups of organisms.[729]

The late Stephen Jay Gould, in a commendable display of candor, remarked that the "extreme rarity of transitional forms in the fossil record persists as the trade secret of paleontology."[730] Gould further revealed that "all paleontologists know that the fossil record contains precious little in the way of intermediate forms; transitions between major groups are characteristically abrupt."[731] Richard Dawkins observes, "From Darwin onwards evolutionists have realized that, if we arrange all our available fossils in chronological order, they do not form a smooth sequence of scarcely perceptible change. We can, to be sure, discern long-term trends of change—legs get progressively more bulbous, and so on—but the trends as seen in the fossil record are usually jerky, not smooth."[732] A college biology textbook notes, "The fossil record is much more complete now than it was in Darwin's day, but fossil series showing graduated changes from older to younger species are still quite rare, considering how extensively life has changed over the geological period."[733] Professor Mayr sees the same record: "All major evolutionary changes seem to occur rather abruptly, not connected by intermediates with the preceding fossil series."[734] Michael Denton, in an excellent critique of Darwinism, observes that "while the rocks have continually yielded new and exciting and even bizarre forms of life, dinosaurs, ichthyosaurs and pterosaurs, in the early nineteenth century, Hallucigensia and Tribrachidium and many others in the twentieth century, what they have never yielded is any of Darwin's myriads of transitional forms."[735]

Nature's greatest leap occurred during what is known as the Cambrian explosion.[736] Darwinian evolutionists believe life began on Earth about 3.5 billion years ago. But fossil records of these early creatures are sparse for the first 3 billion years of evolution. Then, roughly 600 million years ago, a host of animal forms burst onto the scene.[737] Animal forms present today are largely modeled after those that emerged during the Cambrian period.[738] How so many new forms could suddenly appear in the fossil record has been called one of biology's "great mysteries"[739] and "deepest paradoxes."[740] Richard Dawkins remarks that the fossils look "as though they were just planted there, without any evolutionary history."[741] And perhaps they were, for that is what the facts imply.

The almost complete absence of transitional forms both in the living world and in the fossil record show a mind at work in creation, a mind that works by generating form after form, model to model. A fundamental principle of science—and one that separates it from religion—is that science is based upon objective evidence.[742] Real-world testing is science's "primary tool."[743] "Science is a particular way of knowing about the world. In science, explanations are restricted to those that can be inferred from the confirmable data—the results obtained through observation and experiments that can be substantiated by other scientists. Anything that can be observed or measured is amenable to scientific investigation. Explanations that cannot be based upon empirical evidence are not part of science."[744]

If Darwinian evolution were correct, there should be countless transitional forms present in the world and in the fossil record. There is no reason whatsoever for why, out of the billions of purported evolutionary sequences set in motion at life's beginning, the mindless process of natural selection would have molded organisms into discrete forms.

Material scientists, however, cannot rid themselves of their materialistic prejudices when confronting the data. They believe they must either explain (away) the gaps in the fossil record or have no choice but to accept the teachings of religion. Giving in to an alternative explanation, material scientists assume, is tantamount to forfeiting the scientific enterprise. They believe that any theory—no matter how farfetched—is better than the belief system of religion, for at least scientists use their minds.

Well, continue using your mind but do not stop the inquiry at a conclusion that only satisfies your preconceived notions about the world. Once again, there is another choice: interpret the data within a theoretical framework that offers a better explanation for the empirical evidence. The fossil record shows the dream-creating mind fleeing from nothing, spinning out an array of life-forms as it rockets toward the highest form. As the late Professor Mayr put it,

> One of the most characteristic features of science is its openness to challenge. The willingness to abandon currently accepted belief when a new, better one is proposed is an important demarcation between science and religious dogma.[745]

Is not the Real Dream worldview a test of this bedrock principle of science?

Darwinian theories that explain the gaps in the fossil record are difficult to refute. Like the graviton of modern physics, these theories attribute what we cannot find (transitional forms) to a blind spot in our knowledge. We cannot see the gravitons flooding the universe because they operate in the fleeting moment of uncertainty; in the same way, we cannot see the intermediate forms because they came and went quickly, or simply did not leave fossil remains. Darwinians tell us that the intermediate forms existed but we will never find them.

In the mindless and purposeless Darwinian worldview, we must ask why nature should exhibit such an abundance of distinct bodily forms? Why did nature make the living world into a zoological garden instead of a freak show of deformed creatures? In Darwin's world, no artist directs the course of evolution; nature produces variations without rhyme or reason. Adaptation to the environment and reproductive success alone determine survival. Why then did Darwin's isolated species always produce distinct creatures? If evolution proceeds gradually along a smooth continuum, why did not some of the branches lead to what we would call a transitional form, such as a half-dog, half-cat, or half-horse, half-man?

Isn't it peculiar that out of the 10 million existing species, and the millions of additional historic species, almost none are transitional forms? In a world created without an intelligence, should not a high percentage consist of odd creatures or even monsters? In fact, is there any reason to think that distinct forms would be favored? We thought reproductive success was the only criterion for natural selection.[746] Darwinian evolutionists tell us that natural selection is an ordering mechanism, but they cannot say it has the mind of an artist, for they have drained mind from the world.

Darwinian evolution fails because it seeks to build a world of endless order without the only thing that can produce such a world: a Mind. In the fossil record we find evidence for the truth. The fossil record shows neither special creation nor gradual Darwinian evolution. Rather, it reveals the footprints of an infinite mind in the process of building a dream world.

Chapter Forty-One

THE ILLUSION OF NATURAL SELECTION

Even if we assume *as given* a world where a nearly infinite amount of matter bursts from the void and life arises from dead atoms, we still must account for the astounding order of the natural world. We must find a source for the diversity of life and the peculiar manner in which life has adapted to nature.

Darwinian evolutionists find the source for order in natural selection, which Darwin described as follows:

> Owing to the struggle for life, any variation, however slight and from whatever cause proceeding, if it be in any degree profitable to an individual of any specie, in its infinitely complex relations to other organic beings and to external nature, will tend to the preservation of that individual and will generally be inherited by its offspring. The offspring, also, will thus have a better chance of surviving, for, of the many individuals of any specie which are periodically born, but a small number can survive. I have called this principle, by which each slight variation, if useful is preserved, by the term Natural Selection.[747]

The theory of natural selection is the cornerstone of Darwinian evolution. With this theory, scientists believe that they have found a force to organize their mindless, frenzied world. Natural selection, in their eyes, sculpts the living world, though it has no artist's touch, and accounts for the ingenuity of the human brain, though it has no mind.

In this chapter we consider the concept of natural selection. This theory is among the most prized in the material science worldview because scientists believe that natural selection provides a mechanism to account for the order in the living world and the diversity of life-forms. The mechanism is mindless but generates order. This feature makes natural selection the best available solution to the materialistic dilemma of how to build a world of wonder without a guiding intelligence. Put differently, this theory is the best that material scientists can do to explain the rise of the living world. With no other theory available, they circle the wagons, declare evolution a "fact,"[748] and denigrate all who challenge it.[749]

Evolution and natural selection do occur in our world, but not in the way Darwin envisioned. Before discussing how these terms change meanings in a dream world, let us first examine how material scientists believe evolution works.

The Two Steps of Natural Selection

Modern evolutionists refer to natural selection as a two-step process. "The first step consists in the production (through genetic recombination) of an immense amount of new genetic variation, while the second step is the nonrandom retention (survival) of a few of the new genetic variants."[750] In other words, organisms produce variations randomly, and then nature selects those variations best suited for survival. These two steps must be distinguished to understand how Darwinian evolutionists believe that a bacterium could evolve into a human. Let us take them one at a time.

Natural Selection's First Step

The first step of natural selection—the production of variety—is random.[751] By "random," evolutionists mean that changes occur in an organism's offspring "without reference to their future adaptiveness in the environment."[752] Another approach is to say that the "production of any new variation [is] independent of the needs of the organism."[753]

Variations are the raw material upon which natural selection operates.[754] Without variations evolution could not occur,[755] and only bacteria might today inhabit the Earth. But for evolution to work, favorable variations produced in individual generations must be passed on to descendants or inherited.[756] "Heritable variation is the fountainhead of evolution."[757] Unless descendants inherit favorable traits, such as thicker fur, organisms could not increase their adaptiveness to the environment. In addition, since nature makes no leaps in Darwin's world, nature must build favorable traits step-by-step.[758] To complete the building of an eye, for example, separate components must be transferred to the next generation for it to continue the construction project.[759] If a favorable component, such as the cornea, was not inheritable, construction of an eye (or other complex organ) would have to start anew every generation. Even Darwinians would probably agree that nature could not have built an eye in this manner.[760]

Darwin knew physical characteristics were inherited, but he understood neither the carrier of heredity[761] nor how variations arose.[762] Gregor Mendel (1822–1884) is credited for having discovered that physical characteristics (what biologists also call the *phenotype*) are passed across generations in whole packages; they are not blended.[763] The best example of this principle is sex. Offspring are either male or female; they are not androgynous (both male and female).[764]

As noted above, in the first half of the twentieth century, biologists identified the gene as the unit of heredity, which they located in thin strands (chromosomes) found in the cell's nucleus. Looking deep inside the chromosome, researchers hit bottom and discovered the DNA molecule. Here they found a mechanism both to carry heritable information and to produce variation.

The process of DNA replication, where the double-helix unzips and copies itself, provides a physical picture of reproduction.[765] When an error is made in copying DNA or in carrying out its protein-assembly instructions, a mutation arises.[766] Enzymes assembling the new complementary DNA strand may, for example, insert the wrong base code and produce distorted building instructions for the new organism.[767] These mutations supply new raw material for the evolutionary stream.

But mutations that simply distort the message of a DNA molecule will not easily transform a one-celled bacterium into a trillion-celled man, or extend the hundred-letter primordial RNA molecule into the billion-letter human genome. Somehow the message must be lengthened and made more complex. New words for the genetic dictionary must be invented. Also, mutations, according to material science, not only distort a given message, they can shorten or lengthen the building instructions.[768] Copying errors may cause an enzyme to insert an extra base triplet onto the new strand and produce a longer message. Through these copying errors, the genetic message of a bacterium grows into instructions to build a woman, at least according to material science.

Most mutations are useless or detrimental to the organism.[769] But periodically, through the luck of the draw, a mutation will produce instructions for a slightly superior feature, such as thicker fur on an animal in a cold climate, or sharper claws for hunting.[770] These favorable variations, according to Darwin, may better adapt the creature to the environment. If so, these variant animals stand a better chance of survival and will leave more offspring.[771]

Although the frequency of mutations can generally be predicted (about one per million generations), the specific nature of any one mutation cannot be known ahead of time. Darwin's common ancestor had no vision of what it wanted to be and no end in view.[772] If in hindsight it appears advantageous for a fish to have grown legs to walk upon the soil, as Darwinians tell us they did, the fish never knew legs would serve such a beneficial purpose. Darwin's common ancestor stumbles toward man, eyes closed to the future, with survival all that is important.

We are only at the first step of the two-step natural selection process, but already this theory is taking on water. To avoid appeals to God and the miracles of creationism, Darwinians suppose that life arose through sheer chance. But this first organism was no simple thing. At a minimum it must have possessed the ability to copy itself and to pass on body-building instructions to offspring—instructions written in a language still in use 3 billion years later to build elephants, sunflowers, human beings, and millions of other plant and animal species. Scientists have compared these instructions to a computer program, a library, a recipe, a blueprint—descriptions meant literally, not metaphorically. In the material science worldview, the genetic code is truly a code for building living things, in the same sense that a dictionary contains the words for constructing meaningful sentences. Where did the grammar of the genetic code come from?

Material scientists, in their quest to explain the world without resorting to God or miracles, substitute materialistic miracles for spiritual ones. After assuming that the genetic code assembled itself, scientists then proceed to overlook its intrinsic order and proclaim that the cellular machinery generates gibberish. Mutations and genetic recombinations both occur randomly and for no reason; they are directed to no end, and have no thought of building any bodily part, be it wings, legs, fur, beaks, gills, eyes or anything else.

Here material scientists commit a serious inconsistency. Computers, libraries, Morse codes, blueprints, and the other information sources to which they compare DNA do not generate or contain gibberish. Rather, the ordered nature of languages is the direct product of an intelligence—programmer, writer, engineer—that uses the language to create a coherent message, implying of course that the same mind that devised the language uses it to express an intelligible point. Language is the tool of someone who wants to communicate. Words have fixed and known meanings because otherwise communication would not be possible. If we find a dictionary on an alien planet it would be a fair assumption that an intelligent being wrote it. To detach the ordered language from the necessary next step—some being who uses it intelligently—is naïve. But that is what material science does with the genetic code.

According to material science, DNA replication, despite the ordered language of the genetic code, generates nonsense. The genetic code appears intelligently made like any human-based language, but according to material science, this ordered language spins out random, chaotic messages.

Why do material scientists make this assumption? One reason presents itself: material science, having granted itself one miracle, cannot accept any more. It accepts the miracle of a self-replicating molecule walking out of a prebiotic soup, and then reverts to its mindless, disorganized world picture. By emphasizing the random interplay of materialistic forces, these thinkers believe they are being scientific. If so, they are doing so at the expense of logic. True science should begin with no assumptions, and then apply the scientific method. Instead, material science assumes the independent reality of the external world and then begins its work. They want to rely only upon "natural" explanations but forget that we are equipped with a mind that has the power of projecting the appearance of an external world from the deepest part of its being. The power to dream is *natural*. Instead of recognizing this truth, material scientists detach the projected world from its source (the mind) and seek to explain the workings of this world without reference to the mind. Material science's independent-world assumption, in the end, clouds their vision and damages their theories. By assuming nature produces variation randomly, for example, Darwinians are left to explain how these shots in the dark created a woman out of a bacterium. This is no easy task.

So modern biology begins with chaos and jumps to the endless order of life, using luck as its springboard. Then, with the dictionary to building living things established, they say that nature's copying machine generated only chaotic messages, but that this random noise produced the order found in the world today. Chaos (prebiotic soup) to order (genetic code) to chaos (random variation) to order (living things). Would it not make more sense to theorize instead that the force underlying the order in the genetic code is the same force which assures that organisms produce ordered messages? If nature has the ability to write the genetic code, why can it not also assure that this code generates messages in tune with the environment? Computers are programmed for a reason. How do we know that nature did not also program the genetic code for a reason? Furthermore, given the integrated language of the genetic codes and the endless diversity of structured life forms, how do we know that we are looking at something from the inside-out that we should be looking at outside-in? The orchestrated molecular processes of living things are better explained not as random outgrowths from a mindless world, but rather as physical reflections of a three-dimensional dream-form in the process of striving for life.

Natural Selection's Second Step

Darwinian evolutionists, despite the order exhibited by the genetic code, all agree that nature produces the raw material of evolution, variations, randomly.[773] But they also agree that chance alone cannot account for the living world. Professor Futuyama explains, "'Accidents' and 'chance' certainly could not suffice to produce the order and complexity of living things, but no biologist claims that they can."[774] Then what is the source of order and complexity?

Darwinian evolutionists account for the undeniable order of the living world through the second step of the two-step natural selection process. It is the second step, they say, that "shapes order out of mutational chaos."[775] "For Darwin, random variation was presented first and the ordering activity of the environment (natural selection) followed afterward."[776] Displeased with the objection that, having drained God and mind from the world, they are left with no ordering mechanism,[777] Darwinians reply that the second step supplies the missing piece of the puzzle.

"The second step is the nonrandom retention (survival) of a few of the new genetic variants."[778] "Although mutations arise by chance," Darwinians say, "they succeed or fail to become established in a species by natural selection, which is the antithesis of chance."[779] Natural selection is "of course an antichance process,"[780] and is "quintessentially *non*random."[781] "Mutation is random, natural selection is the very opposite of random."[782] Where do we find the ordering mechanism?

The second step of natural selection plays a vital role in Darwinian evolution, for it is the mechanism that replaces God or any other intelligent guiding force. Thus, Darwinians are forced to describe this second step and account for its purported ability to forge order out of chaos without using the terms "God" or "mind." Instead of using these taboo terms, they resort to other words strongly suggestive of an intelligent designer to describe natural selection, but still stop short of using the word "mind." The late Stephen Jay Gould, who himself compared natural selection to an engineer,[783] reports that the concept has been likened to a composer, a poet, a sculptor, and even William Shakespeare.[784] Others prefer the blind watchmaker,[785] unconscious editing process,[786] and tinkerer,[787] all of which personify what is supposed to be a mindless, mechanical process.

But of course Darwinians use these terms metaphorically.[788] Natural selection is really not an engineer or artist; its products only resemble those made by engineers or artists. It is ironic to note that creationists and Darwinians both look out at the same world of infinite order, but one attributes the order to an all-powerful God, and the other to the mindless forces of nature. Indeed, the blind watchmaker must be quite talented if his works are mistaken for those of God.[789]

One and one-half centuries after Darwin[790] devised the concept of natural selection, the same questions remain: Does this concept, stripped of all metaphors, have enough power and talent to perform the job demanded of it? Can the second step of natural selection organize a bacterium's random mutations into a woman, a sixty-four-letter alphabet into the *Encyclopedia Britannica*? The answer is a simple no. Darwinian evolutionists have loaded more responsibility upon natural selection than the concept can bear.

Natural selection has no mind. As noted, in describing natural selection, Darwinian evolutionists use such terms as antichance and nonrandom, implying that this concept is indeed the opposite of chance and randomness. But antonyms of these two terms strongly imply design or deliberateness, two features of a mind. For example, antonyms for "chance" include "design," "purpose," and "plan";[791] antonyms for "random" include "planned," "designed," and "intentional."[792] So Darwinian evolutionists tell us that natural selection is the "antithesis of chance"[793] and "quintessentially nonrandom"[794] while they advise us that natural selection has "no plan for the future" and "no purpose in view."[795]

Therefore, it seems, when Darwinians say that evolution is the opposite of chance, they do not really mean it is the opposite of chance, for this would imply an intelligent designer. They want the benefits of a mind (its organizing ability) but do not want to concede that a mind is at work in nature, for this would imply the presence of an intelligence behind the scene, which science does not allow into its worldview.

Natural selection has no organizing ability. What Darwinians actually mean by the second step is that natural selection is not an artist or designer but rather a set of environmental conditions under which organisms compete for survival.[796] If an organism possesses features better adapted than others to the given "constellation of environmental conditions,"[797] then it will win in the struggle for existence, and probably leave more offspring.[798]

Environmental conditions play a large role in determining who survives.[799] Looking at the possible environmental conditions, however, we see trees, earth, grass, rocks, terrain, temperature, wind, and so on, but no panel of judges, and nothing to do any selecting.

These environmental conditions, however complex they may be, can perform no greater function than furnishing a field of play for living things. To say that these conditions select the best-adapted creatures infuses nature with the mind Darwinians have taken down from heaven.

Darwinians also say that it is the "struggle for existence" that propels living things through the gauntlet of environmental conditions—the high cliffs, frozen tundra, shaded forests. The competition for survival occurs in unique environmental conditions, shaping creatures to adapt to the scenery presented. But suppose we take a natural scene, such as the great plains of the western United States, and ask, What sort of organism would best fit into this scenery? The question is made easier by considering a simple mold, say, of a triangle. If we instead were asked, What type of living thing would best adapt to this world? we'd probably answer, Something shaped like a triangle. When we look at our three-dimensional scene of the grassy plains, our answer might be, Something that can fit all around it, such as air, water, or perhaps jellylike creatures. At least a triangle mold is bounded. But using a three-dimensional, wide-open natural scene as a mold, it is hard to see how nature can shape the form of an animal (such as a prairie dogy) if only a random machine generated the mutations sprayed against the canvas.

We can compare the form-creating ability of barren scenery to an artist who shapes each part of a picture to melt into a flowing scene of symmetry. The artist learns from his errors—the distorted noses, the out-of-shape foreheads and off-color horizons—to create a picture of beauty.

The scene of mindless rocks and dirt, on the other hand, has no such artistic sense and no learning ability.

In short, the environment is not much of a mold, as it is mostly empty space. Darwin contributed to the problem by comparing the workings of natural selection to human animal breeders.[800] He noted that we are able to breed faster racehorses, long- and short-horned cattle, and a host of other specialty plants and animals by regulating the mating process.[801] Here, of course, the animal breeder has an end in view;[802] he may want to breed fast race horses, and thus continuously mates promising fillies with a champion stud.

Professor Mayr recognized that Darwin's use of the word "selection" was unfortunate because it implies an "agent in nature who, being able to predict the future, selects 'the best.'"[803] Mayr explains,

> This, of course, is not what natural selection does. The term simply refers to the fact that only a few (on the average, two) of all the offspring of a set of parents survive long enough to reproduce. There is no particular selective force in nature, nor a definite selecting agent. There are many possible causes for the success of the few survivors. Some survival, perhaps a lot of it, is due to stochastic processes, that is, luck. Most of it, though, is due to a superior working of the physiology of the surviving individual, which permits it to cope with the vicissitudes of the environment better than other members of the population.[804]

Turning to natural selection, we note an obvious distinction: nature, by definition, has no end in view.[805] Nature does not know what it wants to breed. The second step of natural selection, the supposed ordering mechanism, is simply a set of conditions. These conditions are unpredictable and could change dramatically in a year or even overnight.

If nature has no mind, then how can its creations be superior to those of a human artist? Where among the rocks, trees, dirt, and wind do we find the artistic spirit? In the Real Dream, the works of nature are superior to those of an individual because nature is the creation of the united and infinitely free mind. But in Darwin's world, where nature is mindless, any comparison between nature and an artist is at most metaphorical. When the metaphors are stripped away, nature provides simply a set of environmental conditions that does no selecting, has no artistic ability, and is blind to the future.[806]

Where Is the Order-Generating Mechanism?

Looking objectively at natural selection in action, we find two things: an organism randomly generating mutations and barren background scenery. Where is the order generated?

The cellular machinery churns out random mutations. But these mutations are assumed to come from a dictionary with the necessary words to spell out instructions to make any bodily part. In the stewing pot of acids and bases that make up DNA we find hidden instructions to make anything, as if the bodily part was made first and then the film rewound or deconstructed into the language of particles. Material scientists look at the deconstructed bodily parts and believe they have found the secret to life. Instead, they have found the pieces to a dream.

The source for order in Darwinian evolution must either be in the cell or in the environment. We know the cell is intricately ordered, but material scientists tell us that the processes of reproduction and cell division generate only random mutations with no goal in mind.

Shining a light through a picture slide instantly projects a coherent image because the mind created the slide to distribute the light rays into a pattern. As an organism generates mutations, what substance filters these mutations into structured living organisms? The computer chip cannot be in a cell, for that would imply a form of special creation. We know it is not in the external environment because that would imbue the barren scenery with form-creating powers.

So, in Darwin's world, what is the source for order? It is not in the cellular nucleus and it is not out in the natural world. The answer, therefore, is that the source of order is *the mind of the material scientist who simply imagines natural selection as a more powerful order-creating mechanism than it can possibly be.* As we saw in the field of cosmology, material scientists make up with their own imagination what their theories lack in organizing ability. Again, this is more wishful thinking than scientific theory.

In the Real Dream, the external world is the mind, *projected*. It is a three-dimensional translation of our inner needs, thoughts, and emotions. Physical life-forms are the vehicles within which to experience life—the flowing movement on an endless mission to escape from nothing. Life is a combination of the *will to survive* and *infinite creativity*. A power we will never understand answered the call for there to be something; once this happened and the mind became aware of its own dream-creating ability, it locked on to the object of its dream—the physical world—and so began a steady flow of mirrored inspiration as the mind builds a home in the sky, like two paired trees that grow and spread their branches to opposite ends of the forest.

The mind, in the midst of a dream, projects three-dimensional forms. Creation gushes from the source, streaming away from nothingness. This mind possesses a power it does not yet understand nor can fully control; it is the infinite power of the imagination. As the mind flows out of itself, the imagination fills the forms, but upon the initial breakthrough—let there be light?—something else happens: the mind inspires itself, like a poet whose cascading lines of verse flow from the first words, or jazz musicians trading riffs.

We know that reflective evolution did occur, as it explains the close adaptation of animals and plants to their physical environment—why monkeys swing from trees, snakes slither on the ground, fish swim in the sea, and birds fly through the air. Each living thing is a creative source, an image of life in action, striving outward in its own way to lose itself in the Real Dream, escape from nothing, and make itself a home. The imagination spawned the forms; the will to survive filters through and breathes out through the organism, as it experiences the outer world and builds itself a home.

Propelled by the fear of nothing, the imagination flows toward the highest form, but this is a dream occurring in a vivid reality—feet on the ground, in the *now*. Cosmology, the Earth's formation, and the rise of civilization show the footprints of the mind, bootstrapping itself through time. The Real Dream worldview does not change history; it simply gives us a different and deeper perspective from which to view it.

The cosmos did not suddenly spring whole from the mind of God. Rather, the cosmos is the Mind of God in the process of learning about itself and how to manage its remarkable powers.

The Evolution of the Eye

Darwin's theory of mindless evolution meets its greatest obstacle when it seeks to explain how natural selection formed complex organs such as the human eye. The problem is that the eye appears to be an intricate arrangement of interworking parts. Each part, such as the lens, diaphragm, optic nerve, retina, cornea, and muscles, seems ready-made for each other, like the parts to a car. Considered separately, the eye parts have no use, but put together they supply the marvelous sense of sight.

Comparable structures, such as a car, computer, or telescope, reveal the handiwork of a designer who had an idea of the completed object in mind before construction began. The component parts carry out the function of the whole machine and are often useless alone.[807] Darwin himself conceded that, at first glance, to suppose natural selection created an eye seems "absurd in the highest possible degree."[808] Upon further reflection, Darwin managed to convince himself that, given enough time, natural selection might indeed create an eye. It need only be shown, he thought, that each successively formed eyepiece conferred some small advantage on the organism's chances of survival.[809] Richard Dawkins uses the same line of reasoning to argue that through "cumulative selection,"[810] nature alone might have the power to build the eye.

These arguments again show scientists supplying with their imaginations what their theories lack. Dawkins in particular reveals by his argument how some evolutionists have forgotten that "hindsight is always 20-20." He asks, "Could the human eye have arisen directly from something slightly different from itself, something that we may call X?"[811] He answers, "Clearly, *yes*, provided only that the difference between the modern eye and its immediate predecessor X is sufficiently small."[812]

And here comes his supposed clinching argument. If one is still in doubt, he says, keep making the step between the eye and its predecessor smaller and smaller until you are convinced that this now infinitesimally small step is possible. Continue dividing into one thousand, ten thousand, even one hundred thousand steps until you get to no eye at all. There now, he says: Isn't it possible for natural selection to have created an eye?

Using the immense amount of geological time he believes available,[813] Dawkins states that by "more-or-less abstract reasoning, we have concluded that there is a series of imaginable x's, each sufficiently similar to its neighbors that it could plausibly turn into one of its neighbors, the whole series linking the eye back to no eye at all."[814] Thus, according to Dawkins's reasoning, if starting with a fully formed eye, you could imagine tiny steps backward in time to no eye at all, the evolution of an eye is possible.

Among the flaws in Dawkins's reasoning is that he is looking at a process in reverse that had to occur forward. He takes a film of an eye, rewinds it slowly, and then proclaims that natural selection created an eye. But this is not the question. The question is how a picture appeared on the screen in the first place. The creator, whether it was God, the mind, or natural selection, had to start from a blank slate and venture into the unknown. The creative force did not have the advantage of a completed picture in front of it. Of course it is possible to imagine backward steps from a complete picture to nothing, but this exercise is irrelevant to how natural selection works. The organism cannot see ahead and plan for the future; variations are blind to the needs of the organism and the demands of the environment. In Darwin's world, we are not imagining our way backward; we are stumbling blindly forward.

Consistent with the material science worldview, this thing that later became an eye did not know it was becoming an eye during any stage of the building process. Evolution doesn't look ahead and has no end in view.[815] Let's say that the number of steps from no eye at all to a complete eye is ten thousand. Then, let us suppose that the no-eye organism is capable of producing one hundred thousand possible mutations, one of which might be the start of a good eye. The lucky day arrives, and the favorable mutation occurs. Stop. We turn to Dawkins and ask him to explain what advantage this one ten-thousandth of a future eye confers on the organism. He gives a satisfactory answer—perhaps it scares away predators, because it surely cannot be used to see.

So now we have an organism with an infinitesimally small mutation growing out of its head; it now must await a second lucky mutation that will just so happen to fit perfectly on the first one.

How is this going to happen? We find here two serious problems that scientists regularly overlook. First, why does the program for building an eye reside in the genetic code? Why are the right parts in the genetic supply room, and where did the supply room come from in the first place (the origin-of-life problem)?

The second problem is just as serious: even assuming that through some miracle the ingredients for building an eye reside in the cellular nucleus, how did these random chemical processes march out tiny mutations that lined up just so perfectly to form the eye? Calculations show that even making the simplest of protein molecules, such as insulin (consisting of fifty-one chained amino acids), through random processes is 2.25 times 10^{66}.[816] And if it is argued that evolution has millions of years to find the right combinations, we encounter the problem of why the mutations stacked on top of one another in such a way to form an eye— or, for that matter, anything. The source of the problem is that biologists take for granted the intricate processes of the cellular machinery as if the DNA molecule was handed down from the sky, ready to churn out recipes for building living things.

The flaw with the step-by-step approach, therefore, is that unless these lifeless chemicals know where they are going, they will never get there.

But this sightless creature does not know where it is going. No eye is being built, as that would imply foresight. The mutations just happen to pile on each other. The second mutation might have wiped out the first one, or appeared elsewhere on the body. Again we need to know: What advantage did this second mutation confer upon the organism so that it will be preserved? Is this mutation also scaring away predators? If so, is the mutation also scaring away mates, thus lowering the chances this mutant organism will leave offspring?[817]

And we keep repeating the process, remembering that each new variation has to build upon a prior base preserved long enough for just the right new eye fragment to appear randomly at just the right place. The small fragments must stay together and continue conferring advantages that natural selection will favor and offspring will inherit. Through no stage of the process does anything—the organism, the growing mutation, or nature—know it is building an eye. Finally, let's assume that through a string of lucky hits, 5 percent of something that one day might be considered an eye is formed. Suppose, for example, that a transparent membrane appears on an organism's forehead.

Can this membrane be used to see? Dawkins argues that 5 percent of complete vision is better than no vision at all.[818] But Dawkins again misses the point. He positions himself at a completed eye and looks backward toward no eye at all. In his reasoning, he seems to have a complete eye in mind when he asks whether 5 percent of an eye is better than no eye. Whether such a partial feature could even see anything is highly doubtful as a threshold matter.[819] But more importantly, at the time this mutation occurred, it was not 5 percent of an eye; it was a stack of mutations that didn't know what it was. This thing will continue to have an identity crisis each step of the way until it forms an organ that can actually be called an eye—for at no point was an eye ever under construction, according to Darwinian evolution.

After presenting this dubious explanation, Dawkins then tells us to "imagine"[820] our way every step backward from a complete eye to no eye. He seems to believe that if this backward process of imagination is possible, then so is the random forward process of natural selection. But natural selection did no imagining either forward or backward, because it had no mind with which to perform this activity.[821]

We can go further and state that the creation of an organized, harmonious structure—such as a pyramid, human eye, crystal, and any living thing—is not possible without a mind to first conceive of the completed object. Unless an artist or mind has an idea of what the complete picture will look like, the picture cannot be drawn. Organized structures are made with an end in view. Intelligent creatures learn from experience how to make individual parts fit together so that the complete picture makes sense. Random processes by definition cannot see ahead to a final picture and can do nothing other than generate noise . . . paint splashes upon a wall. When material scientists attempt to explain the evolution of complex organs such as the eye, they cannot separate the mind's theorizing function from its creative function. They look out at a world that an infinite mind created, but under their worldview, mind had no role in creation. Thus, the theorist must separate the external world from his own mind (the same mind that helped create the world) and then, using the mind, explain how only mindless forces created the world. No wonder scientists such as Richard Dawkins tell us to use our imagination to become convinced of the truth of Darwinian evolution; our minds must contribute the creativity that natural selection lacks.

Adaptation and the Invisible Hand of Natural Selection

Consistent with the material science worldview, Darwinians say that the second step of natural selection is "completely independent" of the first step (the production of inheritable random variations).[822] The DNA molecule and the world's weather patterns are not in radio contact. Fur does not get thicker as the weather gets colder; bird beaks do not grow as seeds enlarge. Rather, the organism spins out mutations that now and then successfully fold around natural obstacles and barriers. On this point, Darwinians walk into further difficulties. As they advise us that variations are blind to the needs of the organism and the demands of the environment, they also point to an endless assortment of extraordinary adaptations present in the living world. But if variations are so blind, then why do creatures constantly generate just the right feature to adapt to the environment? Examples in nature abound. Insects camouflage themselves from predators by undertaking the appearance of a flower (the flower mantid), a dead leaf (Trinidad tree mantid), and a green leaf (Central American mantid).[823] Birds have developed beaks to fit whatever need presents itself. Some birds have short, wide bills to eat seeds; others a long arched bill for removing nectar from blossoms.

The macaw has a crooked beak that acts as a powerful nutcracker, capable of opening the rock-hard Brazil nut.

The woodpecker's beak bores into tree barks in search of beetles.

Inside the flamingo's hooked beak is a delicate sieve through which it siphons water and gathers small crustaceans.

The sword-billed hummingbird is specially equipped with a beak four times its bodily length to draw nectar hidden deep inside Andean flowers.[824]

Even more amazing are the countless examples of teamwork displayed between flowers and insects in the fertilization process. Flower nectar so delights many insects that they spend all their time feasting on it, while unknowingly collecting pollen on their skins to fertilize new plants. The stapelia plant of southern Africa attracts flies to fertilize itself using rather extreme measures. These plants mimic the odor of decaying flesh; produce flowers with shriveled, brown hairy petals having the appearance of rotting skin; and radiate heat as would a dead animal. This fakery easily fools flies that unwittingly help fertilize the stapelia.[825] Another example is a specie of the orchid that attracts wasps by masquerading as a female; the mimicry, which includes eyes, wings, antennae, and the female mating scent, so completely fools the male that it attempts to have sex with the flower. In the process the male wasp unloads a supply of pollen into the flower, thus fertilizing it.[826]

Adaptation is the rule, not the exception, in the living world. Organisms seem to fit peculiarly into their niche, as a hand in a glove. Darwinians account for adaptation by citing natural selection.[827] But that is the problem. If variations are random and the organism is not in communication with nature, then why is just the right feature seemingly always on hand to respond to the problem posed by the environment? Why do polar bears produce thick white hair and bats sonar? Did all these variations just so happen to reside within the program of the animal's genetic library?

If the range of possible variations were infinite, there would be insufficient time for nature to have produced the correct one. The set of possible variations, however, is said to be constrained by an organism's genetic library.[828] But even though variations are limited, like the colors of paint available to an artist, material scientists still insist that animals are out of touch with the needs of the environment. Here Darwinians go further than the facts warrant. The following example may help illustrate this point.

Suppose a law is passed prohibiting the use of catalytic converters in automobiles because of air pollution problems. As of January 1, 2016, under this law, catalytic converters must be replaced by a special part called a widget. If the part is not replaced by that date, the car cannot be driven on the road; it becomes extinct.

A car with a catalytic converter rolls into a repair shop. But this car has one special feature. It pulls a trailer that contains not only all the replacement parts for the car, but also various defective parts and proto-type components. The mechanic goes to the back of the trailer and pulls out the widget needed to comply with the new law.

In this example, the car (the organism) adapted to a new environ-mental condition (the catalytic converter law) by producing the correct variation (the widget). The mechanic identified the need and replaced the part. He did not go into the repair shop and randomly attach pieces onto the car until one fit. He knew just what part was needed for the car to survive; in fact, so did the driver, since he carried the widget in his trailer.

Darwinians tell us that an organism is unaware of what part is needed to respond to the environmental need. Does nature know? The answer must be no, because nature only works with the raw materials (variations) on hand.[829] But we must then ask: Why is it that just the right feature existed among those the organism produces? Why did the orchid possess the genetic message to mimic a wasp, or the stapelia decaying flesh? Why, in almost every instance when the mechanic goes to the back of the trailer, does the right part just happen to be there? Darwinian evolutionists believe that they have devised a purely objective, mechani-cal theory that relies only upon the production of directionless variations to supply the raw material for natural selection. Mind and purpose they eliminate from life.

But nature does not reflect this picture. Variations may be fired by a shotgun, but the gun is aimed at the target. Again and again an organism's genetic arsenal contains just the right feature to adapt to the environment. Material science may have weakened the link between a living thing and nature, but even within its own theory the chain remains unbroken. Animals and nature still talk to each other even under Darwin's theory.

In the Real Dream, a different explanation for adaptation is available. Mind and the world grow up together, as nature reflects the aspirations of the mind. The actor and world are the bonded couplet. The inanimate world is a backdrop to the dreamer, offering endless inspiration for the mind to improve upon its creation.

We know we can dream. This is an empirical fact. In asking why we dream, we answer, because we are afraid of the dark and of loneliness. We desire companionship. Therefore, the source of the struggle is simply our own deeply rooted desire to break free of the black night; somehow, through one miracle we will never understand, the world has reflected our inner need. Our mind gave us the dream we wanted.

The Real Dream worldview easily explains evolution. The mind has no boundaries; when it strives for existence it has at its disposal unlimited imagination. Therefore, at the same time it is creating the perfect form—the human body—it is exhausting a host of other forms. The living world is the trail of a great comet streaking for the highest form. As the mind enters the dream, we must remember that it continues to strive (or struggle) and continues to create. Like Michelangelo inspired by the works of ancient Rome, the mind's creation inspires it to always reach higher.

Reproduction may be viewed as the dream's incessant striving, overflowing into new forms. The wheel of time throws off bodily forms (people) that do not align themselves with the true nature of being, or with the "way." In other words, the Mind of God, the ground of being, finally selects the survivors. Darwin was thus right about natural selection, but underestimated the depth and scope of its power.

Generations connect to each other like a river of life, each building on their ancestors; the river flows until the end, where the dreamers, finally aware of their responsibility for the dream, act as one to control it. Genes become an artist's conception of the process of reproduction, except here, an infinite dreaming mind is the artist. This mind, in its original creative state, projects the world of nature. In its scientific state, it continues creating, like a motion picture projector mistakenly left on and dropped down a well, the mind continues to project a physical world.

We may want the world to be more than a dream. We may desire it to stand on its own with no help from our mind, but however strong this desire, we can never break the link between the dreaming mind and the world. Rather, we need to recognize that this desire is an expression of the mind's dreaming power that flows from a source we call God.

Chapter Forty-Two

THE BRIDGE TO A BETTER WORLD

I was driving through the English countryside with my daughter Juliet, then aged six, and she pointed out some flowers by the wayside. I asked what she thought wildflowers were for. She gave a rather thoughtful answer. "Two things," she said. "To make the world pretty, and to help the bees make honey for us." I was touched by this and sorry I had to tell her that it wasn't true.
—Richard Dawkins, *Climbing Mount Improbable*

If you could see the miracle of a single flower clearly, your whole life would change.
—Buddha

DARWIN'S THEORY OF EVOLUTION by common descent is crude, archaic, and in the final analysis, grossly flawed. Though it represents scientists' best attempt to explain life without help from God, the theory is wrong on almost every count.

Darwin's first error was the error of the materialistic: he assumed that the world, as well as life, arose from forces external to the mind. Working backward from a physical world he assumes as given, Darwin rewinds the film toward a common organism. Proceeding in reverse seems easy enough, but explaining how this first life-form came from dead particles is among material science's greatest mysteries. Darwin must wait for the impossible to occur before his theory of evolution can start to work. But the impossible never happens.

Curiously, material scientists regularly claim that evolution is a fact and not a theory,[830] when the odds against this threshold event (life from dead particles) boggle the mind. If the strength of a theory is measured by its foundation, then Darwin's theory is enormously weak; it rests upon odds so improbable that if faced with them in any other context we would quickly conclude the claimed event cannot occur.[831]

The odds against life originating from purely material processes are so immense because life did not arise in this manner. Rather, the common ancestor for living things is the one mind of God.[832]

Darwin's common ancestor purportedly arose at a single birthplace and then spread gradually across geographical regions (space) and downward through history (time). The facts do not support this viewpoint. The appearance of identical species on widely separated islands and mountains suggests that leaps across space occurred. Even more troubling for Darwinians is that neither the living world nor the fossil record support the view that organisms change only in infinitesimally small, gradual steps. Both the living world and fossils mark the imprint of a creative force working in leaps, not in slow-moving waves. Leaping from idea to idea, or design to design, is a sign of a mind in action, not Darwin's blind process of natural selection.

With natural selection, we find one of the most overtaxed concepts in science. This miraculous power is considered equivalent to an omnipotent God, yet when the metaphors (engineer, blind watchmaker, artist) are taken away, we find only lifeless environmental conditions. Even the most diehard materialists at times find it hard to believe this mindless force created nature's out-of-mind complexity and stunning beauty. Steven Weinberg, for example, remarks that he sometimes finds "nature more beautiful than strictly necessary."[833] Perhaps we are simply deluded into thinking that nature is beautiful, these materialists say,[834] or maybe through a "natural selection of ideas" we have "gotten it beaten into us that nature is . . . beautiful."[835] Even flowers puzzle these thinkers, with Darwin calling them "an abominable mystery." Natural selection is supposed to be the creative force in nature and Darwin's replacement for God. But this dumb and blind scientific concept does not account for nature's beauty.

Natural selection supposedly ordered aimless variations into a picture-perfect universe. But even if the organisms best adapted to environmental conditions survive, natural selection has no artist's brush to paint nature's scenery, or engineering degree to write the genetic code. The concept of natural selection offers at best weak predictions about the characteristics of future survivors and fails at playing the role of God in the story of life.

What natural selection lacks in explanatory power, material scientists supply with their own imagination. Scientists enter familiar territory when they turn to the imagination to explain life. Unfortunately, material science allows for no contribution from any mind to explain events in the world; mindless particles will never leap as high as the imagination. Life must be understood from the inside out, from the heart and mind out into the world, not under the lens of a microscope.

Darwin, though, was right about one thing: all living things struggle for life. The root of this struggle, however, is not the mindless interplay of dead particles. These particles—atoms, electrons, DNA—could only have one source: our own mind. They are the internal working parts of a three-dimensional dream-form. To suppose that dead particles burst from the dark void and created both the entire universe and the living world is to choose the impossible over the possible, the absurd over the real. Out of our mind issued the world. The struggle to live represents our need for something to do. It is the story of an infinite mind seeking to overcome the eternal darkness. We write the plot to life, not the double-helix.

Today we live at the mercy of our assumption; the independent material world closes in upon us and defines our outlook to the world. This world we assume operates on its own power and determines what we are and where the universe is heading. We have created a monster that turns back to haunt us. We all want an independent world—the world of Einstein—but we do not realize that the intensity of this desire coincides with our dreaming power. Turned back on itself the mind reflects the mistaken view that the world operates on its own, and then off it goes, whirling away to create a world in response to our misguided command.

Scientist after scientist lines up to instruct us about man's hopeless predicament, as if proclaiming the meaninglessness of life is a badge of honor.[836] The world's most famous scientist, Stephen Hawking, informs us that "the human race is just a chemical scum on a moderate-sized planet orbiting round a very average star in the outer suburb of one among a hundred billion galaxies." We are "collections of molecules, like everything else,"[837] they tell us, "naked apes,"[838] "gene machines, with no purpose other than to pass them on,"[839] "chemical machines,"[840] "robot vehicles blindly programmed to preserve the selfish molecules known as genes."[841] People are not the end of evolution[842] and we are deluded if we think we are "special, apart and supreme."[843] Darwin placed us where we belong: on the same tree as rats, insects, and bacteria.

Subject to the mercy of our assumed material world, we become merely "passing, ephemeral phenomena."[844] Someday the sun will run out of fuel, and the stars will stop shining.[845] Planets will fly off into space and galaxies evaporate; black holes will dominate the universe and swallow the last bit of light.[846] Then in the distant future even black holes will decay,[847] and the universe will disintegrate into radiation and nothingness. Earth's death may come more quickly. Interstellar asteroids the size of mountains may bomb the earth and destroy all life[848]—unless, of course, we don't finish the job off much sooner ourselves.

Yes, material scientists say, our world is not a pleasant place. As one Nobel Prize–winning scientist says, "It has to be accepted as it is, not because we like it, but because that is the way the world works."[849] In their world the "road to truth is permanently closed";[850] we live and die by the spin of the roulette wheel.[851]

The material science worldview knows nothing of morality. "Much as we might like to believe otherwise," these scientists say, "unusual love and the welfare of the species as a whole are concepts which simply do not make evolutionary sense."[852] Having separated the mind from its creation, material science has no moral lessons to convey,[853] and so we suffer at the mercy of our own mistaken assumption.

Deep in our minds a fire still burns; something inside cannot be stopped—an outpouring of desire, an endless striving for something. We dream of a better place, a happier place. We know we can think higher thoughts. We dream of a better world far away where the sun does not burn out and the stars glow forever, where people move in harmony with the planets, marching toward a common goal shining overhead—a world of our dreams. Science, undertaken in the Real Dream, builds a bridge to a place where our dreams can finally come true.

PART 4

On to the Real Heaven

Chapter Forty-Three

GUARDIANS OF THE DREAM

None knoweth whence creation has arisen;
And whether he has or has not produced it:
He who surveys it in the highest heaven,
He only knows, or haply he may not know
—From "Hymn of Creation," *Ṛg Veda*

THE MYSTERY OF THE dream is the eternal mystery of God. We know the mind is capable of reflecting its internal states into a three-dimensional world-scene, but how the mind performs this feat we never will know.[854] It is here that we come upon the religious sentiment: We are products of a miracle that does not violate the laws of nature but, to the contrary, takes the form of a lawful natural world. Traditional religion stops its quest for knowledge at God; modern science stops at the laws of nature. Here, we stop at the end of reason, wonderstruck at the mind's dreaming power. The dream baffles us, but we now understand our true role: *We are guardians of the greatest miracle imaginable.*

Material science, in taking the world for granted, has turned the miraculous universe into a laboratory specimen—dry, inert, lifeless; something to study, probe, dismantle, and dissect; a world delivered by a lucky, finely tuned explosion that just happened to scatter particles into organized life-forms competing for survival.

In the beginning, we dove into the world and submerged ourselves within a place that seemed waiting there for us. We took the miracle for granted. Now, awakening, we discover that we have been lost in our own creation, wrongly assuming that the natural world and other people are separate from us. But this apparent separateness is an illusion. We separated only as a way to overcome loneliness, nothing more. And, contrary to the teachings of some belief systems, the goal of life is not to find peace in some otherworldly place, but rather *to achieve in physical form—our living, breathing bodies—the same oneness that exists at the core of Being. We live to express the oneness out in the open, a grand stage where the actors finally get their parts right and unify the story. In other words, the goal of this dream is peace among men and women, the nations and people of the Earth.* For only in peace can the united mind of God carry out the plan to make a real heaven on earth.

The material science worldview supposes that little particles of matter exist apart from the mind and operate beyond its control. Science understaken in this worldview then manipulates these particles in an effort to master the world.

The Real Dream worldview supposes that the entire universe is the mind projected. Science in this worldview seeks to improve the dream by understanding and then mastering ourselves.

According to a leading modern philosopher, Karl R. Popper (1902–1994), idealism (the view that the world is an idea) is without scientific value because it is irrefutable.[855] Popper knows of no test to prove idealism either right or wrong and, therefore, according to him, idealism has no place in science. Like most material scientists, Popper considers idealism as only an abstract notion in a machine-shop world. They see idealism as a vague, whispery thought floating through the air, but never touching down and achieving scientific stature.

Idealism, to begin with, is an inadequate term to describe the Real Dream. "Idealism" implies a concept rather than a hard reality, such as an architect who has a conceptual vision—or idea—of what he wants to build. The mind must necessarily have an idea or concept before taking action. But some power in the mind allows it to fill in the ideal form with a three-dimensional appearance of the idea out in space. This is known as the real world.

In the Real Dream, everything that we *are* is channeled into the dreaming power. We exist in and through the dream; our desire for the world is coextensive with the world. The solidity of the world is a product of our need for something solid to hold on to—something to steady our grip, to gain a foothold, to have a home.

We, and everything we are—heart, body, and soul—are bound up with the world. Therefore, if we drive relentlessly toward a common goal, we will necessarily increase the chances that our common dream will come true. This must be correct, since the entire universe and our bodies are products of the mind's united dreaming power.

Another way to approach this subject is to ask whether you would be willing to give up your belief in an independent material world for a chance at eternal life in the here and now? Of course, the challenge is that because our bodies *are the product of the united mind*, we cannot gain immortality alone, but only by joining with the power of the united mind, or by making peace with our fellow men and women. Uniting the mind harnesses the power of infinity; separating the mind causes it to war against itself, effectively losing the battle through a form of friendly fire.

As in material science, the task of the Real Dream is to understand the world's inner makeup, and then manipulate it to build a better world. Here, though, we look for the control mechanism deep inside our hearts and minds, not within the atomic nucleus. Modern technology will still be at our disposal, but now we will use a modern perspective to control the world from its source. Technology will serve the same purpose it always has: to make our lives more manageable and more enjoyable.

In this new science, we make a simple hypothesis: the mind's ability to control the dream will be proportional to the teamwork the dreamers display. Put another way, the more people who join forces to reach a common dream, the better the chance they will succeed. In the same way that a longboat is more likely to reach its destination if the oarsmen row in the same direction, so we should expect our control to improve as the number of people working for a common goal increases. *But we must change the navigator as soon as possible because the current one, material science, is leading us on a misguided journey to oblivion, and we each only have one chance to get it right.*

As the forces in support of the Real Dream grow, doubt will fall away. The mind will become freer and return to its natural state. No more proofs of God's existence will be necessary because there will be no doubt, based upon the success of the united dreaming efforts, that we are God. And so we spiral ever upward to a yet higher goal.

Teamwork among people (dreamers) returns us to our natural, and most powerful, state as one mind: the same mind that created the world. A mind that creates the world should be capable of altering it, but we need to join forces to do so. Our fates are intertwined, and so we find salvation in each other.

In the Real Dream, the human species' most conspicuous failing—its inability to get along with one other—strikes to the core of Being. With the Real Dream we no longer interact against a nameless background; we are not mere actors moving across a barren stage setting. Rather, we live and breathe against scenery that expresses what we are as a people.

After looking at the puzzle of human existence in a new light, we have come across the truth of an old teaching: *no law stands above brotherhood.* The Upanishads teach,

> As a person acts, so he becomes in life. Those who do good become good; those who do harm become bad. Good deeds make one pure; bad deeds make one impure. You are what your deep, driving desire is. As your desire is, so is your will. As your will is, so is your deed. As your deed is, so is your destiny.[856]

Buddha taught a similar lesson:

> All that we are is the result of what we have thought: it is founded on our thoughts, it is made up of our thoughts. If a man speaks or acts with an evil thought, pain follows him, as the wheel follows the feet of the ox that draws the carriage . . . If a man speaks or acts with a pure thought, happiness follows him, like a shadow that never leaves him.[857]

Confucius said, "If you set your mind on humanity, you will be free from evil." "To master oneself and return to propriety is humanity. If a man (the ruler) can for one day master himself and return to propriety, all under heaven will return to humanity."[858] For Socrates and Plato, "Knowledge is virtue," and the highest ideal is that of the Good.[859] In the Old Testament Moses gives his followers God's ten moral commandments, and in the New Testament, Jesus Christ conveys to his followers the golden rule, "Love your neighbor as yourself,"[860] and teaches that the "kingdom of heaven" will be open only to the righteous few. "For the Muslim . . . the mediator between man and God is righteousness. It is in moral behavior that the human and the divine meet. The eternal word of God is an imperative."[861]

At the turn of a new millennium, a test awaits us: Shall we join together and make a better world once and for all, or shall we give up before we run the experiment? Shall we spend our time feuding among ourselves over old religious sites, parcels of land, and our place in line before God, or shall we seek the common place where dreams really do come true?

In the real world, with our hands, arms, legs, and voices moving about in space, we will carry out the experiment to learn whether the Real Dream is true. We will see if putting down our weapons and making peace improves the world; whether choosing friendship over hatred and fear improves our way of life; whether being positive about our lives and our world lengthens our life spans, reduces illnesses, cures disease, and generates a lasting peace.

This experiment will occur without our vote. It is occurring now, as an act of necessity, a law of nature. As individuals we gain power by acting along the path of the righteous; from the perspective of nature, the one Mind cannot fuel the ways of unbelievers in the dream, because they disconnect themselves from the only source of life—the One Mind of God. To reject this experiment you have to reach one conclusion: that the world actually is the world of material science—a hardened, mechanical place of little ball bearings, spinning, combining, colliding outside of our control.

To prove the Real Dream true it must be tested. Humankind must play as a unit, act out in physical form the oneness that underlies the world in which we live. Morality rules the cosmos, but moral teachings mean nothing unless we carry them out. And now we have the best of all reasons to be good: the Real Dream is not only an idealistic vision of a future world, but also the bedrock principle of a new science.

Chapter Forty–Four

THE SURPASSING EXPLANATORY POWER OF THE REAL DREAM WORLDVIEW

Science is an enterprise of "reasonable men" who use logic, facts, and data in order to arrive at conclusions that compel assent without coercion.
—Israel Scheffler

A KEY TEST OF A scientific theory is explanatory power: Does the theory offer a way to fit natural events into an explanatory framework? Are reasons given? Are they persuasive? If so, does the theory explain phenomena better than competing theories? Are its assumptions necessary? Testable? Do they withstand logical examination?

Einstein's gravitational theory (the general theory of relativity) is considered a better explanation for why physical bodies attract each other than Newton's gravitational theory, because Einstein's theory better accounts for certain observed phenomena, such as slight changes in Mercury's orbit and the bending of light rays toward the sun.[862] The quantum theory is considered a better explanation for subatomic events than the corpuscular theory or plum pudding model because it accounts for black-body radiation, the behavior of the electron, X-rays, the photoelectric effect, and a host of other phenomena. The majority of cosmologists today support the inflationary big bang theory because it explains (away) the horizon and flatness problems. Darwinian evolution is thought to better account for the diversity of life-forms than special creation because it accounts for the adaptation of organisms to the environment and biological change over time. A scientific theory gains favor if it accounts better for happenings in the world.

The Real Dream worldview offers a vastly superior worldview to that of material science because it operates with no assumptions and explains more. Let us compare three competing theories for explaining the world we experience:

How Three Worldviews Explain Worldly Phenomena

Worldy Phenomena	Material Science	Religion	Real Dream
Appearance of external world/creation of matter	Assumed as given	God	Dreaming power of mind. External world, including its solidity, is an illusion (maya), but because we too are an illusion, the world is real to us.
Expansion of universe	Power of big bang	God or current scientific explanation	Dream in motion. Essentially irrelevant.
Spiral galaxies (strict application of law of gravity states they should fly apart)	Dark matter (mysterious unproven attractive force)	God or current scientific explanation	Mind's overriding desire for beauty. Dark matter is a figment of the scientific imagination.

Accelerated expansion of universe	Dark energy (mysterious unproven repulsive force)	God or current scientific explanation	Dream in motion. Essentially irrelevant.
Origin of life	Highly speculative theories about birth from dead matter	God, or current scientific explanation	The mind, becoming aware of itself in an imagined world, adopts a form to find comfort in the dream. The creative mind flows away from nothing and adopts the highest form to lose itself in the dream, imagining that it is something after all. Life is created by "I" and "Thou," subject and object. The contrast between actor and stage, individual and world, creates the tension that moves life onward. Life is a mixture of the will to survive and infinite creativity.
Consciousness	An unknown, unexplained, "emergent property" of particles in the brain	Gift of God or scientific explanation	The mind aware of itself in the dream

Paranormal	Impossible in material world where no physical signal connects different minds or minds and things, and hence nonexistent. All paranormal events can be explained as acts of trickery or simple coincidence.	Signs of God's presence on Earth, such as faith healing, the answering of prayers, visions, and voices from heaven	We are fundamentally one Mind, separated; thus, underlying our day-to-day consciousness is a common mind that can communicate with itself and with nature outside the range of scientific instruments. Paranormal events are rare because we dream for a normal world, not a nightmare of ghosts and goblins.
Origin of species	Darwinian evolution: random variations sorted by natural selection	God	Reflective evolution. Creative force of mind adopts endless life-forms in broad escape from nothing. The opposite poles of life—nature and organism— inspire each other through adaptation with life-forms filling environmental niches. Variations are not randomly generated, but rather, are a product of creative energy applied to an evolving natural world.

Religion	Delusion of religious followers, or ancillary belief system riding sidecar to scientific worldview	Worship of God	Awareness of unmistakable presence of some higher power, greater good, deeper meaning in the universe. Realization that this world should not be, but is. Sensation of deep soul-connection to one Being. Western religion (in general) explained by imagining heavenly father hovering over the world; this is the ultimate dreamer who has not himself awakened. Eastern religion, which posits a One or Brahman, is correct except that it must be connected with the "ultimate dreamer" to complete the puzzle.

Material science worldview	The assumption of an independent material world allows science to carry out the necessary task of empirical testing in a physical setting or laboratory. These thinkers, who equate science with material science, forget that they have contradicted their own principles by assuming something, an independent material world that is unnecessary and cannot be proven.	Largely adopts the material science worldview, thus marginalizing its metaphysical foundation. In adopting the view that an independent world exists external to the mind, religions are left with no logical (or scientific) basis to contest the findings of science or to explain deviations from natural law, such as miracles. For example, the biblical creation is assumed not to be in a dream world, but in the material science world, raising the insolvable problem of how even an all-powerful God created a ball-bearing universe.	Material science, in short, is a product of unenlightened dreamers living in the "bubble" of the dream, before the "breath-maker" or ultimate dreamer (or heavenly father) appears. Imagine here a long breath flowing out of an infinite soul; the forms appearing in the exhausting breath do not know where they come from. Those who believe the world is in the mind are charged with solipsism, or like Berkeley, must appeal to an unknown God. The mystery, then, is insolvable until the ultimate dreamer appears and lays claim to this dream world. With an independent world no longer assumed, the Real Dream lays the foundation for a true science.

In short, once we no longer assume that the physical world was simply handed over to us, whether by an unknown God or a primordial big bang, we come upon the only explanation left standing: it is we who are God, and we who have conjured up the world from a power we do not understand. This world has forced itself out of nothing to answer our deepest cry for something to hold on to—a something that began with a spark of inspiration and ended with the world outside the window.

This viewpoint answers the atheist's question: If God designed the universe, then what designed God?[863] The answer is that nothing designed God. Rather God—the united mind of mankind—is in the process of designing itself using the power of the dream. God and the universe are the same.

We can explain the appearance of the universe as a projection of God, but we will never know how the dreaming power arose. As individual dreamers in the one Mind of God, we can only get glimpses of the true power of the united mind. But even if we were to reach the highest stage of awareness where our thoughts, emotions, and Being were precisely in tune with the pure one Mind, we would still stand back in awe at the power streaming from the root of the soul. Science, even in the Real Dream, cannot explain everything, but then again maybe that is the point: the mystery of the dream leaves us with endless gratitude at being here, now, in reality, riding the crest of an ever-flowing wave, pouring from a magical source. The scientific enterprise ends with religious awe.

The material science worldview and religion can both be explained within the Real Dream: material science is the best that thinkers can do living within the globe or bubble of the dream, before the ultimate dreamer appears. Like a prisoner encased in a sealed glass container, scientists cannot reason their way out of solipsism and so take the world at face value. But the soul of man, trapped within this enclosure, yearns for a better place, a higher standing. The soul empties, expressing the religious sentiment outward; we know we can do better than this, but we do not know how. We project a God above, at the base of the self or the root of Mother Nature. Upon the appearance of the ultimate dreamer, the soul is freed from its imprisonment, as we realize we are God. But with this realization comes the eternal mystery of how we find ourselves here, now. The religious sentiment comes at the end of science, where we learn that the world rests upon a mystery we can never solve. Here we practice true science and true religion. This yearning for something better is the voice within telling us to dream higher thoughts, the dream of the one and only God.

The Problem of Evil and the Existence of God

The problem of evil has been called the strongest argument against the existence of God. The argument is straightforward: if God is all-good and all-powerful, then why do terrible things happen to good people? Why was there a Holocaust, or the events of September 11, 2001? Why do children get cancer? Why is there ethnic cleansing? Genocide? Abandonment of the poor, the homeless, and the helpless? Why do good people live and die in the streets while bad people live like kings?

From the principles we have covered to this point, the answer should be clear: Evil exists because *we* are God. There is no higher authority that is directing the course of human events. Rather, human events show God acting to understand itself. Evil exists because we have not yet understood who we are or taken responsibility for a world that is only ours.

The infinite dreaming power delivers to us a physical universe, but because we wrongly perceive this world and other people as having a source other than our united mind, we believe our own dream stands wholly separate from us, as we take this world picture and proceed to battle over who prays to the more righteous god. These people of Earth, who fight for god-supremacy among themselves, are like cancer cells eating away at the Mind—a mind, a person, a soul at war with itself. The goal is to unite the Mind to the unifying principle of the one dream and thus direct our ambitions toward a common goal.

An infinite moral divide exists between the love of God and the slaughter of innocent people in the name of God. The question of good and evil is a scientific question in the Real Dream worldview: being good means aligning oneself with the united mind, loving each other as yourself for the simple reason that we are one at the core of our beings—whether you want to be or not. Being evil means raising your own personal belief system above the simple scientific truth of oneness and then using that perverse belief to hate, kill, or torture those who think differently from yourself.

Look out at the power of the world, the sky, the grass, trees, the Earth, and the space in between. Close your eyes and imagine the power that formed this world, the power that gives it reality and solidity and moves it forward, the innermost source of being—this is the power of God. The power lies in raw unity. Today, we have crippled that power by acting as disjointed parts of a machine, and there can only be one solution: to put the parts back together by uniting the dream.

Chapter Forty-Five

ONE WORLD

If there is righteousness in the heart, there will be beauty in the character.
If there is beauty in the character, there be harmony in the home. If there is
harmony in the home, there will be in order in the nation. If there is order
in the nation, there will be peace in the world.
—Confucius

IF WE SET THE belief systems of the great religions over against the theories of material science, we find science and religion occupying two different worlds. Material science believes that the human species arose from a primordial swamp, not an early paradise; the universe began with an infinite explosion of matter, space, and time. It did not issue from the mind of Brahman. Creation, to scientists, has evolved over several billion years; no God assembled it in six days. What to material scientists is ultimate reality (matter), to the Indian thinker is illusion. The laws of nature, according to scientists, overrule all accounts of miracles, which science hence proclaims are impossible.[864] And, of course, material science is value-blind: it classifies living and nonliving objects into countless categories but cannot distinguish good from evil.

Science and religion occupy different worlds largely because those who practice religion tend to adopt the material science worldview. God becomes an invisible spirit suspended over a machine-shop world. Because reason cannot explain how God interacts with a machine, we shut off the reasoning process and look to faith: we know God exists, we just don't know where to find God in this world.

For a moment let us take a different approach and instead set religious belief systems over against the Real Dream: here we find ourselves living in one world after all. The world issues out of Brahman, and every individual self shares in the Great Self. This Self is identical to nature—"that are thou." Maya, the world of appearances, is indeed an illusion, though, as argued above, because the body too is maya, body and world are real to each other. As Hinduism teaches, humankind's chief failing is in embracing material objects as ultimate reality, or as the true measures of worldly success. Rather, truth lies inward where the One dwells.

Buddha advanced a way of life for the boundless self imprisoned within a machine-world. Buddha was not a metaphysician,[865] and probably took the physical world at face value. He assumed that humankind, united or not, could not alter its fate within the world. The self was doomed to suffer. In the face of the human predicament, Buddha set forth his eightfold path of morality: a system of living that best adapted the self to the endless suffering endured at the hands of a runaway world. Detaching the self from the withering material world leads to its spiritual liberation in Nirvana. The body cannot escape death, but the self can join the stream of becoming as it flows toward a better place.

To Buddha the self was trapped within a machine preset to run down beyond the self's control. Here, in the Real Dream, we seek an escape route for the self where we can bring the body with us, and thus make our escape complete. The Real Dream does not assume that the world operates beyond our control; rather it believes that the world reflects the state of the dreamer's soul.

As noted above, nature's harmonies, such as the physical constants and Newton's laws of motion, are explained in the Real Dream as representing the limit of order in a physical world. When the mind turns from the scenery to the actors in the dream, we find that the human form represents the mind's best image of a figure to participate in life. In the escape from nothing, the mind desires a companion, and thus the male and female sexes represent the highest forms of complementary images to experience life. (As mentioned above, this line of reasoning can be tested.

Males, try to imagine a better complementary form than the female; females, try the opposite.[866]) When the mind's unlimited creativity is directed toward physical objects, we encounter mathematical symmetries and beauty: spiral galaxies, planetary orbits, chemical proportions, and the rest. When the mind applies its creativity to living things, we encounter a story.

Since the world has evolved as one dream, we should expect the characters to act out such a story. The story line would be a simple one: the world of people grows to learn that they share the same dream. In the beginning, the actors perceive themselves as separate people in a self-operating world. They have the mind of God but in different bodies. Equipped with an unlimited mind but a confining world, many will seek to master the world through physical manipulation. Power is exerted upon the world, not from within it. Over time, however, the mind grows in awareness and realizes that true power lies in unity, for here the mind joins in bodily forms at the dream's end, and experiences love.

The Real Dream allows us to look at the Old Testament (or Hebrew Bible) through different eyes by viewing its stories[867] as those of early dreamers in God's great dream. Adam and Eve stand as images of the first human figures painted against a heavenly background. The images are perfect, but the characters are hollow; Adam and Eve do not understand the story that their descendants will act out: a world of people who struggle to live together under one sky. These people will exhaust every available means—wars, slavery, torture, discrimination, and prejudices—to advance private causes, until learning that true power in this world comes from unity and that they must share as equals both the sky overhead and the world beneath their feet.

At various times throughout history, as noted above, scientists encounter what they call "Eureka!" moments, a time when nature reveals to them one of its secrets. Kepler's music of the spheres, Kekule's dream of the benzene molecule, and Mendelev's periodic table represent examples of these moments. We accounted for this religious-like feeling by supposing that the individual scientist revisits a creative moment first achieved by the one free mind of God. The mind, in a sense, reunites with its own creation, though in a different form. Not every prediction, of course, turns out to be right. But the same feature of our world that allows for the fulfillment of the scientist's inspiration also allows for the fulfillment of the prophet's vision: one person somehow dips into the dream's undercurrent and, for a moment, becomes its messenger and mouthpiece.

Moses, Jesus Christ, and Muhammad are three historic figures who represent this phenomenon from a religious standpoint. Moses brought the Torah (first five books of the Bible) down from Mount Sinai so that the people of Israel would never forget the one true God. Jesus Christ stands as a "living God" whose awareness of the family of man seemed to flood the world, and who spoke of the coming of a better world—a "kingdom of God"—upon the earth.

The Qur'an is said to contain the words of God spoken by the angel Gabriel directly to the illiterate Muhammad over a twenty-two-year period.[868] Muhammad, Muslims believe, was both a messenger and mouthpiece of God. The Qur'an directs us to turn away from the transient pleasures of the daily world and devote full attention to the one true God:

> God it is who created the heavens and the earth and gives the rain that comes down from the heavens, bringing forth fruits in provisions for you. His ordering makes possible the ships that at His command traverse the sea. He made the rivers also to serve you. Sun and moon, likewise, in their constant orbits He recruits to your service, and night and day as well.[869]

"Allah [God]," the Qur'an states, "is bountiful to man, yet most of them do not give thanks."[870]

In modern man's quest to understand the world, religious beliefs have come to occupy an increasingly narrow ridge. Modern science believes it needs no God in its formulas—matter and the laws of nature will be enough for it to explain creation. But once we no longer take matter and the laws of nature for granted, we find the world can be explained as a dream in the mind of God. We return to God when we no longer assume the world. All the world's religions may find a place against the spiritual horizon this approach creates, and not because we have applied a new concept to old beliefs but because we have returned to a concept older than belief.

We reach this standpoint through reason, not faith. As the idealist philosophers showed, when reason is applied to the problem of the external world, we find ourselves limited to knowing only ideas and images in our mind. Our mind cannot escape itself. Viewed in a positive sense we know that the mind has the ability to conjure out of nothing a real-seeming three-dimensional world in dreams and hallucinations.

But idealist philosophers who attempted to reason their way past this point confront the paradox of solipsism: If the world is a dream, then whose dream is it? The Real Dream has a solution that may seem coincidental: the ultimate source of the dream is also the link joining Eastern and Western religions. The Self is Brahman, and the ultimate dreamer, the God-figure who now waits to enter the dream in person.

Chapter Forty-Six

THE REAL HEAVEN

The Kingdom of Heaven is laid upon the earth, but people do not see it.
—Gospel of Thomas

For thousands of years the mind has perceived the world outside as a foreign object. While holding onto this thought we have pushed deep inside the hope that someday the world will better reflect our dreams. For a time, this state of mind comforts us: we have a home to dwell in, and the laws of nature and God to ensure it stays in place.

The assumption that the external world exists independently of the mind is backed by today's most authoritative intellectual discipline, modern science.[871] At this moment, all across the globe—in living rooms, textbooks, classrooms, laboratories, newspapers, and television shows—this assumption frames discussions about the world. It is the given lying in the background of everything we say. It is the most important opinion we hold, and also the one we have least questioned.

But something noteworthy occurs when we do examine this assumption: it fails to withstand the very sort of questioning that science applies to other beliefs. Night dreams and hallucinations find our mind duplicating physical reality with no help from the forces of nature. In some instances, a link appears between mind and body, as in the placebo effect or mind-driven medical cures. Accounts of patients who have been cured of real physical ailments through the power of faith and belief fill medical literature. In material science's eyes, however, faith and belief can have no effect on our machine-made bodies. Feelings and emotions have no currency in science.

Other phenomena suggest a link between separate living things, as with animal instincts, telepathy, or synchronicity. Ants live in colonies, work in teams, wage war, and capture slaves; geese fly in formation to speed their way through the wind; bees assemble a honeycomb as if they work from the same construction manual; human children learn language much quicker than if each had to begin the lesson anew every generation. In each instance, an instinctive reaction seems to spread invisibly across living things and then down through generations, as if one mind had already learned the lesson once and now conveys it to new forms.

At times we seem to sense what other people are thinking and feeling. We sense their mood; they don't want to visit the in-laws, walk the dog; cook dinner, or say goodbye. In other instances, the world itself seems programmed: events seem synchronized as if one author writes life's script. A song is in our mind; it plays on the radio. We think of a friend, she calls. We are down and out on our luck, the phone rings—a friend offers support, a job opportunity arises. On a different scale, the planet Earth balances with the sun and allows life to develop, evolve, and prosper. Fruit grows on trees; vegetables from the ground. Animals of all kinds inhabit the landscape, providing to some a picturesque background, and to others, a means to survive. The world itself works together in harmony as if it always has—a complicated, involved script, but still one story. Order floods the world, from the smallest particle to the most expansive galaxy.

Material science rejects the interconnectedness between the mind and the world because it does not fit science's current model of the world. On other similar occasions where theory no longer accounted for observed facts, science has been given the choice of ignoring the facts or changing the model. Up to this time, science has chosen to ignore the facts and to refuse to let go of its death grip upon the material science worldview.

Material scientists insist on separating mind from matter in their theories, and assume that the entire universe arose from forces external to the mind. Their theories, however, turn silent when explaining the origin of matter, or how it all operates in mathematical harmony. Matter and the laws of nature, they assume. Whether the event is the formation of the solar system out of the big bang or the evolution of life from a one-celled bacterium, the question is the same: How did dead matter arrange itself into the infinite order surrounding us without an intelligent guiding force?

Penetrating into matter, scientists uncover another clue to the world's true nature: matter is composed not of things but of pulsating images and wave packets—precisely what one would expect to find at the bottom of a dream. Entranced by the strange features of the subatomic world, scientists seem to forget that quantum theory supports the view that the world is not the self-powered machine they first imagined, but a dream the imagination builds.

And when we are done asking the questions and examining the evidence, we come upon the truth: it is we—and only we—who have erected the notion that the external world exists beyond the mind. *And this is a strategy the mind must have planned.* We have unknowingly built the mold for a world to live in; the animal instincts of God indeed run deep.

But we now have reached the stage of evolution where we are ready to accept the world for what it must be: a product of our united imagination. This thought is the sky above, the stars overhead, and the invisible canvas covering the world. The material science worldview is a stage in the evolution of God that we now need to pass by. It has fulfilled its purpose. It is time to move on.

We want a world to unfold before us because that is what we dream for. But in misperceiving the natural world, modern science tells us that our own dream is the prison from which we can never escape. We surrender to it before testing whether the belief that brought us to this point is valid. In the end, we have built this misconception, and we are the ones to tear it down.

We must tear it down by the use of discussion, argument, and experiment. This is a scientific revolution that will become a social revolution by an act of necessity. We should start by rewriting a few textbooks and begin breaking down the artificial barriers—religious beliefs, social status, national origin, and color—that separate us.

In the not-too-distant future, the material science worldview will begin to fade away like a mirage, and then we will have cleared a path to a new homeland: a way of looking at the world that will never change because it is rooted in truth.

In this new world we might find it wise to put our faith not in material science's impersonal laws and indifferent machines, but rather in ourselves. Instead of devoting resources to billion-dollar space probes, atom-smashers, space stations, and ever more deadly bombs, we might consider pursuing goals that will produce true benefits in a dream world. We can begin by disarming those who use weapons only to terrorize the poor, the helpless, and the innocent—those who kill and spread fear in the name of God. We must devote our resources to sustaining a way to improve the quality of life for more people, feeding the hungry, sheltering the homeless, comforting the sick, protecting the environment, and educating the masses. We can hardly expect to improve a dream world unless we improve the state of mind of those doing the dreaming.

We do not know how far this thought will take us; there is still much we do not understand. But we know what type of world we produce when the material science worldview controls our mind. Every day the morning newspaper announces the failure of a world where we look at nature and other people as self-operating machines; it should not be hard to do better than this.

So let us embrace the new millennium by adopting a fresh outlook, a new worldview. In the true spirit of science, let us dive into the Real Dream, put it to the test, and see if we have the power to make the new age equal the world of our dreams. Perhaps the experiment fails, and we find that we are self-operating machines after all; then we will have lost nothing. But then again, if we pour everything we have into this quest, we may find that the dream, once buried inside, now shines out in front of us. The natural world that once imprisoned us now expresses what we can be. Mind and nature inspire each other to reach higher, as we take hold of the ladder of the dream and pull ourselves upward to the goal that still shimmers overhead: the highest dream, an eternal home—a place we may someday, with the steadiest of voices, come to call heaven.

INDEX

NOTE: Page numbers followed by an *"n"* indicate an endnote.

ENDNOTES

Chapter One: The Next Scientific Revolution

[1] See Olson, *Short Introduction to Philosophy*, 29–30.

[2] *Webster's New World Dictionary* defines "mind" as "that which thinks, perceives, feels, wills, etc.; seat or subject of consciousness" (2nd college ed., ed. David B. Guralnik [Prentice Hall, 1986], 904).

[3] Professor Olson states that the "external world consists of physical objects existing in space" (*Short Introduction to Philosophy*, 29).

[4] See Chalmers, "The Puzzle of Conscious Experience," in *The Hidden Mind*.

[5] See, e.g., Einstein, Podolsky, and Rosen, "Can Quantum-Mechanical Description of Physical Reality Be Considered Complete?" The authors write in the first paragraph of their paper: "Any serious consideration of a physical theory must take into account the distinction between the objective reality, which is independent of any theory, and the physical concepts with which the theory operates." The late George Gaylord Simpson, one of the twentieth century's most respected paleontologists, writes, "The most successful scientific investigation has generally involved treating phenomena *as if* they were purely materialistic or naturalistic, rejecting any metaphysical or transcendental hypothesis as only as a natural hypothesis seems possible. The method works. The restriction is necessary because science is confined to material means of investigation and so it would stultify its own efforts to postulate that its subject is not material so not susceptible to its methods" (Simpson, *Meaning of Evolution*, 115 [emphasis in original]). "The scientist accepts space-time, along with matter and energy, as the *givens* of the physical world, and their ultimate origin remains a mystery" (Jones, *Physics for the Rest of Us*, 79). "Physicists have traditionally expected that science should give an account of reality as it would be in our absence. . . . Philosophers call this view realism. It can be summarized by saying that the real world out there . . . must exist independently of us" (Smolin, *Trouble with Physics*, 6–7).

[6] "Worldview" is defined as the "collection of beliefs (ideas, images, attitudes, values) that an individual or a group holds about such things as the universe, humankind, God, the future, etc." (Angeles, *Dictionary of Philosophy*), 319.

[7] Campbell, *Biology*, 513–14.

[8] See Mayr, *One Long Argument*, 24–25, 38–39.

[9] See Weinberg, *Dreams of a Final Theory*, 53.

[10] Dawkins, *Selfish Gene*, ix.

[11] See Davies, *God and the New Physics*, 2.

[12] See Lederman, *God Particle*, 192; Davies, *God and the New Physics*, 2.

[13] *Webster's New World Dictionary*, 1275.

[14] Angeles, *Dictionary of Philosophy*, 78.

[15] See Lederman, *God Particle*: "Is this universe real? If so, can we know it? Theorists don't often grapple with this problem. They simply accept objective reality at face value" (63).

[16] Ditfurth, *Origins of Life*, 143–44.

[17] See Mayr, "Concerns of Science."

[18] Ibid.

[19] Paul Davies explains that according to Occam's razor, "the most plausible of a possible set of explanations is that which contains the simplest ideas and the least number of assumptions" (*God and the New Physics*, 173). *Webster's New World Dictionary* defines Occam's razor as the principle under which the "best explanation of an event is the one that is the simplest, using the fewest assumptions, hypotheses, etc" (983). Isaac Newton made much the same point in the "opus that laid the foundation for modern science," *Philosophiae Naturalis Principia Mathematica* (*Mathematical Principles of Natural Philosophy*): "We are to admit no more causes of natural things than such as are both true and sufficient to explain their appearances. To this purpose the philosophers say that Nature does nothing in vain, and more is in vain when less will serve; for Nature is pleased with simplicity, and affects not the pomp of superfluous causes" (quoted from *Scientific American*, March 1994, 32–33).

[20] Davies, *Accidental Universe*, 76, 79.

Chapter Two: A Problem of Perspective

[21] Descartes, *Meditations on First Philosophy*, 24. As Frederick Copleston writes, "If I am deceived, I must exist to be deceived; if I am dreaming, I must exist to dream" Copleston, *History of Philosophy*, book 2, 4:90.

[22] *Meditations on First Philosophy*, 26-27.

[23] Ibid., 75.

Chapter Four: The Connection between Mind and Matter

[24] If scientists view the mind as the brain, then no physical link is apparent between the brain and the outer world. If they view the mind as a nonphysical entity existing on a different plane from the external world (dualism), then again mind and matter have no means to communicate. See generally Fischbach, "Mind and Brain."

[25] See Angeles, *Dictionary of Philosophy*, 237–38; Olson, *Short Introduction to Philosophy*, 21–22.

[26] Weinberg, *Dreams of a Final Theory*, 167. Smolin calls this assumption RWOT, for "real world out there." He writes that the "belief in the RWOT and the possibility of truly knowing it motivates us to do the hard work needed to become a scientist and contribute to the understanding of nature" (*Trouble with Physics*, 7–9).

[27] Weinberg, Dreams of a Final Theory, 45.

[28] Ibid., 49.

[29] In his book *Science and the Supernatural*, John Taylor, after surveying a host of purported paranormal events, writes, "Everything that I investigated turned out either to have a scientific explanation, such as the electrical explanation of certain psychokinetic results, or did not occur at all under careful test conditions. The earlier results of others in these later cases were found to be explicable under the headings of mischief, fraud, credulity, fantasy, memory, cues and fear of death. With this evidence and the fact that all of these phenomena disagreed completely with scientific results, we have to conclude that the paranormal has 'disappeared.' . . . *The paranormal is now totally normal. ESP is dead.* Such disappearance of the supernatural is inevitable if we weigh it against science" (164–65, emphasis in original). See also Lederman, *God Particle*, 192. Like many materialists, Michael Shermer, in *The Believing Brain*,

attributes the belief in the paranormal and spirituality to some innate but foolish tendency to believe odd things without credible proof. Among these odd beliefs, Shermer lists precognitive dreams, heaven, and God. The view that materialism will someday find a particle-based answer for everything has been termed "promissory materialism." See de Quincey, *Radical Nature.*_

[30] See Jahn and Dunne, *Margins of Reality*.

[31] Broughton, *Parapsychology*.

Chapter Five: The Mind's Ability to Dream

[32] Another example is an orgasmic (wet) dream, where a dreamed experience produces real semen; see O'Flaherty, *Dreams, Illusions and Other Realities*, 45. See also Nelson, "Reality Dreams and Their Effects on Spiritual Belief," in which the author quotes from study by P. E. Craig: "What encounters us while dreaming appears to us as tangibly, palpably present. . . . We are hard pressed to find a reliable basis for saying that dreaming experience is any less real for us while dreaming than our waking experience while awake. . . . We actually feel throughout our bodies and beings the ecstasy, terror, passion, rage or humor which overtakes us in response to that which appears. Sometimes, in fact, we actually wake up drenched in sweat, with tears on our cheeks, or with our heart racing wildly" (236, quoting Craig, "Realness of Dreams," 38). "During a dream, one tends to consider dream events as if they were completely real, even though, upon waking, one promptly recognizes them as fabrication" (Ellis, *World of Dreams*, 5).

[33] Freud, *Interpretation of Dreams*, 253–54.

[34] Ellis, *World of Dreams*, 130. Eillis also reports that English philosopher and political theorist, Herbert Spencer (1820-1903), found, in an informal survey, that three of twelve people he asked recalled such clear dreams of flying downstairs, and "were so strongly impressed by the reality of the experience" that they later attempted to duplicate the act when awake, with one of them injuring his ankle in the process.

[35] *Sports Illustrated*, March 7, 1994, 21.

[36] Ibid., 23.

[37] Taken from Ullman and Krippner, *Dream Telepathy*, 6, referencing Hill, *Such Stuff as Dreams*, 30.

[38] Hempel, *Philosophy of Natural Science*, 15–16.

[39] Ibid. See also Weiss and Brown, "Overlooked Parallel to Kekulé's Dream," 770.

[40] Brooks, *Free Radicals*.

[41] This viewpoint is similar to that held by psychologist Carl Jung, among others.

[42] Taken from Knight, ed., *ESP Reader*, 106–7.

[43] Gurney, Myers, and Podmore, *Phantasms of the Living*, case 160, 1:415.

[44] Ibid., case 223, 2:37. On other occasions, the same authors report that the solidity of the phantasm startles the percipient: "On Thursday evening, 14th November, 1867, I was sitting in the Birmingham Town Hall with my husband at a concert, when there came over me the icy chill which usually accompanies these occurrences. Almost immediately, I saw with perfect distinctness, between myself and the orchestra, my uncle, Mr. W., lying in bed with an appealing look on his face, like one dying. I had not heard anything of him for several months, and had no reason to thing he was ill. The appearance was not transparent or filmy, but perfectly solid-looking; and yet I could somehow see the orchestra, not through, but behind it. I

did not try turning my eyes to see whether the figure moved with them, but looked at it with a fascinated expression that made my husband ask if I was ill. I asked him not to speak to me for a minute or two; the vision gradually disappeared, and I told my husband, after the concert was over, what I had seen. A letter came shortly after telling of my uncle's death. He died at exactly the time when I saw the vision."

[45] See Erickson, "Special Inquiry with Aldous Huxley into the Nature and Character of Various States of Consciousness," 58, 70–71.

[46] Gurney, Myers, and Podmore, *Phantasms of the Living*, 1:479.

[47] See Gershon and Rieder, "Major Disorders of Mind and Brain," 126. See also Glaser, "Inhalation Psychosis and Related States"; Evans, *Alternate States of Consciousness*, 224–25.

[48] See Comer, Madow, and Dixon, "Observations of Sensory Deprivation in a Life-Threatening Situation," 164.

[49] See, e.g., *Castaneda, Teachings of Don Juan;* Evans, *Alternate States of Consciousness*, 197–200.

[50] Sacks, *Hallucinations*, 36 and throughout.

[51] In his book, *Consciousness Explained*, Dennett, using a strict materialistic interpretation of consciousness, concludes that hallucinations are not possible.

[52] Gurney, Myers, and Podmore, *Phantasms of the Living*, Case 37.

[53] Jung, *Synchronicity*, 15n26. Other compelling lost-and-found cases appear in Vaughn's book, *Incredible Coincidences*. One story concerns a farmer's wife who lost her wedding ring in a potato field, and forty years later found the ring in a potato that came from the same field.

[54] Vaughn, *Incredible Coincidences*.

Chapter Six: Mind over External World

[55] *Chicago Tribune*, April 9, 1994, Sec. 3, p. 2.

[56] *Chicago Tribune*, April 30, 1992, Sec. 4, p. 1.

[57] Radin, *Conscious Universe*, 173–86.

[58] Radin, *Entangled Minds*, 182–85.

[59] Descartes wrote, "Although I certainly do possess a body with which I am very closely conjoined; nevertheless, because, on the one hand, I have a clear and distinct idea of myself, in as far as I am only a thinking and unextended thing, and as, on the other hand, I possess a distinct idea of body, in so far as it is only an extended and unthinking thing, it is certain that I [that is, my mind, by which I am what I am] is entirely and truly distinct from my body, and may exist without it" (Descartes, *Meditations on First Philosophy*, meditation 6).

[60] "The molecule is to the bioscientist what the quark is to the particle physicist: the fundamental unit, the derangement of which we recognize as chemical disease. For this reason the modern medical model is called the molecular theory of disease causation" (Dossey, *Space, Time and Medicine*, 6–7). "In the classical view, illness had no local origin in the body; it was a general disturbance caused by an imbalance of the four humors (blood, phlegm, yellow and black bile). After the Newtonian revolution in physics, new medical theories attributed disease to disturbances of solid entities in the body, such as the blood vessels, but the basic model remained the same. Disease was the result of a single, underlying condition that affected the entire constitution; however, in any given patient, the factors that brought on this condition were

individual. The entire focus of treatment was on the patient's symptoms, which were regarded not as signs of the disease, but as the disease itself" (Starr, *Social Transformation of American Medicine*, 38–39).

[61] From Kiev, ed., *Magic, Faith, and Healing*, Foreword.

[62] Beecher, "Powerful Placebo," 1602; Shapiro and Shapiro, *Powerful Placebo*.

[63] See generally Shapiro, "Contribution to a History of the Placebo Effect," 109.

[64] A more technical definition of a placebo is "any therapeutic procedure . . . which is given deliberately to have an effect, or unknowingly has an effect on a patient, symptom, syndrome, or disease, but which is objectively without *specific* activity for the condition being treated" (Benson and Epstein, "Placebo Effect," 1226.

[65] Placebos are commonly thought of as pills, but they can also consist of a medical treatment such as surgery, where the patient believes he or she is undergoing surgery but in fact is not. See Beecher, "Surgery as Placebo," 1102.

[66] See Grunbaum, "Explication and Implications of the Placebo Concept," 9. *Webster's New World Dictionary* defines a *placebo* as a "harmless unmedicated preparation given as a medicine to a patient merely to humor him, or used as a control in testing the efficacy of another, medicated substance" (1087). For a thorough discussion of the definition of a "placebo," see White, Tursky, and Schwartz, *Placebo*.

[67] Benson and Epstein, "Placebo Effect," 1226.

[68] Beecher, "Surgery as Placebo," 1102.

[69] Grad, "Laying On of Hands," 118, 134.

[70] Evans, "Expectancy, Therapeutic Instructions, and the Placebo Response."

[71] Ibid.

[72] Roberts, Kewman, Mercier, and Hovell, "Effects in Healing," 375, 385.

[73] Ibid., 377.

[74] Ibid., 386.

[75] Ibid., 387.

[76] Grad, "Laying On of Hands," referencing Bell, " Placebo Effect in Drug Evaluation," 937–39.

[77] Roberts, Kewman, Mercier, and Hovell, "Effects in Healing," 376

[78] Ornstein and Sobel, *Healing Brain*, 77.

[79] Shapiro, "Contribution to a History of the Placebo Effect," 110. Shapiro further reports that in ancient Egypt sick patients were treated with anything from lizard's blood and crocodile dung to the hoof of an ass; viper flesh, the spermatic fluid of frogs, powdered mummies, and even unicorn horns were once prescribed by doctors to treat illnesses. Although today we have no means to determine whether any of these exotic treatments worked, the consensus is that some did because doctors did not fall in disrepute with their patients (111–12).

[80] Dawkins, *Selfish Gene*.

[81] Lipton, *Biology of Belief*.

[82] Sheldrake, *Science Delusion*, 168.

[83] Hall, Revolution Postponed, 60

[84] Ibid..

[85] It seems that material science is clearly heading in that direction. See Ray Moynihan & Alan Cassels, "A Disease for Every Pill," *The Nation*, October 17, 2005.

Chapter Seven: The Origin of the Debate

[86] This is the logical fallacy of affirming the consequent. See Byerly, *Primer on Logic*, 41–42.

Chapter Eight: The Source of the Belief in an Independent World

[87] Locke, *Essay Concerning Human Understanding*, book 2, chap. 8, ¶ 9.

[88] Ibid, ¶ 10.

[89] See *Scientific American*, Secrets of the Senses, special ed., 2006.

[90] Locke, *Essay Concerning Human Understanding*, book 1, chap. 2, ¶ 15. Locke, like empiricists generally, also believed that we gain knowledge from experiencing the operation of our own mind.

[91] Locke writes, "Since the mind in all its thoughts and reasonings hath no other immediate object but its own ideas, which it alone does or can contemplate, it is evident that our knowledge is only conversant about them" (ibid., book 4, chap. 1, ¶ 1). Put differently, Locke looks at his body as a naïve realist (exactly the way it appears with all qualities inhering in the perceived body) and the world external to the body as a representationalist (primary qualities reside in the object; secondary qualities originate in the mind).

[92] As Berkeley writes, "They who assert that figure, motion and the rest of the primary or original qualities do exist without the mind, in unthinking substance, do at the same time acknowledge that colours, sounds, heat, cold, and such-like secondary qualities, do not; which they tell us are sensations, existing in the mind alone, that depend on and are occasioned by different size, texture, and motion of the minute particles of matter. This they take for an undoubted truth, which they can demonstrate beyond all exception. Now, if it be certain that those *original* qualities are inseparably united with the other sensible qualities, and not, even in thought, capable of being abstracted from them, it plainly follows that *they* exist only in the mind" (Berkeley, *Principles of Human Knowledge*, part first, ¶ 10, emphasis in original). To Berkeley, when we speculate upon the possibility that matter might exist external to the mind, we contemplate only ourselves, not external things. All we ever have are ideas of external things; we can never know whether such a thing as independent matter exists. According to Berkeley, the words "*absolute existence of sensible things in themselves*, or *without the mind* . . . mark out either a direct contradiction or else nothing at all."

[93] Ibid., ¶ 20, 134.

[94] "When in broad daylight I open my eyes, it is not in my power to choose whether I shall see or no, or to determine what particular objects shall present themselves to my view: and so likewise as to the hearing and other senses; the ideas imprinted on them are not creatures of *my* will." Ibid., ¶ 29, 139.

[95] Ibid., ¶ 6, 127.

[96] See Copleston, *History of Philosophy*, book 2, 227.

[97] *Webster's New World Collegiate Dictionary*, 1356; Angeles, *Dictionary of Philosophy*, 265.

[98] *Webster's New World Collegiate Dictionary*, 1418; Angeles, *Dictionary of Philosophy*, 277.

[99] Calkins, Introduction to *Berkeley Selections*, xlviii.

[100] Hume, *Treatise of Human Nature*, book 1, section 6, 116.

101 Ibid., book 1, part 4, section 2.

102 Ibid.

103 Ibid., part 4, section 2, 239.

104 Ibid.

105 Ibid., 243. Hume continues, "Whatever convincing arguments philosophers may fancy they can produce to establish the belief of objects independent of the mind, 'tis not by them, that children, peasants, and the greatest part of mankind are induc'd to attribute objects to some impressions, and deny them to others. . . . For philosophy informs us, that every thing, which appears to the mind, is nothing but a perception, and is interrupted, and dependent on the mind; whereas the vulgar confound perceptions and objects, and attribute a distinct continu'd existence to the very things they feel or see" (243).

106 Ibid., 246. The mind, according to Hume, is like a movie screen that receives images by turning toward the projector. If we turn away from the projector, the source for the picture is removed. But even when turned away from the projector (or when no longer perceiving the external object) we nonetheless, according to Hume, forget that our perception has been interrupted and imagine that the object (for example, a tree) has a continued existence even when our mind is not perceiving it. Not only do we pretend the tree exists when unperceived, we deeply believe it is still there (248).

107 Ibid., 259. Hume explains that the "mind is once in the train of observing a uniformity among objects, it naturally continues, till it renders the uniformity as compleat as possible (249). The mind desires uniformity and constancy in perceptions; though real-time perceptions may be interrupted, our mind "like a galley put in motion by the oars, carries on its course without any new impulse" (248). Viewing the matter strictly, Hume concludes neither experience nor reason led to the idea that external objects have a continued and independent existence from our mind. Only the imagination, weaving together perceptions, is the source for the belief.

108 Ibid., 264.

109 Ibid., 238.

Chapter Nine: The Source of the Belief in a Self-Operating World

110 Angeles, *Dictionary of Philosophy*, 75, defining "empiricism" as the "view that all ideas are abstractions formed by compounding (combining, recombining) what is experienced (observed, immediately given in sensation)."

111 As Hume writes, "Our senses inform us of the colour, weight, and consistence of bread; but neither sense nor reason can ever inform us of those qualities which fit it for the nourishment and support of a human body" Hume, *Enquiry Concerning Human Understanding*, section 4, part 2, 33.

112 Hume, *Treatise of Human Nature*, book 1, section 6.

113 Ibid., section 2.

114 Hume, *Enquiry Concerning Human Understanding*, section 5, part 1.

115 Ibid., 46. Hume continues, "All belief of matter of fact or real existence is derived merely from some object, present to the memory or senses, and a customary conjunction between that and some other object. Or in other words; having found in many instances, that any two kinds of objects—flame and heat, snow and cold—have always been conjoined together; if flame or snow be presented anew to the

senses, the mind is carried by custom to expect heat or cold, and to *believe* that such a quality does exist, and will discover itself upon a nearer approach" (49).

116 In his words, "Hitherto it has been supposed that all our knowledge must conform to the objects: but, under that supposition, all attempts to establish anything about them *a priori*, by means of concepts, and thus to enlarge our knowledge, have come to nothing. The experiment therefore ought to be made, whether we should not succeed better with the problems of metaphysics, by assuming that the objects must conform to our mode of cognition, for this would better agree with the demanded possibility of an *a priori* knowledge of them, which is to settle something about objects, before they are given to us" (Kant, *Critique of Pure Reason*, xxxiii).

117 Kant expressed the problem of metaphysics in logical form: How are synthetic a priori propositions possible? This terse and academic statement of the problem tends to mask its importance. To say that the mind knows something about the world without experiencing it means that the mind forms at least part of experience. See Kant, "Prolegomena to Any Future Metaphysics," § 5, 314.

118 See Lavine, *From Socrates to Sartre*, 158, 168.

119 Kant writes, "The existence of an object outside me (if this word 'me' be taken in the intellectual [not the empirical] sense) is never given directly in perception." And again, "I am not, therefore, in a position to *perceive* external things, but can only infer their existence from my inner perception, taking the inner perception as the effect of which something external is the proximate cause" (*Critique of Pure Reason*, A368, 345 [Kemp Smith, trans.]). "For if we regard outer appearances as representations produced in us by their objects, and if these objects be things existing in themselves outside us, it is indeed impossible to see how we can come to know the existence of the objects otherwise than by inference from the effect to the cause; and this being so, it must always remain doubtful whether the cause in question be in us or outside us" (A372, 347). We can have "no knowledge whatsoever" of the thing-in-itself (A393, 360).

120 Ibid., B72.

121 Ibid., chap. 3, §§ 3–7.

122 Ibid., A369, 346 (Kemp Smith, trans).

123 Copleston, *History of Philosophy*, book 3, 3:3.

124 Kant, *Critique of Pure Reason*, A369, 346 (Kemp Smith, trans).

125 Ibid.

126 Ibid., A120–23. Using the movie-theater metaphor might make Kant's system more clear. In naïve realism our mind is like a screen that receives images from a projector located outside the mind. Locke's representative theory placed some qualities out in the projector, and left others (the secondary qualities) to form on the screen, as if the screen contains chemicals that transforms raw data received from the external world into a picture. Berkeley consolidated all qualities—and hence the entire object—in the mind, but invoked an Eternal Spirit as the ultimate projecting source. Although Kant suggests that indeed the mind projects a picture on the screen, he placed a material supporting brace behind the screen to give the perception of permanence.

127 Ibid., A123–27, 114–15 (Muller trans.).

128 Ibid., A129–30, 116–17 (Muller trans.).

129 He writes in the *Critique*, "Objects are given to us through our sensibility. . . . The effect produced by an object upon the faculty of representation. . . . So far as we are affected by it, is called sensation" (A18–20; B32–34).

[130] Olson writes, "Most of us are by turns naïve realists and representationalists without even being aware of the inconsistency" (*Short Introduction to Philosophy*, 25).

Chapter Ten: Idealism Fails to Complete the Puzzle

[131] *Critique*, A853–56; B881–84: "If the reader has been kind and patient enough to follow me to the end along this path, he may judge for himself whether, if he will help, as far as in him lies, towards making this footpath a highroad, it may not be possible to achieve, even before the close of the present century, what so many centuries have not been able to achieve, namely, to give complete satisfaction to human reason with regard to those questions which have in all ages exercised its desire for knowledge, though hitherto in vain."

[132] Bertrand Russell, for example, writes, "Kant's immediate successor, Fichte (1762–1814), abandoned 'things-in-themselves,' and carried subjectivism to a point which seems almost to involve a kind of insanity" (Russell, *History of Western Philosophy*, 718).

[133] Fichte, *Science of Knowledge*, 202.

[134] Fichte, *Vocation of Man*, 74, emphasis in original.

[135] See ibid.

[136] Frederick Copleston quotes from a Fichte lecture: "It is not the individual but the one immediate spiritual Life which is the creator of all phenomena, including phenomenal individuals."(*History of Philosophy*, book 3, 7:44).

[137] Fichte, *Vocation of Man*, 80.

[138] Ibid.,

[139] Ibid., 90.

[140] Fichte writes, ""It is our *interest* in a reality which we desire to produce: in the good, absolutely for its own sake, and the common and sensuous, for the sake of the enjoyment they afford" (ibid.).

[141] Ibid., 83.

[142] "There arises within me the wish, the desire—no, not the mere desire, but the absolute demand—for a better world" (ibid., 100).

[143] Ibid., 137.

[144] Hegel is famous for his version of the dialectic, a term used to describe a method of reasoning as old as philosophy. The Hegelian dialectic is commonly portrayed as involving the movement of reason triggered by the clash of opposites. See Lavine, *From Socrates to Sartre*, 210–13. A statement (thesis) meets its opposite (antithesis) and a synthesis is produced. Others have noted that Hegel himself seldom uses this triad explicitly. See Copleston, *History of Philosophy*, book 3, 177.

[145] Hegel, *Phenomenology of Spirit*, 490–91.

[146] See Hegel, *Reason in History*: "The question of how Reason is determined in itself and what its relation is to the world coincides with the question, *What is the ultimate purpose of the world?*" (ibid., 20, emphasis in original).

[147] Ibid., 16–17. The thinking spirit "must now advance to the intellectual comprehension of that which originally was present only to the feeling and imagining spirit." Hegel's God is closest to the Holy Spirit of the Christian Trinity. It is the highest idea; the absolute synthesis of all opposing concepts; a combination of the actual and the potential (*Phenomenology of Spirit*, 415, 417); Hegel, *Philosophy of History*, 345, 412–16.

[148] Hegel, *Phenomenology of Spirit*, 492–93 (Miller trans.).

[149] See, e.g., Singer, *Hegel*, 73.

[150] Kojève, *Introduction to the Reading of Hegel*, 153.

Chapter Eleven: The Illusion Maker

[151] To German philosopher Arthur Schopenhauer (1788–1860), the world also was idea or representation; see Schopenhauer, *World as Will and Representation*. But in place of the assumed independent world of science or the mind of God, Schopenhauer placed the "one and indivisible will which is the in-itself of all things, and whose graduated objectification is this whole visible world" (ibid., vol. 1, book 2, chap. 26, 138) This includes the human body (vol. 1, book 1, chap 4; book 2, chap. 18, 100; book 3, chap. 30, 169). The will supports the world (vol. 1, book 3, chap. 34, 181). Schopenhauer's emphasis on the inward path to truth reflects his study of Eastern philosophy, and marks perhaps his greatest contribution to the advance of thought

[152] Schopenhauer, *World as Will and Representation*, vol. 1, book 1, chap. 1, 4, quoting from Jones, *On the Philosophy of the Asiatics*, 4:164.

[153] This unification of the pure (or unencumbered) self with the oneness of the universe is a highly personal experience: descriptions become elusive and hence mystical. In describing the ultimate reality of Hinduism, for example, many sources unavoidably use metaphors, allegories, or simply emphasize the inscrutability of the Ultimate Reality: "the Self is described as *not this, not that*" (Brihadaranyaka Upanisad, in *The Upanisads*, 89); see also an excerpt from the teachings of the Zen Buddhist Hsi Yun (circa A.D. 840) published in Burtt, ed., *Teachings of the Compassionate Buddha*, where it is said, "The nature of the mind, when understood, no human words can compass or disclose" (203).

[154] Chandogya Upanisad, chap. 6, from *Sourcebook in Indian Philosophy*, 68–70.

[155] *Song of God: Bhagavad-Gita*, 73.

[156] Taittiriya Upanishad, *Sourcebook in Indian Philosophy*, 59.

[157] *Sourcebook in Indian Philosophy*, 48.

[158] Ibid., 68.

[159] Ibid., 74.

[160] *The Upanisads*, 105–6.

[161] *Sourcebook in Indian Philosophy*, introduction, xxv.

[162] "This whole world the illusion-maker (mayin) projects out of this [Brahman]" Svetasvatara Upanisad, *Sourcebook in Indian Philosophy*, 91, 4.10. "In the beginning there was Existence, One only, without a second . . . He, the One, thought to himself: Let me be many, let me grow forth. Thus out of himself he projected the universe, he entered into every being" (Chandogya Upanisad, *Upanishads*, 68–69). "Truly the self (*atman*) is mind. Truly, the world is mind. Truly, *Brahman* is mind" (Chandogya Upanisad, *Sourcebook in Indian Philosophy*, 8.3.1, 70).

[163] Svetasvatara Upanisad 4.10, *Sourcebook in Indian Philosophy*, 91.

[164] Radhakrishnan, *Indian Philosophy*, 2:454.

[165] See O'Flaherty, *Dreams, Illusion, and Other Realities*, 115.

[166] *Sourcebook in Indian Philosophy*, 328.

[167] Ibid. Excerpts from *The Vimsatika of Vasubandhu*. Another objection: "If, in waking time as well as in a dream, representations may arise although there are no true objects, then, just as the world naturally knows that dream objects are non-existent,

why is it not naturally known of objects in waking time? . . ." Answer: "Before we have awakened we cannot know that what is seen in the dream does not exist." Explanation: "After this, the purified knowledge of the world which is obtained takes precedence; according to the truth it is clearly understood that those objects are unreal. The principle is the same" (ibid., 332).

168 *Sourcebook in Indian Philosophy*, 328.

169 Radhakrishnan, *Indian Philosophy*, 456.a

170 Samkara is said to have been taught by Govinda, one of Gaudapada's students (ibid., 452).

171 Ibid., 456, 491–92, 497.

172 "The entire complex of phenomenal existence is considered as true as long as the knowledge of the Brahman being the Self of all has not arisen; just as the phantoms of a dream are considered to be true until the sleeper wakes. For as long as a person has not reached the true knowledge of the unity of the Self, so long it does not enter his mind that the world of effects with its names and objects of right knowledge and its reality of actions is untrue . . . The case is analogous to that of a dreaming man who in his dream sees manifold things, and, up to the moment of waking, is convinced that his ideas are produced by real perception without suspecting the perception to be a merely apparent one" (*Sourcebook in Indian Philosophy*, 527–28).

173 Ibid., 534.

174 Ibid., 526.

175 Radhakrishnan, *Indian Philosophy*, 498.

176 "Now, when one is sound asleep, composed, serene, and knows no dream, that is the Self (Atman). . . . That is the immortal, the fearless. That is Brahman" (*Sourcebook in Indian Philosophy*, Chandogya Upanisad, 8.11.1, 68).

177 At this point, both Hinduism and Buddhism, like religions in the West, are not altogether clear or consistent about whether this liberation from the wheel of rebirth is a spiritual journey only, or whether the purpose of life is to perfect the physical body on earth and therefore gain personal immortality. The Upanishads suggest that personal immortality is the ultimate goal, while Buddhism appears to support the perfection of the spiritual self through karma and reincarnation (Humphreys, *Buddhism*, 103–7).

178 Wilson, *Buddhism*, 188; *The Dhammapada*, chap. 14, "The Awakened One."

179 "The ignorant are awake in their sense-life, which they think is daylight: To the seer it is darkness" (*Bhagavad-Gita*, 43).

180 In trying to disprove the illusory character of the world, some Indian thinkers take the tack of an empiricist. Professor O'Flaherty mentions a criticism of idealism made by a clown in a Tibetan text, "All that you teach is untrue; what we perceive with the five senses is not an illusion" (*Dreams, Illusion, and Other Realities*, 116). As noted above in the discussion on the British empiricists, this statement is true in relation to the body and the five senses.

Chapter Twelve: The Origin of Scientific Theory

181 Stephen Hawking writes, "I shall take the simple-minded view that a theory is just a model of the universe, or a restricted part of it, and a set of rules that relate quantities in the model to observations that we make. It exists only in our minds and does not have any other reality (whatever that might mean). A theory is a good theory if

it satisfies two requirements: It must accurately describe a large class of observations on the basis of a model that contains only a few arbitrary elements, and it must make definite predictions about the results of those observations" (Hawking, *Brief History of Time*, 9).

[182] In discussing the worldview of the atomists, Drew A. Hyland writes, "In keeping with the aims of modern science, the atomists offer a thoroughgoing mechanistic account of the universe. No gods or universal Mind arranged the atoms or first set things in motion; there is no teleological claim that the atoms are or ought to be arranged according to what is 'best,' but conglomerations of atoms form into and dissolve from things and qualities 'according to necessity,' which under the circumstances seems to mean very much the same as 'by chance' (Hyland, *Origins of Philosophy*, 286 [footnote omitted]).

[183] Physics Nobel laureate Steven Weinberg believes the advances of modern science have uncovered the universe's lack of direction. In his book *The First Three Minutes* he writes, "The more the universe seems comprehensible, the more it also seems pointless." (Weinberg, *First Three Minutes*, 154). Addressing comments on this remark in a later book, he writes, "It does not seem to me to be helpful to identify the laws of nature as Einstein did with some sort of remote and disinterested God. The more we refine our understanding of God to make the concept plausible, the more it seems pointless." (Weinberg, *Dreams of a Final Theory*, 256). In his book *The Creation of Matter*, physicist Harald Fritzsch makes a similar point in a chapter titled "God and the Absurd Universe": "We do not even know the reason for the big bang, nor do we know whether there was a reason at all. Questions like these and about what happened before the big bang are pointless. Looked at from the vantage point of objective knowledge, the universe makes no sense: it is absurd" (*Creation of Matter*, 274).

[184] See, e.g., Trefil, *Moment of Creation*: "According to the big-bang theory, the universe began as a singular point of infinite density some 10 to 20 billion years ago and pulsed into being in a vast explosion that continues to this day." See also Silk, Szalay, and Zel'dovich, "Large-Scale Structure of the Universe."

[185] See Dawkins, *Blind Watchmaker*. Dawkins writes, "Natural selection, the blind, unconscious, automatic process which Darwin discovered, and which we now know is the explanation for the existence and apparently purposeful form of all life, has no purpose in mind. It has no mind and no mind's eye" (5).

Chapter Thirteen: From Naïve Realism to the big bang

[186] See Angeles, *Dictionary of Philosophy*, 20. Angeles explains, "In general, atomism is the materialistic view that the universe consists of ultimately simple, independent, and irreducible entities that are only contingently interrelated (as opposed to necessarily interrelated) to form objects."

[187] Hyland, *Origins of Philosophy*, 285.

[188] Ibid., 286.

[189] See Lederman, *God Particle*.

[190] Silk, Szalay, and Zel'dovich, "Large-Scale Structure of the Universe," 37; Barrow and Silk, "Structure of the Early Universe," 21; Hawking, *Brief History of Time*, 46, 49–50.

[191] Wilczek, "Cosmic Asymmetry between Matter and Antimatter," 164, 166.

[192] Barrow and Silk, "Structure of the Early Universe," 27; Weinberg, *Dreams of a Final Theory*, 173.

[193] Barrow and Silk, "Structure of the Early Universe," 21.

[194] Hawking, *Brief History of Time*, 46.

[195] Lederman, *God Particle*, 1 (first emphasis in original; second added).

[196] Simpson, *Meaning of Evolution*, 115. "The scientist accepts space-time, along with matter and energy, as the *givens* of the physical world, and their ultimate origin remains a mystery" (Jones, *Physics for the Rest of Us*, 79).

[197] Mayr, "Concerns of Science."

[198] Smolin, in *The Trouble with Physics*, writes that the belief in a "real world out there" motivates scientists "to do the hard work needed to become a scientist and contribute to the understanding of nature" (9). Similarly, Lisa Randall, in her book, *Knocking on Heaven's Door*, writes that because science "relies on objects interacting through mechanical causes and their effects," the "materialist view is . . . essential" (55).

[199] See Kelly, *Human Hologram*; Farrell, *Manifesting Michangelo*; Lipton, *Biology of Belief*.

[200] Maddox, *What Remains to Be Discovered*, 58.

[201] Mather and Boslough, *The Very First Light*, 7.

[202] Ibid., 69.

[203] Rees, *Before the Beginning*, 161.

[204] Fritzsch, *Creation of Matter*, 3.

[205] Seife, *Alpha and Omega*, 65.

[206] Gamov, *Creation of the Universe*.

[207] Ibid., Preface to second printing.

[208] See Wilczek and Devine, *Longing for the Harmonies*. The authors write, "We have found a hint that our rich and varied world can arise, *not quite from nothing*, but from just one very simple and definite thing—namely energy. For, *given* energy alone, we have seen how nature in her fecundity will *give* us material . . . that, rearranged and combined in complicated ways, can certainly generate a rich and varied world" (188 [emphasis added]). Thus, if material scientists are *given* infinite energy they believe the world can be explained. But as we have seen, this approach assumes more than it explains.

Chapter Fourteen: The Big Bang Explodes

[209] Pasachoff and Filippendko, *The Cosmos*, 330-31.

[210] Physicists compare this phenomenon to an expanding balloon; at any point on the balloon an observer sees other points moving away at a uniform rate.

[211] Gamov's coworkers Ralph A. Alpher and Robert Herman contributed to this inference. See Barrow and Silk, "The Structure of the Early Universe," 25, *Particle Physics in the Cosmos*.

[212] Ibid.

[213] "COBE Causes Bang in Cosmology," *Science News* (May 2, 1992), 292.

[214] Barrow and Silk, "The Structure of the Early Universe," 25; Silk, Szalay, and Zel'dovich, "Large-Scale Structure of the Universe," 37; Rees, *Before the Beginning*, 50 ("The only plausible explanation for the microwave background is that it has survived from an epoch when our entire universe was hot, dense, and opaque.");

Hogan, *Little Book of the Big Bang*, 77 ("This light, called the 'cosmic background microwave background radiation' is left over from the Big Bang."); Halliwell, "Quantum Cosmology and the Creation of the Universe," 76 (the hot big bang model predicts "the glow of radiation left over from the initial explosion, which permeates the universe").

[215] Material scientists prefer not to associate the big bang with what we think of as an explosion. Rather, they say that it was really a sudden expansion—or inflating—of space itself, similar to a balloon. For our purposes, it makes no difference whether scientists hypothesize the big bang as an explosion or some other cataclysmic event.

[216] Hogan, *Little Book of the Big Bang*, 84.

[217] Galileo is attributed with the observation that the "laws of nature are written in the language of mathematics." Many scientists have made note of the "unreasonable effectiveness of mathematics" in explaining this random and mindless material world. See Wigner, "Unreasonable Effectiveness of Mathematics in the Natural Sciences"; see also Weinberg, *Dreams of a Final Theory* ("It is very strange that mathematicians are led by their sense of mathematical beauty to develop formal structures that physicists only later find useful, even where the mathematician had no such goal in mind") (157).

[218] See Goldsmith, *Runaway Universe*, 2–3, 31–32; Hogan, *Little Book of the Big Bang*, chap. 4. Hubble made the discovery by noting that the light spectra coming from distant galaxies shifted to longer wavelengths than those found by similar source of light on Earth. Galaxies farther away showed more of a shift to the longer (or redder) wavelengths, thus leading Hubble to conclude that the more distant galaxies are receding at a faster rate. See Peterson, "State of the Universe," 232.

[219] Goldsmith, *Runaway Universe*, 34. Despite the supposed uniformity of the cosmic expansion, it applies only to the universe on the largest of scales. Clearly, individual clumps of matter are not expanding; neither is the solar system, the Milky Way galaxy of which we are a part, or even collections of galaxies. Rather, large clouds of galaxies are gradually flying away from each other (Hogan, *Little Book of the Big Bang*, 48).

[220] Barrow and Silk, "The Structure of the Early Universe," 23.

[221] See Krauss and Turner, "Cosmic Conundrum," 66, 70.

[222] Ibid., 71.

[223] See Sincell, "Eight Great Mysteries."

[224] See Krauss and Turner, "Cosmic Conundrum," 66, 70.

[225] See Krauss, "Cosmological Antigravity."

[226] Ibid., 33.

[227] Krauss and Turner, "Cosmic Conundrum," 66, 70.

[228] Randall, *Knocking on Heaven's Door*, 374–75.

[229] Ibid., 375; Ellis, Does the Multiverse Really Exist?, 38, 42.

[230] Randall, *Knocking on Heaven's Door*, 375.

[231] Ellis, Problems with the Multiverse; Weinberg, Living in the Multiverse, in Bernard Carr (ed.), *Universe, or Multiverse?*

Chapter Fifteen: The Flatness and Horizon Problems

[232] Pasachoff and Filippenko, *The Cosmos*, 378–81; Guth, *Inflationary Universe*, 21–26; Goldsmith, *Runaway Universe*, 50–51.

[233] Pasachoff and Filippenko, *The Cosmos*, 378–81; Guth, *Inflationary Universe*, 21–26; Goldsmith, *Runaway Universe*, 50–51.

[234] Paul Davies presents a similar example in his book *The Accidental Universe*, 91.

[235] Pasachoff and Filippenko, *The Cosmos*, 379.

[236] See Goldsmith, *Runaway Universe*, 51.

[237] Pasachoff and Filippenko, *The Cosmos*, 403.

[238] Krauss, "Dark Matter in the Universe," 3, 10.

[239] Davies, *Accidental Universe*, 91.

[240] Guth, *Inflationary Universe*, 24.

[241] Gribbin, *In Search of the Big Bang*, 348.

[242] Krauss and Turner, "Cosmic Conundrum," 71.

[243] Guth and Steinhardt, "Inflationary Universe," 179.

[244] Guth, *Inflationary Universe*, 183.

Chapter Sixteen: The Amazing Inflating Universe

[245] Nadis, "Inflation Comes of Age," 33, 34.

[246] See Pasachoff and Filippenko, *The Cosmos*, 405. The size of the universe at this very early age is still too large for light—the faster conveyer of information—to have traveled between opposite ends.

[247] Ibid.

[248] Maddox, *What Remains to Be Discovered*, 54.

[249] Nadis, "Inflation Comes of Age," 34.

[250] Stenger, "Anthropic Design" ("The inflationary big bang offers a plausible, natural scenario for the uncaused origin and evolution of the universe, including the formation of order and structure—without the violation of any laws of physics") (42).

[251] See Veltman, "Higgs Boson," 76.

[252] Guth, *Inflationary Universe*, 238 (emphasis in original).

[253] Nadis, "Inflation Comes of Age."

[254] Guth and Steinhardt, "Inflationary Universe," 191.

[255] Peebles, "Making Sense out of Cosmology."

[256] Maddox, *What Remains to Be Discovered*, 55.

[257] Lindley, *End of Physics*, 182.

[258] Timothy Ferris, in his book, *The Whole Shebang*, compares the fine-tuning of parameters required by inflation to the "Canadian Royal Air Force games in which you manipulate a board that tilts on two axes to maneuver a ball bearing through a maze without letting it fall through one of the many holes that dot the board" (238).

[259] Lindley, *End of Physics*, 182.

[260] Steinhardt, "Inflation Debate," 36.

[261] See, e.g., Pasachoff and Filippenko, *The Cosmos*, 406.

[262] Scientists themselves show no hesitation in acknowledging the absurd universe their theories describe. See, e.g., Turner, "Absurd Universe "; Fritzsch, *Creation of Matter*, chap. 17 ("God and the Absurd Universe").

Chapter Seventeen: A Material World That Should Not Be

[263] See Wilczek, "Cosmic Asymmetry between Matter and Antimatter," 164.

[264] Professor Wilczek writes, "A particle and its antiparticle have often been discovered simultaneously when the two were created as a pair by high-energy collision in a

particle accelerator. Such collisions always seem to yield matter and antimatter in equal quantities" (ibid., 164); Wilczek and Devine, *Longing for the Harmonies*, 178.

[265] Zee, *Fearful Symmetry*, 39.

[266] Trefil, *Moment of Creation*, 36–37.

[267] Zee, *Fearful Symmetry*, 39.

[268] Trefil, *Moment of Creation*, 30–31.

[269] Professor Wilczek writes, "It was long assumed that the laws of nature express no preference for matter or antimatter" ("Cosmic Asymmetry," 164).

[270] Ibid., 168. Other scientists express genuine surprise that the universe is made of matter. James S. Trefil writes, "Although we cannot yet send probes to great distances outside of our solar system, we can nonetheless sample the material elsewhere in our galaxy by examining cosmic rays. . . . Therefore, even though we are temporarily locked into our own neighborhood of space, we constantly receive visitors [i.e., cosmic rays] from elsewhere. By studying these visitors, we can learn something of the region from which they came. As far as the matter-antimatter question is concerned, such studies yield an unambiguous result: our galaxy, and most likely all the galaxies in our region, are composed of matter" (*Moment of Creation*, 64). Similarly, Professor Wilczek reports, "The prevailing opinion among astronomers and astrophysicists is that matter dominates over anti-matter in the present universe" ("Cosmic Asymmetry," 166). Thus, after years of study, physicists have reached an unsurprising conclusion: the world is made out of matter.

[271] Wilczek, "Cosmic Asymmetry," 166.

[272] Halliday and Resnick, *Fundamentals of Physics*, 1127; Hawking, *Brief History of Time*, 76.

[273] Trefil, *Moment of Creation*, 41.

[274] Ibid., 115.

[275] Weinberg, "Decay of the Proton," 115.

[276] Ibid.

[277] Wilczek, "Cosmic Asymmetry," 167-68.

[278] Halliday and Resnick, *Fundamentals of Physics*, 1131.

[279] Weinberg, "Decay of the Proton," 110–11.

[280] Trefil, *Moment of Creation*, 174; Guth, *Inflationary Universe*, 108–9.

[281] Trefil, *Moment of Creation*, 174–75.

[282] Ibid., 175.

Chapter Eighteen: Twenty Invisible Universes

[283] Goldsmith, *Runaway Universe*, 66; Pasachoff and Filippenko, *The Cosmos*, 327–28, 398–99. The current breakdown appears to be this: About 4.4 percent of the total matter in the universe is normal matter but only about 1 percent is actually visible. About 23 percent is dark matter, which cannot be detected, and the rest—73 percent—is dark energy, which cannot be detected either (398).

[284] The three laws are as follows: (1) planets orbit the sun following elliptical paths with the sun at one focus, (2) a line connecting the sun and any planet sweeps out equal areas in equal times, and (3) the square of the period of a planet's revolution around the Sun is proportional to the cubes of their mean distance from the Sun. See *The Cosmos*, 86-87.

[285] Pasachoff and Filippenko, *The Cosmos*, 325.

[286] Singh, *Big Bang*, 378.

[287] Rubin, "Dark Matter in Spiral Galaxies," 96.

[288] Ibid., 98.

[289] Ibid. A similar prediction is that the spiral should flatten out into a bar.

[290] Ibid., 96.

[291] In light of the wild goose chase for dark matter, astronomer Warren Brown of the Harvard-Smithsonian Center of Astrophysics is quoted as observing, "Is [dark matter] really out there? We certainly see evidence of something that cannot be explained by our understanding of gravity, but the more time goes on, the more I worry we have the wrong theory" ("Chasing Dark Matter," 10).

Chapter Nineteen: This Accident Never Happened

[292] Davies, *God and the New Physics*, 168-69.

[293] Black holes are collapsed stars that generate gravity so powerful nothing can escape, including light. See Hawking, *Brief History of Time* chap. 6.

[294] Davies, *God and the New Physics*, 178; Penrose, *Emperor's New Mind*, 354.

[295] This number is based on a lottery having a one in 10 million chance of winning, or one in 10. The laws of probability state that to find the odds of winning x days in a row, the odds are squared x times, or in this instance, the exponents are added x times.

[296] See, e.g., Weinberg, *First Three Minutes*; Trefil, *Moment of Creation*, 74.

[297] Cooper, *Introduction to the Meaning and Structure of Physics*, 404.

[298] Veltman, "Higgs Boson," 76.

[299] Ibid.

[300] Ibid.

[301] See Halliday and Resnick, *Fundamentals of Physics*, 1126.

[302] Davies, *Accidental Universe*, 55.

[303] Halliday and Resnick, *Fundamentals of Physics*, 1126.

[304] Cooper, *Introduction to the Meaning and Structure of Physics*, 235.

[305] Zee, *Fearful Symmetry*, 157.

[306] Barrow and Silk, "Structure of the Early Universe," 35.

[307] Jones, *Physics for the Rest of Us*, 243.

[308] Ibid.

[309] See Dyson, "Disturbing the Universe," 52.

[310] Trefil, *Moment of Creation*, 74.

[311] Paul Davies suggests that what may lie at the base of the universe is a simple mathematical principle that physics can describe. He writes, "Physics is proclaimed 'necessary' in the same way that God is proclaimed necessary by theologians. Should we then conclude that *God is physics* as some philosophers (such as Plato) seem to have done?" (*God and the New Physics*, 55).

[312] Pagels, *Dreams of Reason*, 157–58.

[313] Paul Davies writes, "Given the laws of physics, the universe can create itself. Or, stated more correctly, the existence of a universe without an external first cause need no longer be regarded as conflicting with the laws of physics. . . . Given the laws, the existence of the universe is not itself miraculous. This makes it seem as if the laws of physics act as the 'ground of being' of the universe. Certainly, as far as most scientists

are concerned, the bedrock of reality can be traced back to these laws. They are the eternal truths upon which the universe is built" (*Mind of God*, 73).

314 "Pantheism" is the "doctrine that God is not a personality, but that all laws, forces, manifestations, etc. of the self-existing universe are God" (*Webster's New World Dictionary*, 1026).

315 Steven Weinberg, quoting from an Einstein interview, notes that Einstein believed in "Spinoza's God who reveals Himself in the orderly harmony of what exists, not in a God who concerns himself with fates and actions of human beings" (*Dreams of a Final Theory*, 245 [from an interview in the *New York Times*, April 25, 1929]). Spinoza observes, "Nature . . . is always the same and everywhere one. . . . Her laws and rules, according to which all things are and are changed from form to form, are everywhere and always the same, so that there must also be one and the same method of understanding the nature of all things whatsoever, that is to say, by the universal laws and rules of Nature" (*Ethics*, 128).

Chapter Twenty: Creation against the Tide of Entropy

316 Cooper, *Introduction to the Meaning and Structure of Physics*, 104–9.

317 See Jones, *Physics for the Rest of Us*, 105.

318 Cooper, *Introduction to the Meaning and Structure of Physics*, 107–10.

319 See Halliday and Resnick, *Fundamentals of Physics*, 525.

320 Ibid.

321 Ibid.

322 See Jones, *Physics for the Rest of Us*, 104–5.

323 *Introduction to the Meaning and Structure of Physics*, 103.

324 Ibid. See also Davies, *Mind of God*, 47.

325 Greene, *Fabric of the Cosmos*, 173–74 (emphasis in original).

326 See Chaisson, *Cosmic Evolution*.

Chapter Twenty-One: Material Science's Mathematical Laws

327 See Cooper, *Introduction to the Meaning and Structure of Physics*, 53.

328 Ibid., 54.

329 Ibid., 55. Kepler could not contain his pleasure. He writes, "What sixteen years ago I urged as a thing to be sought—that for which I joined Tycho Brahe—at last I have brought to light, and recognize its truth beyond my fondest expectations. The die is cast, the book is written, to be read either now or by posterity, I care not which—it may well wait a century for a reader, as God has waited six thousand years for an observer" (Kepler, *De Harmonia Mundi*, quoted in *Introduction to the Meaning and Structure of Physics*, 54). See also Boorstein, *The Discovers*, 305–12.

330 See, e.g., Weinberg, *Dreams of a Final Theory*; Zee, *Fearful Symmetry*.

331 Cooper, *Introduction to the Meaning and Structure of Physics*, 56–60.

332 It is because gravity is proportional to mass that objects of different weight fall at the same rate in a vacuum (ibid., 62).

333 Ibid., 187–88.

334 Ibid., 535.

Chapter Twenty-Two: The Melody Came First

[335] Although we address Darwinian evolution in more detail in section 3, it must be understood that the validity of Darwinian evolution depends upon the truth of the big bang model. Darwinian evolution is by definition materialistic and mindless. It hopes to explain the rise of the living world without recourse to God or a Mind, much like a young man (or God?) who strikes off on his own desiring to find his way through life, without the crutch of a father.

[336] As Paul Davies writes in the *Accidental Universe*, "If gravity were stronger, stars would burn out faster. An increase in G [force of gravity] by a factor of ten would totally alter the structure of the solar system over the time scale of its present history. The Earth, for example, would no longer exist, having been vaporized as the sun approaches its red giant phase at the end of its hydrogen consumption" (55).

[337] Ibid., 39.

[338] Barrow, "Inconstant Constants," 57; Barrow, *Constants of Nature*; Davies, *Accidental Universe*.

[339] Barrow, *Constants of Nature*, 142.

[340] Barrow, "Inconstant Constants," 58.

[341] Barrow and Tipler, in their book *The Anthropic Cosmological Principle*, define the so-called Weak Anthropic principle as follows: "The observed values of all physical and cosmological quantities are not equally probable but they take on values restricted by the requirement that there exist sites where carbon-based life can evolve and by the requirement that the Universe be old enough for it to have already done so" (16).

[342] Vilenkin, "Anthropic Predictions: The Case of the Cosmological Constant;" Weinberg, "Living in the Multiverse," both in Carr, *Universe or Multiverse?*

[343] Chalmers, "The Higgs? Damn . . . ," 34, 37.

[344] Ellis, "Does the Mulitverse Really Exist?" 38, 43.

[345] See Davies, "Universes Galore: Where Will It End?" in *Universe or Multiverse?*

Chapter Twenty-Three: Material Science's Last Model

[346] Rosenblum and Kuttner, *Quantum Enigma*, 81.

[347] Greene, *Elegant Universe*, 118–19.

[348] Ibid., 129.

[349] Ibid., 203.

[350] As Nobel Prize–winning physicist Richard Feynman observed, "Science is what we have learned about how to keep from fooling ourselves." See Deutsch, *Beginning of Infinity*.

[351] Smolin, *Trouble with Physics*, xiv–xv. See also Woit, *Not Even Wrong*; Woit writes, "The fundamental reason that superstring theory makes no predictions is that it isn't really a theory, but rather a set of reasons for hoping that a theory exists." (175). Further, "As long as no one quite knows exactly what string theory is, its proponents are able to hold very optimistic views about it." (185).

Chapter Twenty-Five: Freezing a Phantom World

[352] See Hyland, *Origins of Philosophy*, 115.

[353] Ibid. 122.

[354] Ibid. 153.

[355] Copleston, *History of Philosophy*, vol. 1, part 1, 79.

356 Hyland, *Origins of Philosophy*, 285–86, 297–98.

357 Robert Boyle is famous for discovering the inverse square law of gases. This law states that the volume of gas is inversely proportional to the pressure applied to it. See Partington, *Short History of Chemistry*, 70–73; see also March, *Physics for Poets*, 157. The atomic theory nicely accounts for Boyle's law. The increased pressure is viewed as compressing atoms in the gas.

358 Partington, *Short History of Chemistry*, 164.

359 Ibid., 153.

360 Ibid., 153–54.

361 Ibid., 169.

362 See March, *Physics for Poets*, 154–56.

363 Quoted from Partington, *Short History of Chemistry*, 153–54.

364 See March, *Physics for Poets*, 155.

365 A total of 106 elements are known, of which 83 occur naturally and 23 that have been manufactured in the scientific laboratory (Asimov, *Atom*, 7).

366 Hawking, in *A Brief History of Time*, equates the discovery of a complete theory of the universe with knowing the mind of God (175). See also Davies, *Mind of God*.

367 Asimov, *Atom*, 21.

368 See *Ascent of Man*, vol. 10 (television series).

369 Dorin, *Chemistry: The Study of Matter*, 308.

370 Ibid., 308–9.

371 Ibid., 310. It may be noted that the atomic number or ranking of an element on the table was later found to correspond with the number of electrons in the atom. Ibid. Material scientists, using the reductionist form of reasoning, say that these electrons explain the periodic table and the variety in the elements (Ne'eman and Kirsh, *Particle Hunters*, 10). To the contrary, the correlation between atomic number, which is simply the ranking of an element on a table, and the number of electrons exhibit no necessary relation. Using electrons to explain the properties of atoms continues material science's habit of explaining the operation of big particles by the operation of small particles. This approach may reduce the physical size of the object requiring explanation, but it marks no progress at explaining why these particles, of whatever size, decided to arrange themselves in mathematical patterns.

Chapter Twenty-Six: To the Center of the Atom Hypothesis

372 Cathode rays are created when an electric current is passed between opposite electric charges in a nearly airless glass tube. The negatively charged terminal is called the cathode, and the positive terminal the anode (Cooper, *Introduction to the Meaning and Structure of Physics*, 309–10). When pierced screens are inserted in the tube to focus the ray, a glow forms at the positively charged end of the tube, as if the rays are coming from the negative terminal. These are cathode rays, better known as the source responsible for the television picture tube.

373 Ibid., 310.

374 See March, *Physics for Poets*, 163–64.

375 Ibid., 164–65.

376 Cooper, *Introduction to the Meaning and Structure of Physics*, 313.

377 Ibid., 314–15.

378 Ibid., 322–23.

379 Once again, the experiment concerned shooting particles at metal sheets. This time, alpha particles were sent through thin gold foil to measure the angle of deflection. Rutherford found that although most of the particles went through the foil undisturbed, some rays were deflected at large angles. This result indicated that the alpha particles had struck a more massive particle. "It was almost as incredible as if you fired a 15-inch shell at a piece of tissue paper and it came back and hit you" (statement of Rutherford, quoted in Cooper, *Introduction to the Meaning and Structure of Physics*, 318).

380 Davies, *Accidental Universe*, 45, 79.

381 Ibid., 45, table 4.

382 Ne'eman and Kirsh, *Particle Hunters*, 8.

383 Cooper, *Introduction to the Meaning and Structure of Physics*, 323.

384 Ibid.

385 Eddington, *Nature of the Physical World*, xii, xiii, xvi.

Chapter Twenty-Seven: The Voyage Stops at the Quantum

386 March, *Physics for Poets*, 169.

387 *Introduction to the Meaning and Structure of Physics*, 323.

388 Professor Cooper observes, "It would be hard to say why any two atoms would be alike, for there would be no reason for two hydrogen atoms, even if they each consisted of a single electron orbiting about a single positive charge, to have their electrons in exactly the same orbits" (ibid., 324).

389 Professor Cooper describes a black body as a "little oven which has been so designed that any light emitted from its inside surface bounces back and forth many times before it is permitted to leave a hole built into the oven" (ibid., 325). The important point about the little oven is that according to the continuous-energy theory, radiation should be emitted from the oven in all possible wavelengths that would fit through the hole. Since energy was assumed to be continuous, there should be an infinite number of wavelengths between the size of the oven's hole and 0. For example, in a dimmer switch there is typically no first notch; the knob moves continuously from 0 to light. Because energy from the oven should be distributed evenly among all possible wavelengths, most of the light should be emitted in radiation having the shortest wavelengths, or in the ultraviolet spectrum. But the hole did not glow violet as this theory predicted; it glowed like most ovens do—first a dull red, then bright red, to white and blue (ibid., 325).

390 Ibid., 535.

391 Ibid., 177.

392 energy (E) = Planck's constant (h) x frequency of light (v)

393 Cooper, *Introduction to the Meaning and Structure of Physics*, 326–27.

394 Ibid.

395 Ibid., 325. Here another one of science's coincidences quietly enters the picture. To fix the spacing of the allowed orbits, Bohr chose none other than Planck's constant (ibid., 333). This constant, which had been invented to account for the way heated bodies glow, now fixes the electron's orbit around the nucleus. But why should these two values be related?

Chapter Twenty-Eight: From Matter to Waves and Back Again

[396] A *standing wave* is a wave, such as that formed on a guitar string, which acts between two fixed points. Because the endpoints are fixed, the only allowable waves are those with wavelengths that fit between them in whole number integers. In other words, the length of the wave must fit totally across the string, or in whole-number fractions—one-half, one-third, one-quarter, etc. See March, *Physics for Poets*, 86–87.

[397] Cooper, *Introduction to the Meaning and Structure of Physics*, 343–45.

[398] March, *Physics for Poets*, 80.

[399] Ibid., 208–9.

[400] Cooper, *Introduction to the Meaning and Structure of Physics*, 170–75.

[401] Colliding particles, such as a cue ball breaking the rack in billiards, bounce off each other in predictable ways. The colliding balls do not merge together to form one larger particle or cause other balls to disappear at the moment of collision. Colliding waves, however, under the right conditions, do join together and cancel each other. If the crest (bump) in one wave meets the crest (bump) of another wave, the two waves will form a wave twice as high as they pass through each other. This event is known as *constructive interference*. In contrast, if the trough (dip) of one wave meets the crest (bump) of another wave, the two waves cancel each other out, provided the wave heights are the same. For example, if the waves are water, the water will be still at the point where the opposite waves meet. This event is called *destructive interference* (see March, *Physics for Poets*, 84–85). When Young passed light through the two holes on his screen, interference patterns formed on the photographic plate.

[402] Cooper, *Introduction to the Meaning and Structure of Physics*, 174–77.

[403] In Young's time this now obvious point was controversial because Newton held the view that light was a particle (ibid., 170–72).

[404] Ibid., 328–30; Halliday and Resnick, *Fundamentals of Physics*, A19–A20. In the photoelectric effect, Einstein explained the peculiar manner in which light ejected electrons from a metal plate by postulating that light was emitted in discrete packets called *photons*. Waves could not bump things out of metal, but these light-things could.

[405] Hey and Walters, *Quantum Universe*, 5–12; March, *Physics for Poets*, 227.

[406] The experimental results are the same for photons.

[407] Hey and Walters, *Quantum Universe*, 10–11.

[408] See, e.g., Jones, *Physics for the Rest of Us*, 164; Heisenberg, *Physical Principles of the Quantum Theory*, 10.

[409] Jones, *Physics for the Rest of Us*, 332.

[410] Al-Khalili, *Quantum: Guide for the Perplexed*, 66.

[411] Davies and Gribbin, *Matter Myth*.

[412] Heisenberg, Debate between Plato and Democritus, in Wilber (ed), *Quantum Questions*

[413] Rosenblum and Kuttner, *Quantum Enigma*.

[414] Laughlin, *Different Universe*, 55.

[415] Stapp, *Mindful Universe*, 9.

[416] D'Espagnat, "Quantum Theory and Reality."

[417] Lindley, *End of Physics*, 62.

[418] Wigner, "Remarks on the Mind-Body Question."

[419] Henry, "Mental Universe," 29.

420 Rosenblum and Kuttner, *Quantum Enigma*.

Chapter Twenty-Nine: The Many-Worlds Interpretation

421 See, e.g., Lindley, *Boltzman's Atom*, 168, 170, 228–29.

422 Ditfurth, *Origins of Life*, 177.

423 See Wolf, *Taking the Quantum Leap*, 119.

424 Al-Khalili writes, "Most physicists believe . . . that we are not tracking the motion of an electron; its wave function is all we have at our disposal to describe it. More than that: the electron itself doesn't even exist as a simple classical particle with a definite location at each time. Its influence is spread out over space. How this can be we can never find out. All we have is the wave function, and that is just a set of numbers (with physical significance, of course). As soon as we look the wave function is said to 'collapse' and the electron becomes a localized particle" (*Quantum*, 67). "At each point in space the wave function is defined by two numbers known as its real and imaginary parts. Joining all the "real" numbers together produces one wave and the "imaginary" numbers another, and the full wave function is a combination of the two" (68).

425 Byrne, "Many Worlds of Hugh Everett," 98.

426 Weinberg, *Dreams of a Final Theory*, 82–84; 232. Weinberg, after pointing out some of the inconsistencies of the Copenhagen interpretation, expresses his preference for the "realist approach to quantum mechanics of Hugh Everett [the originator of the many-worlds interpretation] and others, [where] there is just one wave function describing all phenomena, including experiments and observers, and the fundamental laws are those that describe the evolution of this wave function" (232).

427 Byrne, "Many Worlds of Hugh Everett," 102–3.

428 Davies, *God and the New Physics*, 116.

429 DeWitt, "Quantum Mechanics and Reality."

430 Ibid., 101.

431 Davies reports that "bizzare though the theory may seem, it is supported, in one version or another, by a large number of physicists as well as by some philosophers" (*Mind of God*, 217).

432 As Herbert explains, "A human being . . . dwells in just one of these universes (at a time) and cannot perceive the other[s]. . . . Likewise the inhabitants of the other . . . universes are not aware of their parallel partners" (*Quantum Reality*, 173). See also Davies, *Mind of God*, 190. "Scientifically, the many-universes theory is unsatisfactory because it could never be falsified: what discoveries would lead a many-worlder to change her/his mind?"

Chapter Thirty: The World's Most Accurate Theory

433 Davies and Gribbin, *Matter Myth*, chap. 6, "Quantum Weirdness."

434 Jones, *Physics for the Rest of Us*, 164.

435 Richard P. Feynman, in a published lecture, states, "Working out another system to replace Newton's laws took a long time because phenomena at the atomic level were quite strange. One had to lose one's common sense in order to perceive what was happening at the atomic level. Finally in 1926, an 'uncommon-sense' theory was developed to explain the 'new type of behavior' of electrons in matter. It looked

cock-eyed, but in reality it was not: it was called the theory of quantum mechanics" (Feynman, *QED: The Strange Theory of Light and Matter*, 5).

[436] *QED*, 8.

[437] Jones, *Physics for the Rest of Us*, 291.

[438] Professor Feynman, using a somewhat more conservative measure of accuracy (one part in a billion), puts these numbers in perspective by explaining that if the distance from Los Angeles to New York was measured with the same accuracy, "it would be exact to the thickness of a hair" (*QED*, 7).

[439] In Plato's *Republic*, the great thinker pictured men imprisoned in a cave with their vision fixed staring only at shadows on the wall. This shadow-world was all they knew. At some point, prisoners are led out of the cave and into the sunlight to see reality in all its three-dimensional color and fullness. It was Plato's view that the common person, blinded by the prejudices and unquestioned teachings of the day, lives in a world of secondary reality, and the goal of philosophy is to help people ascend the path out of the cave into the ideal world of the forms and eventually to the highest form, that of the Good (Hamilton and Cairns, eds., *Collected Dialogues of Plato*).

[440] See generally Weyl, *Symmetry*.

Chapter Thirty-One: The Particle Zoo

[441] Professor Stephen Goldman, in his Teaching Company lecture series, *Science Wars: What Scientists Know and How They Know It*, advances the idea that scientists ultimately pursue not ultimate reality, not what truly *is*, but what he calls scientific objects, models of physical reality that scientists use to map the world. As scientific knowledge progresses and thinking evolves, these objects become more refined and elaborate; we move from Democritus's atoms to Thompson's plum pudding, to the Bohr solar system, to quantum waves-particles and quarks. What is finally real? Ultimately, only our ability to dream. Outside of the dreaming power there is nothing. In the mind-created home that we made for ourselves, we can perhaps continue mapping the inner workings of our dream-world with increasingly accurate mental pictures. But eventually, and perhaps the time is now, we stop and realize that we have reached the end of this particular science project. We have gone as far down into the puzzle as we need to in order to put the picture together. We do not need to grind the pieces any further.

[442] See Kane, "Dawn of Physics beyond the Standard Model," 66; Kane, *Particle Garden*, chap. 4.

[443] Kane, "Dawn of Physics Beyond the Standard Model," 70.

[444] See, e.g., Dawkins, *God Delusion*.

[445] See Schwarz, *Tour of the Subatomic Zoo*; Kane, *Particle Garden*; Steven Pollock, lecture, "The Particle Zoo," in Teaching Company course, "*Particle Physics for Non-Physicists: A Tour of the Microcosmos*" (2003); Asimov, *Atom*.

[446] See Kane, *Particle Garden*, 29–33; Quigg, "Elementary Particles and Forces," 3, 5; Harari, "Structure of Quarks and Leptons."

[447] Quigg, "Elementary Particles and Forces," 3, 5. *Hadrons* are a family of particles that are subject to the strong force. Particles not subject to the strong force are called *leptons*. See Glashow, "Quarks with Color and Flavor," 19.

[448] Particle spin is what one would think it is—the rotation of a particle upon its axis, like a top. Spin was originally devised to account for certain observed properties of

the electron; see Cooper, *Introduction to the Meaning and Structure of Physics*, 392–93. Today spin is listed as a property of all elementary particles, along with mass and electrical charge (see ibid., 455, table 46.1). All particles spin in integer multiples of a basic rotation rate. For example, the rotation rate of the proton is 10 times per second (Trefil, *Moment of Creation*, 56).

[449] Halliday and Resnick, *Fundamentals of Physics*, 1134–35.

[450] See Harari, "Structure of Quarks and Leptons," 204.

[451] http://en.wikipedia.org/wiki/Standard_Model.

[452] Lederman, *God Particle*.

[453] Kane, "Dawn of Physics Beyond the Standard Model," 70.

[454] Halliday and Resnick, *Fundamentals of Physics*, 1, 139.

[455] Trefil, *Moment of Creation*, 76, 83; *Introduction to the Meaning and Structure of Physics*, 144.

[456] Trefil, *Moment of Creation*, 76, 83; Georgi, "Unified Theory of Particle and Forces."

[457] Schwartz, *A Tour of the Subatomic Zoo*, 20.

[458] Kane, "Dawn of Physics Beyond the Standard Model," 70.

[459] Kane, *Particle Garden*, 63.

[460] "Perhaps the best way to think of W's and Z's is as objects like photons but very heavy, whose effects are crucial for the sun to shine, and that cause most quarks and leptons to be unstable" (ibid., 64).

[461] Trefil, *Moment of Creation*, 78, 82; Zee, *Fearful Symmetry*, 163–67; Jones, *Physics for the Rest of Us*, 288–90.

[462] Georgi, "Unified Theory of Particle and Forces," 56–57.

[463] See Cooper, *Introduction to the Meaning and Structure of Physics*, 372. "The brunt of Heisenberg's argument is that it is not possible with the material in fact available, to measure the position and momentum simultaneously; it is the nature of the world that the experiment conceived by the classicists . . . is not actually something that can be done."

[464] Georgi, "Unified Theory of Particle and Forces," 57.

[465] Heisenberg writes, "We cannot completely objectify the result of an observation, we cannot describe what 'happens' between this observation and the next" (*Physics and Philosophy*, 50).

[466] See Lederman, *God Particle*, 278.

[467] Georgi, "Unified Theory of Particle and Forces," 57.

[468] Lederman, *God Particle*, 278.

[469] Georgi, "Unified Theory of Particle and Forces," 57.

[470] Professor Hooft writes, "In effect a virtual particle borrows or embezzles a quantity of energy, but it must repay the debt before the shortage can be noticed." See "Gauge Theories of the Forces between Elementary Particles," 82.

[471] James S. Trefil writes, "But one thing that we have learned from quantum mechanics is that there is no such thing as empty space with nothing whatsoever in it. The uncertainty principle . . . guarantees that even in the best vacuum, virtual particles and antiparticles will be created and annihilated continuously" (*Moment of Creation*, 205).

[472] See Jones, *Physics for the Rest of Us*, 289.

[473] Kane, "Dawn of Physics beyond the Standard Model," 74.

[474] Trefil, *Moment of Creation*, 83.

[475] Ibid. Some believe that "there are strong theoretical grounds for thinking" they actually exist (Weinberg, "Decay of the Proton," 110); others concede the particles are "conjectured" (Quigg, "Elementary Particles and Forces," 5); and still others seem to take the graviton as established. Stephen Hawking, for example, states the "gravitational force between the sun and the earth is ascribed to an exchange of gravitons between the particles that make up these two bodies" (*Brief History of Time*, 70).

[476] Trefil, *Moment of Creation*, 83, 199.

[477] Professor Lederman writes, "In this view, so-called empty space can be awash with these ghostly objects: virtual photons, virtual electrons and positrons, quarks and anti-quarks, even (with oh god how small a probability) virtual golf balls and anti-golf balls" (*God Particle*, 278).

Chapter Thirty-Two: The God Particle

[478] Lederman, *God Particle*, 21.

[479] See, e.g., Greene, *Elegant Universe and Hidden Reality*; Randall, *Warped Passages*; Kaku, *Physics of the Future*; Ferris, *Whole Shebang*; Davies, *God and the New Physics*; Kirshner, *Extravagant Universe*; Hawking, *Brief History of Time*.

[480] See, e.g., Ferris, *Whole Shebang*: "Particles can thus be viewed as evidence of symmetry-breaking events that took place in the big bang. . . . In this sense the cosmos has *de*volved from a state of perfect (or nearly perfect) symmetry to the rubble heap of broken symmetries we find around us today" (214–16) (emphasis in original).

[481] An electron volt equals the "energy gained by an electron in passing from a point of low potential to a point one volt higher in potential" (*Webster's New Third International Dictionary*, 733).

[482] Kane, "Mysteries of Mass," 44. A "giga" equals 1 billion.

[483] Randall, *Knocking on Heaven's Door*, 287.

[484] Lederman, God Particle.

[485] Veltman, "Higgs Boson." John Maddox, in *What Remains to Be Discovered*, writes that the "importance of the Higgs particle cannot be exaggerated. It is exclusively an invention of the standard model." ("Higgs Boson," 83).

[486] Veltman, "Higgs Boson," 76. According to one Nobel Prize–winning scientist, "The Higgs boson is thought to generate the masses of all the fundamental particles; in a manner of speaking, particles 'eat' the Higgs boson to gain weight."

[487] Another bizarre feature of the Higgs field is that the mathematical equation underlying the theory incorporates a value that, when squared, is a negative number. Most of us know that a positive number multiplied by itself always equals a positive number; the same is true for negative numbers. To suppose that nature conforms itself to imaginary mathematical values seems to be pushing things a bit, to put it mildly. See Kane, *Supersymmetry*, 149–52.

[488] Weinberg, *Dreams of a Final Theory*, 196–200.

[489] Veltman writes, "From a physical point of view little is gained by proposing that the Higgs boson accounts for mass. It is not known, for example, why the Higgs field should couple more strongly to some particles than it does to others. Nor do investigators understand how the mass of the Higgs boson itself (which is not known) comes about, although it is generally presumed to be dominantly through a self-interaction with the Higgs field. In this sense ignorance about the origin of particle

masses is replaced by ignorance about particle-Higgs couplings, and no real knowledge is gained" ("Higgs Boson," 78).

[490] Riordan, Tonelli, and Wan, "The Higgs at Last," 66, 70.

[491] Slezak, "New Particle, New Questions," 6; http://blogs.scientificamerican.com/observations/2013/03/15/its-official-weve-found-the-higgs-boson-but-which-one/

[492] Riordan, Tonelli, and Wan, "The Higgs at Last," 69.

[493] In the 1980s, material scientists obtained U.S. government funding to build an $8 billion, ten-mile-long particle accelerator known as the "Superconducting Supercollider" to track down the Higgs particle. After spending about $2 billion of the budget, in 1993 Congress shut off the funding to the dismay of the material science community. Meanwhile, several European nations combined resources to fund the multibillion-dollar Large Hadron Collider, originally scheduled for start-up in 2008 but only recently brought on line. For more information see http://en.wikipedia.org/wiki/Superconducting_Super_ColliderWikipedia.com.

[494] See Folger, "Higgs: What Causes the Weight of the World."

[495] See Kane, "Mysteries of Mass," 41.

[496] Weinberg, *Dreams of a Final Theory*, 219.

[497] See Sheldrake, *Science Set Free*.

[498] Turner, "Absurd Universe."

Chapter Thirty-Three: The Universe That Appeared between Picture Frames

[499] Guth and Steinhardt, "Inflationary Universe," 193. In this article, both "absolutely nothing" and "almost nothing" are used to describe the beginning of it all. See also Tryon, "Is the Universe a Vacuum Fluctuation?" 396; Gribbin, *In Search of the Big Bang*, 372–78.

[500] Gribbin, *In Search of the Big Bang*, 372.

[501] Hawking, *Brief History of Time*, 105–6.

[502] One of the odd—and deceptive—features of some modern science writers is the manner in which they convert wild speculation into fact over a few pages of a book. In *A Universe from Nothing*, for example, Lawrence Krauss writes that "*if* inflation is indeed responsible for all the small fluctuations in the density of matter and radiation that would later result in the gravitational collapse of matter into galaxies and stars and planets and people, then it can be truly said that we are all here today because of quantum fluctuations" (98). Buried in this passage are a number of enormous assumptions including (a) whether a quantum wave actually exists independent of consciousness, (b) whether inflation occurred, and (c) how these mindless forces created a world of endless order. In the very next chapter, however, Krauss's high-order speculation suddenly becomes an established fact. He writes, "The structures we can see, like stars and galaxies, were all created by quantum fluctuations from nothing" (105).

[503] Guth, *Inflationary Universe*, 12.

[504] Barrow and Silk, "Structure of the Early Universe," 32.

[505] Davies and Gribbin, *Matter Myth*, 143; Barrow and Silk, "Structure of the Early Universe," 32.

[506] Through various mathematical calculations, these scientists imagine that the universe has zero energy (itself an interesting coincidence) where the total gravitational energy exactly counterbalances the mass energy. When this zero net energy system

meets up with a vacuum of some larger area in which the universe is contained, the vacuum fluctuates, presumably forcing the virtual particles into reality. Tryon, "Is the Universe a Vacuum Fluctuation?" 397; Barrow and Silk, "Structure of the Early Universe," 32; see Thomsen, "New Inflationary Nothing Universe"; Davies and Gribbin, *Matter Myth*, 164–65.

[507] Guth and Steinhardt, "Inflationary Universe," 194.

[508] Tryon, "Is the Universe a Vacuum Fluctuation?" 397.

Chapter Thirty-Four: Where Did the Struggle Begin?

[509] "Creation and evolution, between them, exhaust the possible explanations for the origin of living things" (Futuyma, *Science on Trial*, 197).

[510] Mayr, *This is Biology: The Science of the Living World*, 33.

[511] *Kitzmiller v. Dover Area School District*, 400 F. Supp.2d 707 (M.D. Pa. 2005).

[512] Mayr, *This is Biology*, 34.

[513] See, e.g., Morris, ed., *Scientific Creationism*.

[514] In the *Kitzmiller* decision, Judge Jones agreed with the plaintiff's lead expert, Dr. Miller, that "from a practical perspective, attributing unsolved problems about nature to causes and forces that lie outside the natural world is a 'science stopper'" (*Kitzmiller*, 736).

[515] One scientist writes, "Science 'discovers' truth by a never ending process of elimination; the single logical possibility still standing after careful scrutiny of all available data and all competing hypotheses becomes—for as long as it withstands new challenges—the theory upon which new research builds" (Berra, *Evolution and the Myth of Creationism*, 3). "It is in the spirit of science to reject views of the old masters when new evidence sheds doubt on established views" (Byerly, *Primer of Logic*, 47). "Nothing in science is ever proven; we merely achieve greater and greater confidence in the validity of our hypotheses as more data support or fail to support them" (Futuyma, *Science on Trial*, 222). "At its best, science challenges not only nonscientific views but established scientific views as well" (ibid., 163).

[516] "We are very complex organisms; but everything in us, including what constitutes a brain, is built of pretty ordinary stuff" (Berra, *Evolution and the Myth of Creationism*, 77); Ernst Mayr writes, "Even at the molecular level, the macromolecules that characterize living beings do not differ in principle from the lower-molecular-weight molecules that are the regular constituents of inanimate nature, but they are much larger and more complex. This complexity endows them with extraordinary properties not found in inert matter" (*Toward a New Philosophy of Biology*, 14).

[517] See Mayr, *Toward a New Philosophy of Biology*, "An Analysis of the Concept of Natural Selection," 95–113.

[518] See Futuyma, *Science on Trial*, 223–24.

[519] Darwin, *Origin of the Species by Means of Natural Selection*, 117. Darwin also recognized that despite the "geometric increase" of individuals, populations remained constant (see Mayr, *One Long Argument*, 72, fig. 1). These facts suggested that individuals necessarily compete for limited food sources in the struggle for life. Ibid. Darwin was clearly inspired by the ideas of Thomas Malthus, who, with respect to the human population, had theorized that unless reproduction rates were checked by war, famine, disease, and other factors, population growth would exceed food supply.

See Malthus, *Essay on the Principle of Population*. See also Mayr, *One Long Argument*, 71–80, for a discussion of Darwin's debt to Malthus.

[520] Darwin, *Origin of the Species*, 115.

[521] Ibid.

[522] Mayr, *Toward a New Philosophy of Biology*, 96: "Selection simply is the fact that in every generation a few individuals among the hundreds, thousands, or millions of offspring of a set of parents survive and are able to reproduce because these individuals happened to have a combination of characteristics that favored them under the constellation of environmental conditions they encountered during their lifetime."

[523] Ibid., 13–17.

Chapter Thirty-Five: An Imperfect Darwinian World

[524] Morris, ed., *Scientific Creationism*, 208, 247.

[525] See Mayr, *One Long Argument*, 12–25.

[526] Ibid.

[527] *Origin of the Species*, 455; Mayr, *One Long Argument*, 24.

[528] Morris, ed., *Scientific Creationism*, 11–13.

[529] Mayr, *One Long Argument*, 58–60.

[530] Ernst Mayr writes that by the 1940s, "no competent biologist . . . was left who still believed in any final causation of evolution" (*One Long Argument*, 65–66). "Finalism is no longer part of any respectable philosophy." (66).

[531] Mayr, *Toward a New Philosophy of Biology*, 96.

[532] Morris, ed., *Scientific Creationism*, 203, 207.

[533] Mayr, *One Long Argument*, 69.

[534] Mayr, *Toward a New Philosophy of Biology*, 176.

[535] Ibid. Darwin writes in the *Descent of Man*, "The main conclusion here arrived at . . . is that man is descended from some less highly organized form. The grounds upon which this conclusion rests will never be shaken, for the close similarity between man and the lower animals in embryonic development, as well as in innumerable points of structure and constitution . . . are facts which cannot be disputed. . . . The great principle of evolution stands up clear and firm. . . . He who is not content to look, like a savage, at the phenomena of nature as disconnected, cannot any longer believe that man is the work of a separate act of creation. He will be forced to admit that the close resemblance of the embryo of man to that, for instance, of a dog—the construction of his skull, limbs, and whole frame on the same plan with that of other mammals . . . all point in the plainest manner to the conclusion that man is the co-descendant with other mammals of a common progenitor" (excerpted from Appleman, *Darwin*, 196-96).

[536] Tax, ed., *Evolution after Darwin*, vol. 1, "The Evolution of Life"; Simpson, "History of Life,"117, 135.

[537] Mayr, *Toward a New Philosophy of Biology*, 202. "Soon it was demonstrated that even animals and plants, seemingly so different from each other, could be derived from a common, one-celled ancestor."

[538] Berra, *Evolution and the Myth of Creationism*, 75–78.

[539] See, e.g., Eigen, "Origin of Genetic Information," 18.

[540] Darwin capitalized "nature" at times. See, e.g., *Origin of the Species*, 117.

[541] Dawkins, *Ancestor's Tale*, 141–42, 167.

[542] Asimov, *Atom*, 17. After questioning the sanity of any scientist who doubts the existence of atoms, Asimov goes on to say that the theory of evolution is "under constant attack from people who are either ignorant of science or, worse, who allow their superstitions to overcome what knowledge they might have." See *also* Dawkins, *Ancestor's Tale*, 13 ("Beyond all sane doubt, . . . our history is evolutionary, and . . . all living creatures are cousins").

[543] Dawkins calls Darwinism biology's a "grand unifying theory" (Dawkins, *Ancestor's Tale*, 1).

Chapter Thirty-Six: Darwin's Common Ancestor

[544] Darwin, *Origin of the Species*, 455.

[545] Mayr, *One Long Argument*, 24. Professor Futuyma concurs: "Almost all scientists hold that . . . the first simple living things developed from inanimate matter, through natural chemical and physical processes. All species that have ever lived—bacteria, viruses, plants, and animals—are descended from these first forms of life (almost certainly from a single ancestral form" (*Science on Trial*, 10).

[546] Berra, *Evolution and the Myth of Creationism*, 70–74.

[547] Monod, *Chance and Necessity*, vii.

[548] Campbell, *Biology*: "Reductionism—reducing complex systems to simpler components that are more manageable to study—has been the most powerful strategy in biology" (4).

[549] Berra, *Evolution and the Myth of Creationism*, 72–73.

[550] Campbell, *Biology*, 92.

[551] Dawkins, *Blind Watchmaker*, 115.

[552] See Campbell, *Biology*, chap. 6.

[553] Cells do not have a gender. The use of the word "daughter" is traditional. See Campbell, *Biology*, 229.

[554] Ibid., 228–29. "The ability of organisms to reproduce their kind is the one phenomenon that best distinguishes life from inanimateness. . . . The perpetuation of life is based on the reproduction of cells. . . . What is most remarkable about cell division is the fidelity with which genetic programs are passed along, without dilution, from one generation of cells to the next." See also chap. 14 in Campbell's volume, "The Chromosomal Basis of Inheritance."

[555] Ibid.

[556] Cairns-Smith, *Seven Clues to the Origin of Life*, 9.

[557] Dawkins, *Blind Watchmaker*, 172.

[558] Lampton, *DNA and the Creation of New Life*.

[559] Dawkins, *Ancestor's Tale*, 184–85. Dawkins explains that a toolbox subroutine is a pre-set sequence of instructions for performing certain computer operations, such as hiding the cursor when it's not needed. The nucleus of a cell, he believes, contains the toobox of DNA routines for carrying out a variety of biochemical functions. He writes, "Different cells, for example, liver cells, bone cells and muscle cells, string 'calls' of these routines together in different orders and combinations when performing particular cell functions including growing, dividing, or secreting hormones."(ibid).

[560] Ayala, "Mechanisms of Evolution," 58.

561 See Edey and Johanson, *Blueprints: Solving the Mystery of Evolution*, for a clear discussion of the history of evolution theory and the DNA molecule.

562 Campbell, *Biology*, 311.

563 Theodosius Dobzhansky, excerpts from "The Nature of Heredity," in Appleman, *Darwin*, 270.

564 Crick, "Genetic Code: III," 94.

565 An enzyme is a protein molecule that acts as a catalyst in biological processes (Berra, *Evolution and the Myth of Creationism*, 167). They are "chemical agents that change the rate of a reaction without being consumed by the reaction" (Campbell, *Biology*, 102). In this section they are referred to as "worker molecules" because they carry out the activities involved in molecular processes.

566 Campbell, *Biology*, 335. Scientists found that the four chemical bases in the DNA molecule spell out sixty-four possible three-letter words. Sixty of the words code for one of the twenty amino acids, which necessarily means that some words specify the same amino acid. One word tells cell processes to start protein synthesis, and the remaining three words act as signals to stop.

567 Campbell, *Biology*, 74–76.

568 Ayala, "Mechanisms of Evolution," 59; ohttp://en.wikipedia.org/wiki/List_of_organisms_by_chromosome_count

569 Campbell, *Biology*, 326.

570 Ibid.

571 Dobzhansky, "Nature of Heredity," 271.

572 Campbell, *Biology*, 330.

573 Ibid.

574 Cell processes add roughly fifty nucleotides per second to the new DNA strand (ibid., 316).

575 Ibid., 318–19.

576 This account is greatly simplified. Further cell processes regulate how much of given protein the cell should make, where to put the protein, and numerous other processes.

577 See, e.g., Dawkins: "At some point a particularly remarkable molecule was formed by accident. We will call it the replicator. It may not necessarily have been the biggest or the most complex molecule around, but it had the extraordinary property of being able to create copies of itself. This may seem a very unlikely sort of accident to happen. So it was. It was exceedingly improbable" (*Selfish Gene*, 16).

578 Mayr, *Growth of Biological Thought*, 583–84.

579 Darwin, *Origin of the Species*, 223–24; Mayr, *One Long Argument*, 44–46.

580 Dawkins, *Blind Watchmaker*, 43.

581 Ibid., 249.

582 See Mayr, *Toward a New Philosophy of Biology*, Essay 14, "The Concept of Finality."

583 Dawkins, *Blind Watchmaker*, 50.

Chapter Thirty-Seven: How Material Science Believes Life Began

584 This thought, that material scientists need only an initial supply of matter to explain the entire universe, is reflected in thinkers as diverse as the eighteenth-century German philosopher Immanuel Kant and Professor Alan Guth, the originator of the inflationary universe model. As Kant said, "Give me matter, and I will construct a

world out of it!" (Kant, "Universal Natural History and Theory of the Heavens").
Alan H. Guth, in turn, writes that he only needs one "speck" of matter to begin the
wild ride of his inflationary model. *Quoted in* Nadis, "Inflation Comes of Age."

585 Dawkins, *Ancestor's Tale*, 563 and following.

586 de Duve, *Vital Dust*, 9.

587 Mayr, *One Long Argument*, 104.

588 Campbell, *Biology*, 513.

589 Ibid., 513–14; Eigen, Gardiner, Schister, and Winkler-Oswatitsch, "Origin of
Genetic Information," 15.

590 Quoted from Dawkins, *Ancestor's Tale*, 560.

591 Dickerson, "Chemical Evolution and the Origin of Life."

592 Ibid.

593 Ibid.

594 Cairns-Smith, *Seven Clues to the Origin of Life*, 6.

595 Eigen et al., "Origin of Genetic Information," 88.

596 Futuyma, *Science on Trial*, 223; Berra, *Evolution and the Myth of Creationism*, 73–74.

597 Berra, *Evolution and the Myth of Creationism*, 74: "There is no doubt that all of the
building blocks of life can be accounted for with the various simulation experiments."

598 Campbell, *Biology*, 15–19; Berra, *Evolution and the Myth of Creationism*, 74.

599 Shapiro, *Origins*, 104.

600 Ibid.

601 Ibid.

602 Ibid.

603 Dickerson, "Chemical Evolution and the Origin of Life," 36.

604 Shapiro, *Origins: A Skeptic's Guide to the Creation of Life on Earth*, 105.

605 Ibid., 116.

606 Dickerson, "Chemical Evolution and the Origin of Life," 35.

607 Campbell, *Biology*, 513, 518.

608 Hazen, *Genesis—The Scientific Quest for Life's Origin*, 93.

609 Shapiro, *Origins: A Skeptic's Guide to the Creation of Life on Earth*, 128.

610 This estimate assumes odds of 1 in 10 of winning the lottery on a given day.

611 Ditfurth, *Origins of Life*, 29.

612 Ibid.

613 See, e.g., Campbell, *Biology*, 18 (from interview with Stanley Miller).

614 Davies, *God and the New Physics*, 69. Davies goes on to cite the work of I. Prigogine
as suggestive of a way out of this predicament. Prigogine believes that living things,
including humans, can be viewed as *dissipative structures*. This term means a being
that stays out of thermal equilibrium, and therefore disorder, by transforming energy
into order. This theory, however, is like using the law of gravity to explain the Big
Dipper; the order exhibited in the world is much too deep and pervasive, if not
artistic, to be explained by the general notion that living things convert energy to
order. In our world, it is here argued that order comes from an intelligent source (the
mind) that also serves as the ultimate source of energy (the will to live).

615 Shapiro, *Origins: A Skeptic's Guide to the Creation of Life on Earth*, 108.

616 See Eigen et al., "Origin of Genetic Information;" Campbell, *Biology*, 516–17;
Dawkins, *Ancestor's Tale*, 570–74.

617 Mayr, *Growth of Biological Thought*, 354, 361.

[618] Manfred Eigen and his colleagues write, "Darwinian competition evaluates the fitness of each mutant RNA according to its rate and accuracy of self-replication and its stability" ("Origin of Genetic Information," 106). See also Campbell, *Biology*, 518.

[619] Eigen et al., "Origin of Genetic Information," 99.

[620] Ibid., 91.

[621] See Cairns-Smith, *Seven Clues to the Origin of Life*, 42–44.

[622] Freeman, "Handmade Cell," *Discover* 46, 48.

[623] Ibid. See also Waldrop, "Finding RNA Makes Proteins Gives 'RNA World' a Big Boost," *Science* 1397; Campbell, *Biology*, 516-17.

[624] See Freeman, "Handmade Cell," 48.

[625] Ibid.

[626] Ibid.

[627] Ibid., 52.

[628] Campbell, *Biology*, 518; Hoyle, *Intelligent Universe*.

[629] See Crick, *Life Itself*, 116.

[630] Campbell, *Biology*, 518.

[631] Crick, *Life Itself*, 129.

[632] See Johnson, *Darwin on Trial*, 100–111.

[633] See National Research Council, Limits of Organic Life in Planetary Systems.

[634] Cairns-Smith, *Seven Clues to the Origin of Life*; see Dawkins, *Ancestor's Tale*, 567.

[635] Cairns-Smith, *Seven Clues to the Origin of Life*, 66.

[636] Ibid. 107.

[637] See, e.g., Casti, *Paradigms Lost*, 140-42; Dawkins, *Ancestor's Tale*, 567.

Chapter Thirty-Eight: The Melody Came First

[638] See, e.g., Smith and Szathmary, *Origins of Life*; Wills and Bada, *Spark of Life*; de Duve, *Vital Dust and Life as a Cosmic Imperative*; Lahav, *Biogenesis*; Hazen, *Genesis—The Scientific Quest for Life's Origin*; and Schopf, ed., *Life's Origin*.

[639] Lederman, *God Particle*, 1.

[640] Dawkins, *Ancestor's Tale*, 1, 13.

[641] See Berra, *Evolution and the Myth of Creationism*.

[642] *Kitzmiller v. Dover Area School District*, 400 F. Supp.2d 707 (M.D. Pa. 2005).

[643] See Stenger, "Anthropic Design."

Chapter Thirty-Nine: Darwin's Common Ancestor Populates the Globe

[644] Berra writes, "Since life evolved from non-living matter, at some point we must arbitrarily draw a line and say that everything past that point is alive" (*Evolution and the Myth of Creationism*, 75).

[645] Darwin, Origin of the Species, 348.

[646] Ibid., 349.

[647] Ibid., 309.

[648] Ibid., 115.

[649] See Mayr, *Toward a New Philosophy of Biology*, 96: "The Concept of Natural Selection."

[650] Darwin, *Origin of the Species*, 348.

[651] Ibid., chaps. 10, 11; Campbell, *Biology*, 434; Mayr, *One Long Argument*, 22–23.

[652] Darwin, *Origin of the Species*, 344.

[653] Ibid.

[654] Ibid., 346–47.

[655] The branching of organisms from a common source also fits well with the existing "tree of life" classification scheme (Campbell, *Biology*, 435).

[656] Darwin, *Origin of the Species*, 435.

[657] Campbell, *Biology*, 434.

[658] Ibid., 435; Darwin questioned why the "hand of a man, formed for grasping, that of a mole for digging, the leg of the horse, the paddle of the porpoise, and the wing of the bat, should all be constructed on the same pattern, and should include the same bones, in the same relative positions?" (*Origin of the Species*, 415; see also Berra, *Evolution and the Myth of Creationism*, 20–21).

[659] Campbell, *Biology*, 435.

[660] Ibid.

[661] Darwin, *Origin of the Species*, 419.

[662] Campbell, *Biology*, 436.

[663] Ibid.

[664] Campbell, *Biology*, 437; see Dawkins, *Ancestor's Tale*, 19–22.

[665] Darwin, *Origins of the Species*, 350.

[666] Mayr, *Toward a New Philosophy of Biology*, 202.

[667] Mayr, *One Long Argument*, 94, 99.

[668] Darwin, *Origin of the Species*, 357.

[669] Ibid., 366–67.

[670] Ibid., 367–68.

[671] Mayr, *Growth of Biological Thought*, 452.

[672] Dawkins, *Ancestor's Tale*, 141–43, 166–67. Dawkins acknowledges the improbability of these animals crossing the ocean via conveniently available mangrove rafts, but concludes that despite the "massive improbability," it "only had to happen once" (142).

[673] Darwin, *Origin of the Species*, 384.

[674] Bert James Loewenberg notes that Darwin was "rarely inhibited by epistemological reservations. Darwin accepted the facts of nature as provisionally given; he did not begin his inquiry with the problem of knowledge. He was in no sense an aggressive empiricist; he simply was not concerned with metaphysics" ("Mosaic of Darwinian Thought," in Appleman, *Darwin*, 214).

[675] Mayr, *Growth of Biological Thought*, 450. Professor Mayr notes that during the "heyday," of this theory, "there was no ocean that was not crisscrossed by land bridges."

[676] Darwin, *Origin of the Species*, 357, 376.

[677] Ibid., 359.

[678] Mayr, *Growth of Biological Thought*, 447.

[679] Dawkins, *Ancestor's Tale*, 142–44, 167.

[680] Ibid., 451–52.

Chapter Forty: Darwin's Gradual Leaps

[681] Professor Mayr explains that there are two types of evolution: vertical and horizontal. "Vertical evolutionism deals with adaptive changes in the time dimension, while horizontal evolutionism deals with the origin of new diversity in the space dimension,

that is, with the origin of incipient species and new species as populations move into new environmental niches" (Mayr, *One Long Argument*, 20).

[682] Wald, "Origins of Life."

[683] Darwin, *Origin of the Species*, 439. Professor Futuyma agrees: "To pass from primordial molecules to the first cell, and from the first cell to complex animals and plants had to take time—billions of years" (*Science on Trial*, 207).

[684] Mayr, *Toward a New Philosophy of Biology*, 170.

[685] Abell, "Ages of the Earth and the Universe."

[686] Berra, *Evolution and the Myth of Creationism*, 78.

[687] See Attenborough, *Life on Earth*, 18.

[688] The scientific dating of the universe actually could correspond to the age of the dream, but I doubt it. Considering the maturation of our civilization, this seems like a young world.

[689] See Gish, *Evolution: The Challenge of the Fossil Record*, 35.

[690] Ibid., 44.

[691] Mayr, *One Long Argument*, 18–19.

[692] Ibid., 19.

[693] Darwin, *Origin of the Species*, 223–34.

[694] Mayr, *One Long Argument*, 44–47.

[695] *Origin of the Species*, 219.

[696] Ibid.

[697] See Dawkins, *Blind Watchmaker*, chap. 3.

[698] Mayr, *The Growth of Biological Thought*, 517; Mayr, *One Long Argument*, 100.

[699] Mayr, *One Long Argument*, 100–101.

[700] Ibid., 36.

[701] Ibid. Professor Mayr defines evolution as the theory that the "world is not constant or recently created nor perpetually cycling but rather is steadily changing and that *organisms are transformed in time*" (36) (emphasis added).

[702] See ibid., 44-47.

[703] Darwin, *Origin of the Species*, 142; Dawkins, *Blind Watchmaker*, 232.

[704] Though the speed of the transition between a specie and its predecessor may vary, there should nonetheless be a continuum linking the two forms. See Mayr, *Toward a New Philosophy of Biology*, 205, 457 (Essay 26).

[705] Darwin, *Origin of the Species*, 444.

[706] Mayr, *The Growth of Biological Thought*, 352.

[707] Mayr, *One Long Argument*, 44.

[708] Professor Mayr explains that the term "random . . . when applied to variation, means that it is not in a response to the needs of the organism" (*One Long Argument*, 143).

[709] Ayala, "Mechanisms of Evolution," 56, 59.

[710] See, e.g., Dayhoff, "Computer Analysis of Protein Evolution," 111, 118; Edey and Johanson, *Blueprints*, 360.

[711] See Edey and Johanson, *Blueprints*, 353 (tree showing descent of man from apes).

[712] Berra, *Evolution and the Myth of Creationism*, 171, 174.

[713] See, e.g., Edey and Johanson, *Blueprints*, 353.

[714] Dayhoff, "Computer Analysis of Protein Evolution," 118.

[715] Ibid.

[716] Darwin, *Origin of the Species*, 438.

[717] Ibid., 297.

[718] Ibid., 293·

[719] Ibid., 292.

[720] The story is told how Thomas H. Huxley admonished Darwin for "loading up" his theory of evolution with "an unnecessary difficulty in adopting *Natura non facit saltum* [Nature makes no jumps] so unreservedly" (Mayr, *One Long Argument*, 46).

[721] Darwin, *Origin of the Species*, 438 (emphasis in original).

[722] Darwin said, "But, as by this theory innumerable transitional forms must have existed, why do we not find them embedded in countless numbers in the crust of the earth?" (ibid.).

[723] Darwin said that the reason transitional forms are not found in the fossil record "mainly lies in the record being incomparably less perfect than is generally supposed." (ibid., 206).

[724] Ibid., 438.

[725] Ibid.

[726] Ibid., 341.

[727] See Gish, *Evolution: The Challenge of the Fossil Record*.

[728] Berra, in *Evolution and the Myth of Creationism*, states, "This lavish fossil record speaks loudly and clearly to the fact that evolution has occurred" (46).

[729] Raup, "Geological and Paleontological Arguments of Creationism," 147, 156 (emphasis added).

[730] Gould, *Panda's Thumb*, 181.

[731] Ibid., 189.

[732] Dawkins, *Blind Watchmaker*, 229.

[733] Campbell, *Biology*, 484.

[734] Mayr, *One Long Argument*, 153.

[735] Denton, *Evolution: A Theory in Crisis*, 162.

[736] See Levinton, "Big Bang of Animal Evolution," 84; Simpson, *Meaning of Evolution*, 14–22.

[737] Levinton, "Big Bang of Animal Evolution," 84.

[738] Ibid.

[739] Campbell, *Biology*, 636.

[740] Levinton, "Big Bang of Animal Evolution," 84.

[741] Quoted from Johnson, *Darwin on Trial*, 54.

[742] Frazier, "Science and Religion—Conflicting or Complementary?"

[743] Mayr, "Concerns of Science."

[744] *Kitzmiller*, 736.

[745] Mayr, *This is Biology*, 33-34.

[746] Simpson, *Meaning of Evolution*, 15; Ayala, "Mechanisms of Evolution," 56; Futuyma, *Science on Trial*, 116; Mayr, *Toward a New Philosophy of Biology*, 96.

Chapter Forty-One: The Illusion of Natural Selection

[747] Darwin, *Origin of the Species*, 115.

[748] Mayr, *What Evolution Is*, 14 ("given the fact of evolution").

[749] Dawkins, *Ancestor's Tale*, 14 (arguing that "beyond all sane doubt . . . our history is evolutionary").

[750] Mayr, *One Long Argument*, 88; *Toward a New Philosophy of Biology*, 98.

[751] Mayr, *Toward a New Philosophy of Biology*, 99; Ayala, "Mechanisms of Evolution," 59.

[752] Ayala, "Mechanisms of Evolution," 59.

[753] Mayr, *Toward a New Philosophy of Biology*, 98–99.

[754] Ayala, "Mechanisms of Evolution" 56; Mayr, *Toward a New Philosophy of Biology*, 98.

[755] Mayr, *Toward a New Philosophy of Biology*, 98.

[756] Ibid., 219, 226.

[757] Dobzhansky, "Evolution and Environment," 409.

[758] Dawkins advocates cumulative selection in his book *The Blind Watchmaker.*

[759] See ibid., chap. 3, "Accumulating Small Change."

[760] Ibid.

[761] Darwin, *Origin of the Species*, 76.

[762] Mayr, *Toward a New Philosophy of Biology*, 226; Dobzhansky, "Evolution and Environment," 409.

[763] Ayala, "Mechanisms of Evolution," 56. Mendel found, by the intensive study of pea plants, that offspring inherit traits in whole packages; traits are not blended. A yellow pea plant fertilized with a green pea plant will produce either a yellow pea plant or a green pea plant; it will not produce chartreuse peas.

[764] See Edey and Johanson, *Blueprints*, chap. 5.

[765] When the double-helix splits, the new DNA molecule copies the body-building instructions contained in the parent molecule. This inherited code then directs the construction of an organism duplicating the parent. Provided no errors are made in the copying process, the daughter cell replicates the parent exactly. See Dobzhansky, "Nature of Heredity," 271–72.

[766] A mutation is an "error in the replication of DNA prior to its translation into protein" (Ayala, "Mechanisms of Evolution," 58); Campbell, *Biology*, 448–49.

[767] See Futuyma, *Science on Trial*, 136.

[768] Ayala, "Mechanisms of Evolution," 59-60.

[769] Campbell, *Biology*, 448; Dobzhansky, "Evolution and Environment," 409.

[770] See Futuyma, *Science on Trial*, 136.

[771] See Mayr, *Toward a New Philosophy of Biology*, 135, 146. Though mutations are the ultimate source of new raw material in the gene pool, the process of sexual reproduction, in which chromosomes from the two sexes mix together into new combinations, produces the most variety upon which natural selection can act. Mutations add new ingredients to the recipe; recombination mixes existing ingredients into new living things.

[772] See Dawkins, *Blind Watchmaker*, 5.

[773] See, e.g., Ayala, "Mechanisms of Evolution," 59; Mayr, *Toward a New Philosophy of Biology*, 99; Dawkins, *Blind Watchmaker*, 47; Gould, *Ever Since Darwin.*

[774] Futuyma, *Science on Trial*, 114.

[775] Ibid., 136.

[776] See Mayr, *The Growth of Biological Thought*, 354; Mayr, *Toward a New Philosophy of Biology*, 98–99.

[777] See Mayr, *Toward a New Philosophy of Biology*, 97–98. Professor Mayr rebukes critics who claim natural selection is wholly a chance process.

[778] Mayr, *One Long Argument*, 88.

[779] Futuyma, *Science on Trial*, 224.

[780] Ibid., 147.

781 Dawkins, *Blind Watchmaker*, 49 (emphasis in original).

782 Ibid., 41.

783 Gould, *Ever Since Darwin*, 42.

784 Ibid. 44.

785 Dawkins, *Blind Watchmaker*.

786 Dawkins, *Selfish Gene*, 34.

787 The description is attributed to Nobel Prize–winning molecular biologist Francois Jacob. See Lewin, *Thread of Life*, 66.

788 Gould, *Ever Since Darwin*, 44.

789 Dawkins writes, "Natural selection is the blind watchmaker, blind because it does not see ahead, does not plan consequences, has no purpose in view. Yet the living results of natural selection overwhelmingly impress us with the appearance of design as if by a master watchmaker, impress us with the illusion of design and planning" (*Blind Watchmaker*, 21). Dawkins here illustrates how the material science world-view can distort one's thought process. Faced with a world of infinite order, but no mind to explain it, Dawkins concludes that the order is really an illusion. In the Real Dream, in contrast, the order is as real as the world and responds to our infinite need for regularity.

790 Alfred Lord Wallace, a contemporary of Darwin, is actually recognized as a coinventor of the concept of natural selection (Dawkins, *Ancestor's Tale*, 265).

791 Devlin, *Dictionary of Synonyms and Antonyms*, 48.

792 Ibid., 254.

793 Futuyma, *Science on Trial*, 224.

794 Dawkins, *Blind Watchmaker*, 48.

795 Ibid., 5, 21.

796 See Futuyma, *Science on Trial*, 116. Professor Futuyama uses the term "initial conditions" to describe the ordering mechanism of the second step. Professor Mayr explains, "The theory of natural selection has enormous heuristic value and permits so-called predictions under specified environmental conditions" (Mayr, *Toward a New Philosophy of Biology*, 96).

797 Mayr, *Toward a New Philosophy of Biology*, 96.

798 Ibid.; Futuyma, *Science on Trial*, 116. "Selection is an *a posteriori* phenomenon—that is, it is the survival of a few individuals who are either luckier than the other members of the population or have certain attributes that give them superiority in the particular context" (Mayr, *One Long Argument*, 87). Professor Futuyama provides the following example: Experimenters place two different strains of bacteria in a glass vessel containing a nutritious broth, which is continuously replenished. The two types of bacteria multiply and are removed at a regular rate. Over time, it will be found that one type of bacteria performs better in the specific broth mixture, overtakes the other strain, and eventually accounts for all the bacteria left in the vessel. In this example, the broth mixture is the environmental condition that constitutes the second step of natural selection. Professor Futuyama explains, "The outcome of competition between the bacteria isn't a matter of chance; it is a predictable consequence of the difference in their biochemical capacities. Chance may well dictate whether these bacteria find themselves in an environment that is low in sugar; chance may well determine whether a population of bacteria contains a genetic mutant that can metabolize sugar more rapidly; but if what a mathematician would call the initial conditions exist—if there is little sugar, and an efficiently metabolizing genotype of

bacteria is present—then the more efficient genotype will predictably replace the other." In other words, if the environmental conditions are known, then biologists believe they generally can predict which organisms will fare better and leave more offspring (Futuyama, *Science on Trial*, 116).

799 Ibid., 88.

800 Darwin, *Origin of the Species*, 115.

801 See ibid., 77.

802 See Johnson, *Darwin on Trial*, 17–18, for a similar discussion. Darwin, after discussing animal breeders, describes natural selection as if it were a super–animal breeder: "We have seen that man by selection can certainly produce great results, and can adapt organic beings to his own uses, through the accumulation of slight but useful variations, given to him by the hand of Nature. But Natural Selection . . . is a power incessantly ready for action, and is as immeasurably superior to man's feeble efforts, as the works of Nature are to those of Art" (*Origin of the Species*, 117).

803 Mayr, *One Long Argument*, 86.

804 Ibid., 86–87.

805 Dawkins, *Blind Watchmaker*, 5.

806 In *Descent of Man*, Darwin notes that in early editions of *Origin of the Species*, he might have "attributed too much to the action of natural selection or survival of the fittest" (Appleman, *Darwin*, 173). He acknowledges that he had been unable to eliminate fully his former belief in special creation, and perhaps overstated the abilities of natural selection. But he had a worthwhile end in view: the overturning of the "dogma of special creation." Darwin's candor is commendable, but now it is his own dogma that needs to be overthrown. Darwin's nature is no artist.

807 Another example is the contrast between cans of different colored paint and a painting. Sitting undisturbed in the can, the paint has no form. But placed at the tip of an artist's brush, small portions of unformed paint may combine to create a masterpiece.

808 Darwin, *Origin of the Species*, 217.

809 Ibid.

810 Dawkins, *Blind Watchmaker*, 49, 77–79.

811 Ibid., 77.

812 Ibid. (emphasis added).

813 Ibid., 78.

814 Ibid.

815 Ibid., 5.

816 Woodpecker/mathbasc.htm.

817 Darwin also believed that sexual (as opposed to natural) selection was partly responsible for certain features of living things. Under this theory, certain physical features, such as the plumes on birds of paradise, have little or no adaptive significance; these beautiful feathers do not aid in survival. Darwin believed that if these nonadaptive, though appealing, characteristics did not assist in survival, perhaps they served to attract mates. Accordingly, the more beautiful or attractive a given feature, such as a peacock's tail, the more potential mates it would attract and the more offspring it would leave behind who would inherit beautiful tails. Thus, under this theory, nature favors the beautiful by producing more of them. Because reproductive ability is the ultimate measure of success in Darwin's world, this theory explains beauty simply as a means to facilitate reproduction. Beauty apparently serves no other purpose,

such as to please the eye or satisfy the heart. Current thinkers seem to differ over the role of sexual selection in evolution. Some of the problem is attributed to the reduction of evolution to molecules and blind forces, which have little use for beauty. See *Biology*, 455-56; *Toward a New Philosophy of Biology*, 104, 504-05. It does seem, however, that Darwin's theory concerning the gradual development of a complex organ works against sexual selection; these partially formed organs cannot help attract mates. In terms of the logical coherency of sexual selection, it is subject to most of the same flaws of natural selection. It also presumes that beauty serves only reproductive significance, which is materialism at its worst. Beauty is an end in itself, and represents physical arrangements most pleasing to our mind.

[818] Dawkins, *Blind Watchmaker*, 81.

[819] See Johnson, *Darwin on Trial*, 35-36.

[820] Dawkins, *Blind Watchmaker*, 78.

[821] Dawkins himself advises us that natural selection "has no mind and no mind's eye" (*Blind Watchmaker*), 5.

[822] Mayr, *Toward a New Philosophy of Biology*, 98.

[823] Campbell, *Biology*, 13.

[824] These examples are taken from Attenborough's fine book *Life on Earth*. He states, "The list of odd bills is virtually endless and ample proof of the malleability of the keratin beak" (178).

[825] Ibid., 84.

[826] Ibid.

[827] Campbell, *Biology*, 13; Mayr, *Toward a New Philosophy of Biology*, "Adaptation and Selection."

[828] Mayr, *One Long Argument*, 116; *Toward a New Philosophy of Biology*, 106–9.

[829] Mayr, *One Long Argument*, 164.

Chapter Forty-Two: The Bridge to a Better World

[830] For example, Professor Mayr writes, "The basic theory of evolution has been confirmed so completely that modern biologists consider evolution simply a fact." Mayr, *One Long Argument*, 162; Ditfurth, *The Origins of Life*, 268; Gould, *Hen's Teeth and Horse's Toes*, 253.

[831] Physicist Eugene P. Wigner provided a perceptive explanation for this state of affairs. He said, "One may well wonder how materialism, the doctrine that 'life could be explained by sophisticated combinations of physical and chemical laws,' could so long be accepted by the majority of scientists. The reason is probably that it is an emotional necessity to exalt the problem to which one wants to devote a lifetime" ("Remarks on the Mind-Body Question," 168, 174).

[832] Louis Agassiz, a contemporary of Darwin, is considered one of the great natural scientists in history, but is regularly criticized by modern biologists for believing that "the history of life reflects a preordained, divine plan and that species are the created incarnations of ideas in God's mind." See Gould's essay "Agassiz in the Galapagos" in *Hen's Teeth and Horse's Toes*, 107, 108; Mayr, *One Long Argument*, 41–42.

[833] Weinberg, *Dreams of a Final Theory*, 250.

[834] Dawkins writes, "Natural selection is the blind watchmaker, blind because it does not see ahead, does not plan consequences, has no purpose in view. Yet the living results of natural selection overwhelmingly impress us with the appearance of design

as if by a master watchmaker, impress us with the illusion of design and planning" (*Blind Watchmaker*, 21).

835 Weinberg, *Dreams of a Final Theory*, 158.

836 In relating the history of how natural selection has come to dominate biology, Professor Mayr writes as if Darwin was a hero who eliminated purpose from the world: "Darwin could have never adopted natural selection as a major theory, even after he had arrived at the principle on a largely empirical basis, if he had not rejected essentialism and physicalism. But there was one other impeding ideology Darwin had to refute in order to be able to adopt natural selection, and that was the finalistic or teleological worldview" (*One Long Argument*, 49–50).

837 Dawkins, *Blind Watchmaker*, 112.

838 Morris, *Naked Ape*.

839 Dawkins, *Selfish Gene*, 78.

840 Monod, *Chance and Necessity*, 45.

841 Dawkins, *Selfish Gene*, ix.

842 Ditfurth, *The Origins of Life*, 5

843 Margulis and Sagan, *Microcosmos*, 16.

844 Ditfurth, *The Origins of Life*, 5.

845 Dicus, Letaw, Teplitz, and Teplitz, "Future of the Universe," 197, 200–201.

846 Ibid., 204.

847 Ibid., 204–5.

848 "The Science of Doom," *Newsweek*, November 23, 1992.

849 Weinberg, *Dreams of a Final Theory*, 53.

850 Ditfurth, *The Origins of Life*, 260.

851 Monod, *Chance and Necessity*.

852 See Dawkins, *Blind Watchmaker*, 2–3.

853 Ibid., 328.

Chapter Forty-Three: Guardians of the Dream

854 This is the same mystery explored in the great source books of Indian philosophy and religion, the *Rg Veda*, the *Upanishads* and the *Bhagavad-gita*.

855 "The doctrine that the world is my dream—that is, the doctrine of idealism—is irrefutable" (Popper, *Realism and the Aim of Science*, 82).

856 Brihadaranyaka Upanisad 4:5.

857 *Teachings of the Compassionate Buddha*, 52.

858 *Sourcebook in Chinese Philosophy*: The Analects of Confucius, 25; 38 (¶ 4:4; ¶ 12:1).

859 Plato, *Republic*, book 6; *Protagoras*.

860 Matthew 22:39.

861 Smith, *Islam in Modern History*, 25.

Chapter Forty-Four: The Surpassing Explanatory Power of the Real Dream Worldview

862 Passachoff and Filippenko, *The Cosmos*, 211-12.

863 Dawkins, *God Delusion*, 109.

Chapter Forty-Five: One World

[864] The "classic" case against miracles is made by Hume in the *Enquiry Concerning Human Understanding*, Sec. X, Pt. 1, 126; see also Davies, *God and the New Physics*, 190. Hume, as we have seen, argued that the necessary connections that guarantee the regularity of natural events originate in the mind's needs and beliefs, not in external things. Therefore, his argument that miracles are impossible because they violate the laws of nature seems inconsistent with his own philosophy. If the order originates in the mind, then under the right circumstances, the mind can disrupt this order. This position is also that of the eighteenth-century philosopher George Berkeley. See Berkeley, *Principles of Human Knowledge*.

[865] *Sourcebook in Indian Philosophy*, 272.

[866] Homosexuality shows a variation from this simple dichotomy.

[867] I am not saying that these stories are historically accurate. I am saying that the Real Dream worldview allows us to consider them in a new light.

[868] See Faran.

[869] Cragg, *Readings from the Qur'an*, Surah 14.32–34, 100.

[870] Surah 10:60.

Chapter Forty-Six: The Real Heaven

[871] No number of scientists will ever make this assumption true, though they may make it harder to uproot.

BIBLIOGRAPHY

Abbot, Leonard Dalton, ed. *Masterworks of Economics*. McGraw-Hill, 1973.

Abell, George O. "The Ages of the Earth and the Universe." In Godfrey, *Scientists Confront Creationism*.

Al-Khalili, Jim. *Quantum: Guide for the Perplexed*. Weidenfeld and Nicolson, 2003.

Angeles, Peter A. *Dictionary of Philosophy*. Barnes and Noble Books, 1981.

Appleman, Philip. ed. *Darwin*. Norton Critical Edition. 2nd ed. W. W. Norton, 1979.

Ascent of Man, The. Television series. BBC. (1973 –).

Asimov, Isaac. *Atom*. Truman Talley, 1991.

Astronomy. Special edition. Origin and Fate of the Universe (2004).

Attenborough, David. *Life on Earth*. Little Brown, 1979.

Ayala, Francisco J. "The Mechanisms of Evolution." *Scientific American* 239 (1978).

Barrow, John D. *The Constants of Nature*. Vintage Books, 2002.

———, and John K. Webb. "Inconstant Constants," *Scientific American* 292 (2005).

———, and Joseph Silk. "The Large-Scale Structure of the Universe." In Carrigan and Trower, *Particle Physics in the Cosmos*.

———. "The Structure of the Early Universe." In Carrigan and Trower, *Particle Physics in the Cosmos*.

Barrow, John D., and Frank J. Tipler. *The Anthropic Cosmological Principle*. Oxford University Press, 1986.

Beecher, Henry K. "The Powerful Placebo." *Journal of the American Medical Association* 159 (1955).

———. "Surgery as Placebo." Journal of the American Medical Association 176 (1961).

Begley, Sharon. "The Science of Doom." *Newsweek*, November 23, 1992.

Bell, J. S. "The Placebo Effect in Drug Evaluation." *Applied Therapeutics* 6 (1964).

Benson, Herbert, and Mark D. Epstein. "The Placebo Effect: A Neglected Asset in the Care of Patients." *Journal of the American Medical Association* 232 (1975).

Berkeley, George. *Principles of Human Knowledge*. 1710. In *Berkeley Selections*. Ed. Mary Calkins. Charles Scribner's Sons, 1929.

Berra, Tim M. *Evolution and the Myth of Creationism*. Stanford University Press, 1990.

Boorstein, Daniel J. *The Discovers*. Random House, 1983.

Brooks, Michael. *Free Radicals: The Secret Anarchy of Science*. Overlook Hardcover, 2012.

Broughton, Richard S. *Parapsychology: The Controversial Science*. Ballantine Books, 1991.

Brown, Warren. "Chasing Dark Matter." *Discover* (July–August 2009).

Byerly, Henry C. *Primer on Logic*. Harper and Row, 1973.

Byrne, Peter. "The Many Worlds of Hugh Everett." *Scientific American* 297 (2007).

Cairns-Smith, A.G. *Seven Clues to the Origin of Life*. Cambridge University Press, 1985.

Campbell, Neil A. *Biology*. Benjamin/Cummings Publishing, 1990.

Carr, Bernard, ed. *Universe or Multiverse?* Cambridge University Press, 2007.

Carrigan, R.A., Jr., and W. P. Trower, eds. *Particle Physics in the Cosmos: Readings from Scientific American Magazine*. W. H. Freeman, 1989.

———. *Particles and Forces at the Heart of Matter: Readings from Scientific American Magazine*. W. H. Freeman, 1990.

Castaneda, Carlos. *The Teachings of Don Juan: A Yaqui Way of Knowledge*. Pocket Books, 1968.

Casti, John L. *Paradigms Lost*. Avon Books, 1989.

Chaisson, Eric J. *Cosmic Evolution: The Rise of Complexity in Nature*. Harvard University Press, 2001.

Chalmers, David J. "The Puzzle of Conscious Experience." In *The Hidden Mind, Scientific American* (2002).

Chalmers, Matthew. "The Higgs? Damn." *New Scientist* 216 (2012).

Chan, Wing-Tsit. *A Sourcebook in Chinese Philosophy*, Princeton University Press, 1963.

"COBE Causes Bang in Cosmology." *Science News* 141 (1992).

Comer, N.L., L. Madow, and J. J. Dixon. "Observations of Sensory Deprivation in a Life-Threatening Situation." *American Journal of Psychiatry* 124 (1967).

Cooper, Leon N. *An Introduction to the Meaning and Structure of Physics*. Harper & Row, 1970.

Copleston, Frederick. *A History of Philosophy*. Image Books, 1985.

Cragg, Kenneth. *Readings from the Qur'an*. Collins Liturgical Publications, 1988.

Craig, P.E. "The Realness of Dreams." In Russo, *Dreams Are Wiser Than Men*.

Crick, F.H.C. "The Genetic Code: III." 1966. In Folsome, *Life—Origin and Evolution*.

———. *Life Itself*. Simon and Schuster, 1981.

Darwin, Charles. *The Origin of the Species by Means of Natural Selection*. 1859. Penguin Books, 1982.

Davies, Paul. *Accidental Universe*. Cambridge University Press, 1982.

———. *God and the New Physics*. Simon and Schuster, 1983.

————. *The Mind of God*. Simon and Schuster, 1992.

————. "Universes galore: where will it end?" In Carr, *Universe or Multiverse?*

————, and John Gribbin. *The Matter Myth*. Touchstone, 1992.

Dawkins, Richard. *Ancestor's Tale: A Pilgrimage to Dawn of Evolution*. Mariner Books, 2005.

————. *The Blind Watchmaker*. W. W. Norton, 1987.

————. *The God Delusion*. Houghton Mifflin, 2006.

————. *The Selfish Gene*. Oxford University Press, 1976.

Dawood, N.J., trans. *The Koran*. 4th ed. Penguin Books, 1974.

Dayhoff, Margaret Oakley. "Computer Analysis of Protein Evolution." In Folsome, *Life—Origin and Evolution*.

de Duve, Christian. *Vital Dust: Life as a Cosmic Imperative*. Basic Books, 1995.

Dennett, Daniel. *Consciousness Explained*. Penguin Adult, 1993.

Denton, Michael. *Evolution: A Theory in Crisis*. Adler and Adler, 1986.

de Quincey, Christian. *Radical Nature: Soul of Matter*. Park Street Press, 2010

Descartes, Rene. *Meditations on First Philosophy*. 1641. Trans. L. J. LaFleur. Bobbs-Merrill, 1960.

D'Espagnat, Bernard. "The Quantum Theory and Reality." *Scientific American* 241 (1979).

De Spinoza, Benedict. *Ethics*. 1675. Rev. by Amelia Hutchinson Stirling, based on trans. by William Hale White. Ed. James Gutman (1894, 1899). Hafner Publishing, 1949.

Deutsch, David. *The Beginning of Infinity*. Viking, 2011.

DeWitt, Bryce S. "Quantum Mechanics and Reality." In DeWitt and Graham, eds. *The Many-Worlds Interpretation of Quantum Mechanics*. Princeton University Press, 1973.

Dhammapada. Trans. Eknath Easwaran. Nilgiri Press, 1986

Dickerson, Richard E. "Chemical Evolution and the Origin of Life." In Folsome, *Life—Origin and Evolution*.

Dicus, Duane A., John R. Letaw, Doris C. Teplitz, and Vigdor L. Teplitz. "The Future of the Universe." In Carrigan and Trower, *Particle Physics in the Cosmos*.

Ditfurth, Hoimar V. *The Origins of Life*. Harper and Row, 1982.

Dixon, Bernard, ed. *From Creation to Chaos*. Basil Blackwell, 1989.

Dobzhansky, Theodosius. "Evolution and Environment." In Tax, *Evolution after Darwin*.

————. "The Nature of Heredity." In Appleman, *Darwin*.

Dorin, Henry. *Chemistry: The Study of Matter*. CEBCO–Allyn and Bacon, 1987.

Dossey, Larry. *Space, Time, and Medicine*. Shambhala, 1982.

Dyson, Freeman. "Disturbing the Universe." In Dixon, *From Creation to Chaos*.

Ebon, Martin, ed. *The Signet Handbook of Parapsychology.* New American Library, 1978.

Eddington, Arthur. 1958. *The Nature of the Physical World.* Ann Arbor Paperbacks, 1968.

Edey, Maitland A., and Donald C. Johanson. *Blueprints: Solving the Mystery of Evolution.* Penguin Books, 1989.

Eigen, Manfred, William Gardiner, Peter Schuster, and Ruthild Winkler-Oswatitsch. "The Origin of Genetic Information." *Scientific American* 244 (April 1981).

Einstein, Albert, Boris Podolsky, and Nathan Rosen. "Can Quantum-Mechanical Description of Physical Reality Be Considered Complete?" In Wheeler and Zurek, *Quantum Theory and Measurement.*

Ellis, George F. R. "Does the Multiverse Really Exist?" *Scientific American* 305 (August 2011).

———. "Multiverses: description, uniqueness and testing." In Carr, *Universe or Multiverse?*

Ellis, Havelock. *The World of Dreams.* Houghton-Mifflin, 1922.

Erickson, Milton H. "A Special Inquiry with Aldous Huxley into the Nature and Character of Various States of Consciousness." In Tart, *Altered States of Consciousness.*

Evans, Frederick J. "Expectancy, Therapeutic Instructions, and the Placebo Response." In White et al., *Placebo.*

Evans, Hilary. *Alternate States of Consciousness.* Aquarian Press, 1989.

Faran, Caesar E. *Islam: Beliefs and Observances.* Barron's Educational Series, 1970.

Farrell, Joseph Pierce. *Manifesting Michelangelo.* Atria Books, 2011.

Ferris, Timothy. *The Whole Shebang.* Simon and Schuster, 1997.

Feynman, Richard P. *QED: The Strange Theory of Light and Matter.* Princeton University Press, 1985.

Fichte, Johann Gottlieb. 1794. *Science of Knowledge.* Trans. and ed. Peter Heath and John Laths. Cambridge University Press, 1982.

———. 1800. *The Vocation of Man.* Trans. William Smith. Ed. Robert M. Chisholm. Library of Liberal Arts–Bobbs-Merrill, 1956.

Fischbach, Gerald D. "Mind and Brain." *Scientific American* 267 (1992).

Folger, Tim. "Higgs: What Causes the Weight of the World?" *Discover* (January–February 2013).

Folsome, C., ed. *Life—Origin and Evolution: Readings from Scientific American Magazine.* W. H. Freeman, 1979.

Frazier, Kendrick. "Science and Religion: Conflicting or Complementary?" In *Skeptical Inquirer. Special Issue. Science and Religion: Conflict or Conciliation?*

Freeman, David H. "The Handmade Cell." *Discover* (August 1992).

Freud, Sigmund. *The Interpretation of Dreams.* 1900. Trans. A. A. Brill. First Modern Library Edition. Random House, 1950.

Fritzsch, Harald. *The Creation of Matter.* Basic Books, 1984.

Futuyma, Douglas J. *Science on Trial*. Pantheon Books, 1983.

Gackenbach, L., and A. A. Sheikh, eds. *Dream Images: A Call to Mental Arms*. Baywood Publishing, 1991.

Gamov, George. *The Creation of the Universe*. Mentor Books, 1952.

Georgi, Howard. "A Unified Theory of Particle and Forces." In Carrigan and Trower, *Particle Physics in the Cosmos*.

Gershon, Elliot S., and Ronald O. Rieder. "Major Disorders of Mind and Brain." *Scientific American* 267 (1992).

Gish, Duane T. *Evolution: The Challenge of the Fossil Record*. Creation-Life Publishers, 1985.

Glaser, Frederick B. "Inhalation Psychosis and Related States." In Tart, *Altered States of Consciousness*.

Glashow, Sheldon Lee. "Quarks with Color and Flavor." In Carrigan and Trower, *Particles and Forces at the Heart of Matter*.

Godfrey, Laurie M., ed. *Scientists Confront Creationism*. W. W. Norton, 1983.

Goldman, Stephen. "Science Wars: What Scientists Know and How They Know It." The Great Courses, The Teaching Company, 2006.

Goldsmith, Donald. *The Runaway Universe*. Perseus Books, 2000.

Gould, Stephen Jay. *Ever Since Darwin*. W. W. Norton, 1977.

———. *Hen's Teeth and Horse's Toes*. W. W. Norton, 1983.

———. *The Panda's Thumb*. W. W. Norton, 1980.

Grad, Bernard. "The Laying On of Hands." In *The Signet Handbook of Parapsychology*. Ed. Martin Ebon.

Greene, Brian. *The Elegant Universe*. W. W. Norton, 1999.

———. *The Fabric of the Cosmos*. Alfred A. Knopf, 2004.

———. *The Hidden Reality*. Alfred A. Knopf, 2011.

Gribbin, John. *In Search of the Big Bang*. Bantam, 1986.

Grunbaum, Adolf. "Explication and Implications of the Placebo Concept." in White et al., *Placebo*.

Gurney, Edmund, Frederic W. H. Myers, and Frank Podmore. *Phantasms of the Living*. 1886. Scholars' Facsimiles and Reprints, 1970.

Guth, Alan H. *The Inflationary Universe*. Helix Books, 1997.

———, and Paul J. Steinhardt. "The Inflationary Universe." In Carrigan and Trower, *Particle Physics in the Cosmos*.

Hall, Stephen S. "Revolution Postponed." *Scientific American* 303 (2010).

Halliday, David and Robert Resnick, *Fundamentals of Physics*. John Wiley & Sons, 1988.

Halliwell, Jonathon J. "Quantum Cosmology and the Creation of the Universe." *Scientific American* 265 (1991)

Hamilton, Edith, and Huntington Cairns, eds. *The Collected Dialogues of Plato*. Princeton University Press, 1961.

Harari, Haim. "The Structure of Quarks and Leptons." In Carrigan and Trower, *Particles and Forces at the Heart of Matter*.

Hawking, Stephen. *A Brief History of Time*. Bantam Books, 1988.

Hazen, Robert M. "Genesis: The Scientific Quest for Life's Origin." In
Schopf, *Life's Origin.*

———. *Genesis: The Scientific Quest for Life's Origin.* Joseph Henry Press,
2005.

Hegel, G.W.F. *Phenomenology of Spirit.* 1807. Trans. A. V. Miller, with analysis
of text and Foreword by J. N. Findlay. Oxford University Press, 1977.

———. *The Philosophy of History.* 1937, Trans. J. Sibree. Dover Publications,
1956.

———. *Reason in History.* 1837. Trans. and Introduction by R. S. Hartman.
Library of Liberal Arts–Bobbs-Merrill, 1953.

Heisenberg, Werner. "The Debate between Plato and Democritus." In Wilber,
Quantum Questions.

———. *Physical Principles of the Quantum Theory.* 1930. Trans. C. Eckart and
F. C. Hoyt. Dover Publications, 1949.

———. *Physics and Philosophy.* Harper and Row, 1958.

Hempel, Carl G. *Philosophy of Natural Science.* Prentice-Hall, 1966.

Henry, Richard Conn. "The Mental Universe." *Nature* 436 (2005).

Herbert, Nick. *Quantum Reality.* Anchor Books Doubleday, 1985.

Hey, Tony, and Patrick Walters. *The Quantum Universe.* Cambridge University
Press, 1987.

Hogan, Craig. *The Little Book of the Big* Bang. Copernicus, 1998.

Hill, R., ed. *Such Stuff as Dreams.* R. Hart-Davis, 1967.

Hooft, G.'t. "Gauge Theories of the Forces between Elementary Particles." In
Carrigan and Trower, *Particle Physics in the Cosmos.*

Hoyle, Fred. *The Intelligent Universe.* Holt, Rinehart, and Winston, 1983.

Hume, David. *A Treatise of Human Nature.* 1739–40. Penguin Books, 1969.

———. *An Enquiry Concerning Human Understanding.* 1777. Open Court
Publishing , 1966.

Humphreys, Christian. *Buddhism.* 3rd ed. Penguin Books, 1962.

Hyland, Drew. *The Origins of Philosophy.* Capricorn Books, 1973.

Jahn, Robert G., and Brenda J. Dunne. *Margins of Reality.* Harcourt Brace
Jovanovich, 1987.

Johnson, Phillip E. *Darwin on Trial.* Regnery Gateway, 1991.

Jones, Roger S. *Physics for the Rest of Us.* Contemporary Books, 1992.

Jones, W. "On the Philosophy of the Asiatics." *Asiatic Researches, Vol.* 4, 1799.

Jung, Carl G. *Synchronicity.* Princeton University Press, 1973.

Kaku, Michio. *Physics of the Future.* Doubleday, 2011.

Kane, Gordon. "The Dawn of Physics beyond the Standard Model." *Scientific
American* 288 (2003).

———. "The Mysteries of Mass." *Scientific American* 293 (2005).

———. *The Particle Garden.* Basic Books, 1995.

———. *Supersymmetry.* Helix Books, 2001.

Kant, Immanuel. *Critique of Pure Reason.* 1781. Trans. Norman Kemp Smith.
St. Martin's Press, 1965.

————. *Critique of Pure Reason.* 1781. Trans. F. Max Muller. Anchor Edition, 1966.

————. *Prolegomena to Any Future Metaphysics.* 1783. In Wolff, *Ten Great Works of Philosophy.*

————. *Universal Natural History and Theory of the Heavens.* 1755. In *Kant's Cosmogony.* Trans. W. Hastie. James Maclehose & Sons,1900.

Kelly, Robin. *Human Hologram.* Energy Psychology Press, 2011.

Kiev, A., ed. *Magic, Faith, and Healing.* Foreword by Jerome D. Frank. Free Press, 1964.

Kirshner, Robert. *The Extravagant Universe.* Princeton University Press, 2002. 7. 400 F. Supp.2d 707 (M.D. Pa. 2005).

Knight, David C., ed. *The ESP Reader.* Grosset and Dunlap, 1969.

Kojève, Alexandre. *Introduction to the Reading of Hegel.* Cornell University Press, 1980.

Krauss, Lawrence. "Cosmological Antigravity." In *The Once and Future Cosmos.* Special edition of *Scientific American* (2002).

————. "Dark Matter in the Universe." In Carrigan and Trower, *Particle Physics in the Cosmos.*

————. *A Universe from Nothing.* Free Press, 2012.

————, and Michael S. Turner. "A Cosmic Conundrum." In *The Frontiers of Physics.* Special edition of *Scientific American* (February 2006).

Lahav, Noam. *Biogenesis.* Oxford University Press, 1999.

Lampton, Christopher. *DNA and the Creation of New Life.* Arco Publishing, 1983.

Laughlin, Robert. *A Different Universe.* Basic Books, 2005.

Lavine, T.Z. *From Socrates to Sartre: The Philosophic Quest.* Bantam Books, 1984.

Lederman, Leon. *The God Particle.* Houghton Mifflin, 1993.

Levinton, Jeffrey S. "The Big Bang of Animal Evolution." *Scientific American* 267 (1992).

Lewin, Roger, *The Thread of Life,* Smithsonian Books, 1989.

Lindley, David. *Boltzman's Atom.* Free Press, 2001.

————. *The End of Physics: The Myth of a Unified Theory.* Basic Books, 1993.

Lipton, Bruce H. *The Biology of Belief.* Hay House, 2006.

Locke, John. *An Essay Concerning Human Understanding.* 1690. Ed. A. D. Woozley. Meridian Books, 1974.

Loewenberg, Bert James. "The Mosaic of Darwinian Thought." In Appleman, *Darwin.*

Maddox, John. *What Remains to Be Discovered.* Free Press, 1998.

Malthus, Thomas Robert. An Essay on the Principle of Population. 1798. In Abbot, *Masterworks of Economics.*

March, Robert H. *Physics for Poets.* Contemporary Books, 1983.

Margulis, Lynn, and Dorion Sagan. *Microcosmos.* Touchstone Books–Simon and Schuster, 1986.

Mather, John, and John Boslough. *The First Very Light*. Basic Books, 1996.

Mayr, Ernst. "The Concerns of Science." In *Skeptical Inquirer*. Special Issue. Science and Religion: Conflict or Conciliation?

————. *The Growth of Biological Thought*. Belknap Press, 1982.

————. *This is Biology: The Science of the Living World*. Belknap Press, 1998.

————. *Toward a New Philosophy of Biology*. Harvard University Press, 1988.

————. *One Long Argument*. Belknap Press, 1991.

————. *What Evolution Is*. Basic Books, 2001.

Monod, Jacques. *Chance and Necessity*. Alfred A. Knopf, 1971.

Morris, Desmond. *The Naked Ape*. Dell, 1972.

Morris, Henry M., ed. *Scientific Creationism*. 2nd ed. Master Books, 1985.

Moynihan, Ray and Alan Cassels, "A Disease for Every Pill," *The Nation* (Oct. 2005).

Nadis, Steve. "Inflation Comes of Age." In *Origin and Fate of the Universe*. Special edition of *Astronomy* (2004).

National Research Council. *The Limits of Organic Life in Planetary Systems*. The National Academies Press, 2007.

Ne'eman, Yuval, and Yoram Kirsh. *The Particle Hunters*. Cambridge University Press, 1986.

Nelson, Tore A. "Reality Dreams and Their Effects on Spiritual Belief: A Revision of Animism Theory." In Gackenbach and Sheikh, *Dream Images*.

Newton, Issac. *Philosophiae Naturalis Principia Mathematica (Mathematical Principles of Natural Philosophy)*. 1687. Trans. A. Motte. B. Motte 1729.

O'Flaherty, Wendy Doniger. *Dreams, Illusion, and Other Realities*. University of Chicago Press, 1984.

Olson, Robert G. *A Short Introduction to Philosophy*. Harcourt, Brace, and World, 1967.

Ornstein, Robert, and David Sobel. *The Healing Brain*. Simon and Schuster, 1987.

Pagels, Heinz. *The Dreams of Reason*. Bantam Books, 1984.

Partington, J.R. *A Short History of Chemistry*. 3rd ed., revised and enlarged. Dover Publications, 1989.

Pasachoff, Jay M., and Alex Filippenko. *The Cosmos: Astronomy in the New Millennium*. 2nd ed. Tomson, 2004.

Peebles, P. James E. "Making Sense out of Cosmology." In *The Once and Future Cosmos*. Special edition of *Scientific American* (2002).

Penrose, Roger. *The Emperor's New Mind*. Penguin Books, 1989.

Peterson, Ivars. "State of the Universe: If Not with a Big Bang, Then What?" *Science News* 139 (1991).

Plato, *Republic*, 360 B.C.E. in *The Collected Dialogues of Plato*, Edith Hamilton and Huntingon Cairns eds. Princeton University Press, 1961.

Pollock, Steven. "Particle Physics for Non-Physicists: A Tour of the Microcosmos." The Great Courses, The Teaching Company, 2003.

Popper, Karl R. *Realism and the Aim of Science*. 1983. Routledge 1992.

Quigg, Chris. "Elementary Particles and Forces." Carrigan and Trower, *Particles and Forces at the Heart of Matter.*

Radhakrishnan, Sarvepalli. *Indian Philosophy.* 1923. Unwin Hyman, 1989.

———, and Charles A. Moore, eds. *Sourcebook in Indian Philosophy.* Princeton University Press, 1957.

Radin, Dean. *The Conscious Universe.* HarperOne, 1997.

———. *Entangled Minds.* Paraview Pocket Books, 2006.

Randall, Lisa. *Knocking on Heaven's Door.* HarperCollins, 2011.

———. *Warped Passages.* Harper Perennial, 2005.

Raup, David M. "The Geological and Paleontological Arguments of Creationism." In Godfrey, *Scientists Confront Creationism.*

Rees, Martin. *Before the Beginning.* Helix Books, 1999.

Riordan, M., G. Tonelli, and S. L. Wan. "The Higgs at Last." *Scientific American* 307 (2012).

Roberts, Alan H., Donald G. Kewman, Lisa Mercier, and Mel Hovell. "Effects in Healing: Implications for Psychosocial and Biological Treatments." *Clinical Psychology Review* 13 (1993).

Rosenblum, Bruce, and Fred Kuttner. *Quantum Enigma.* 2nd ed. Oxford University Press, 2011.

Rubin, Vera. "Dark Matter in Spiral Galaxies." *Scientific American* 248 (1986).

Russell, Bertrand. *A History of Western Philosophy.* 1945. Simon and Schuster, 1972.

Russo, R.A., ed. *Dreams Are Wiser Than Men.* North Atlantic Books, 1987.

Sacks, Oliver. *Hallucinations.* Alfred A. Knopf, 2012.

Schopenhauer, Arthur. *The World as Will and Representation.* 1818. Trans. E. F. J. Payne. Dover, 1958.

Schopf, J. William, ed. *Life's Origin.* University of California Press, 2002.

Schwarz, Cindy. *A Tour of the Subatomic Zoo: A Guide for the Perplexed.* 2nd ed. AIP, 1997.

Scientific American. Special ed. Secrets of the Senses. 2006.

Seife, Charles. *Alpha and Omega.* Penguin, 2003.

Shapiro, Arthur K. "A Contribution to a History of the Placebo Effect." *Behavioral Science* 5 (1960).

———, and Elaine Shapiro. *The Powerful Placebo.* Johns Hopkins University Press, 1997.

Shapiro, Robert. *Origin: A Skeptic's Guide to the Creation of Life on Earth.* Bantam Books, 1987.

Sheldrake, Rupert. *The Science Delusion.* Coronet, 2012, republished in U.S. as *Science Set Free.* Deepak Chopra Books, 2012.

Shermer, Michael. *The Believing Brain.* Times Books, 2011.

Signet Handbook of Parapsychology. New American Library, 1978. Martin Ebon ed.

Silk, Joseph, Alexander S. Szalay, and Yakow B. Zel'dovich. "The Large-Scale Structure of the Universe." In Carrigan and Trower, *Particle Physics in the Cosmos.*

Simpson, George Gaylord. "The History of Life." In Tax, *Evolution after Darwin.*

———. *The Meaning of Evolution.* Bantam Books, 1971.

Sincell, Mark. "Eight Great Mysteries." In *Origin and Fate of the Universe.* Special edition of *Astronomy* (2004).

Singer, Peter. *Hegel.* Oxford University Press, 1983.

Singh, Simon. *Big Bang: The Origin of the Universe.* Fourth Estate, 2004.

Skeptical Inquirer. Special Issue. Science and Religion: Conflict or Conciliation? (1999).

Slezak, M. "New Particle, New Questions." *New Scientist* 215 (July 14, 2012).

Smith, Maynard, and E. Szathmary. *The Origins of Life.* Oxford University Press, 1999.

Smith, Wilfred Cantwell. *Islam in Modern History.* Mentor Books, 1957.

Smolin, Lee. *The Trouble with Physics.* First Mariner Books, 2007.

Song of God: Bhagavad-Gita. Trans. Swami Prabhavananda and Christopher Isherwood. Mentor Books, 1951.

Stapp, Henry. *The Mindful Universe.* 2nd ed. Springer, 2011.

Starr, Paul. *The Social Transformation of American Medicine.* Basic Books, 1982.

Steinhardt, Paul J. "The Inflation Debate." *Scientific American* 304 (2011).

Stenger, V.J. "Anthropic Design: Does the Cosmos Show Evidence of Purpose?" In *Skeptical Inquirer.* Special Issue. *Science and Religion: Conflict or Conciliation?*

Tart, Charles T., ed. *Altered States of Consciousness.* 3rd ed. HarperCollins, 1990.

Taylor, John. *Science and the Supernatural.* E. P. Dutton, 1980.

Tax, Sol, ed. *Evolution after Darwin.* University of Chicago Press, 1960.

Teachings of the Compassionate Buddha. Ed. and commentary by E. A. Burtt. Mentor, 1982.

Thomsen, Dietrick E. "The New Inflationary Nothing Universe." *Science News* 123 (February 12, 1983).

Trefil, James S. *The Moment of Creation.* Collier Books, 1983.

Tryon, Edward P. "Is the Universe a Vacuum Fluctuation?" *Nature* 246 (December 14, 1973).

Turner, Michael S. "Absurd Universe." In *Origin and Fate of the Universe.* Special edition of *Astronomy* (2004).

Ullman, Montague, and Stanley Krippner with Alan Vaughan. *Dream Telepathy: Experiments in Nocturnal ESP.* 2nd ed. McFarland, 1989.

Upanishads, The. Trans. S. Prabhavananda and F. Manchester. Mentor–Vedanta Society of Southern California, 1957.

Upanishads, The. Trans. E. Easwaran. Nilgiri. 2007.

Vaughn, Alan. *Incredible Coincidences: The Baffling World of Synchronicity*. J. B. Lippincott, 1979.

Veltman, Martinus J.G. "The Higgs Boson." *Scientific American* 255 (1986).

Vilenkin, Alexander, "Anthropic Predictions: The Case of the Cosmological Constant," in *Universe or Multivere?* edited by Bernard Carr, Cambridge University Press, 2007.

Wald, George. "The Origins of Life." In Folsome, *Life—Origin and Evolution*.

Waldrop, M.M. "Finding RNA Makes Proteins Gives 'RNA World' a Big Boost." *Science* 256 (1992).

Weinberg, Steven. "The Decay of the Proton." In Carrigan and Trower, *Particle Physics in the Cosmos*.

———. *Dreams of a Final Theory*. Pantheon, 1992.

———. *The First Three Minutes*. Updated ed. Basic Books, 1988.

———. "Living in the multiverse." In Carr, *Universe or Multiverse?*

Wei Shih Er Shih Lun, or The Treatise in Twenty Stanza on Representation-only. Trans. Clarence H. Hamilton. American Oriental Series 13. American Oriental Society, 1938.

Weiss, Ulrich, and Ronald A. Brown. "An Overlooked Parallel to Kekulé's Dream." *Journal of Chemical Education* 64 (1987).

Weyl, Hermann. *Symmetry*. Princeton University Press, 1952.

Wheeler, John Archibald, and Wojciech Hubert Zurek, eds. *Quantum Theory and Measurement*. Princeton University Press, 1983.

White, Leonard, Bernard Tursky, and Gary Schwartz, eds. *Placebo: Theory, Research, and Mechanisms*. Guilford Press, 1985.

Wigner, Eugene P. "Remarks on the Mind-Body Question." In Wheeler and Zurek, *Quantum Theory and Measurement*.

———. "The Unreasonable Effectiveness of Mathematics in the Natural Sciences." In *Communications in Pure and Applied Mathematics*. 13 John Wiley and Sons, 1960.

Wilber, Ken, ed. *Quantum Questions*. New Science Library, 1984.

Wilczek, Frank. "The Cosmic Asymmetry between Matter and Antimatter." In Carrigan and Trower, *Particle Physics in the Cosmos*.

———, and Betsy Devine. *Longing for the Harmonies*. W. W. Norton, 1988.

Wills, C., and J. Bada. *The Spark of Life*. Perseus Publishing, 2000.

Wilson, N.W. *Buddhism: A Way of Life and Thought*. Vintage Books, 1980.

Woit, Peter*bh*. Basic Books, 2006.

Wolf, Fred Alan, *Taking the Quantum Leap*. Perennial Library, 1989.

Wolff, Robert Paul, ed. *Ten Great Works of Philosophy*. Mentor Books, 1969.

Zee, A. *Fearful Symmetry: The Search for Beauty in Modern Physics*. Collier, 1986.

ABOUT THE AUTHOR

PHILIP COMELLA is a lawyer, visionary futurist, and host of the popular radio show *Conversations Beyond Science and Religion*, podcast at *www.webtalkradio.net*. His book, *The Collapse of Materialism: Visions of Science, Dreams of God*, is the culmination of decades of work committed to developing a new and credible scientific paradigm to unify the physical world of science with the metaphysics of religion. He lives with wife and daughter in Glen Ellyn, Illinois.

RELATED TITLES

If you enjoyed *The Collapse of Materialism*, you may also enjoy other
Rainbow Ridge titles. Read more about them at
www.rainbowridgebooks.com.

The Cosmic Internet: Explanations from the Other Side by Frank DeMarco

Conversations with Jesus: An Intimate Journey by Alexis Eldridge

Dance of the Electric Hummingbird by Patricia Walker

Coming Full Circle: Ancient Teachings for a Modern World by Lynn Andrews

*Consciousness: Bridging the Gap Between Conventional Science
and the New Super Science of Quantum Mechanics* by Eva Herr

Jesusgate: A History of Concealment Unraveled by Ernie Bringas

Messiah's Handbook: Reminders for the Advanced Soul by Richard Bach

Blue Sky, White Clouds by Eliezer Sobel

Inner Vegas: Creating Miracles, Abundance, and Health by Joe Gallenberger

Flames and Smoke Visible by Danny Lliteras

When the Horses Whisper: The Wisdom of Wise and Sentient Beings
by Rosalyn W. Berne, Ph.D.

Lessons in Courage by Bonnie Glass-Coffin and don Oscar Miro-Quesada

The Big Book of Near-Death Experiences by P.M.H. Atwater

Channeling Harrison by David Young

Rainbow Ridge Books publishes spiritual, metaphysical, and self-help titles,
and is distributed by Square One Publishers in Garden City Park, New York.

To contact authors and editors, peruse our titles, and see submission
guidelines,please visit our website at *www.rainbowridgebooks.com.*

For orders and catalogs, please call toll-free: (877) 900-BOOK.